Explorations in Theology 5

Explorations in Theology 5

DONALD MACKINNON

MA, DD Aberdon., FBA

SCM PRESS LTD

334 01975 3

First published 1979
by SCM Press Ltd
58 Bloomsbury Street, London WC1

Phototypeset in V.I.P. Palatino by
Western Printing Services Ltd, Bristol
Printed in Great Britain by
Richard Clay (the Chaucer Press) Ltd
Bungay, Suffolk

Contents

Introduction

The materials assembled together in this volume have different origins, even as they are concerned with different subjects. But of the thirteen papers, eight (nos. 3–8, 11 and 12) were presented at the annual meetings in January of the Colloquium on the philosophy of religion, initiated by the late Professor Enrico Castelli of the Institute of Philosophy in the University of Rome. It has been my good fortune to attend these meetings annually since 1967, and the papers which I have given have been published in Europe, both in French in the official reports of the gatherings, brought out by Aubier of Paris, often in Italian, and more or less completely in successive editions of the well-known German series *Kerygma und Mythos*. Four of them (nos. 4, 5, 6 and 8) have in fact appeared in English in the last named (series VI, vols 7 and 8, 1976). [Paper 6 also appeared in the *Epworth Review* for the same year, vol. 3 no. 2.] Any who have consulted the volumes of proceedings in libraries will know how very many learned men of international reputation have contributed to them, and what a privilege it has been for me to be associated with their work. To some extent the variety of the subjects dealt with in the papers here gathered together reflects the variety of topics with which the meetings in Rome have dealt.

Of these eight papers, that on the concept of *raison d'état* was presented in a somewhat different form to a group concerned with the theory of international politics in 1974 and later, more or less as it was submitted in Rome, to the meeting of the Society for the Study of Theology in Oxford in the spring of 1976. The paper presented in Rome in January 1977 on the theological resonance of the controversy between realism and idealism has been modified and, in some respects, expanded.

The other papers include both previously published an unpublished materials. The second paper, on 'Lenin and Theology', based on a lecture given in Cambridge in April 1970 and published in *Theology* for March 1971, has been very considerably worked over and expanded. The address on the problems raised by the personal lives and commitments of Frege, Kittel and Tillich has not been published, and the same is true of the lecture on 'Ethics and Tragedy', given before the University of Stirling in February 1971. The tenth paper in this volume, the Presidential Address to the Aristotelian Society, delivered in London in October 1976, was published in the Society's *Proceedings* for 1976–1977 and is reprinted here by courtesy of the Editor of the Society.

As I reflect on this collection, I am aware that the material reflects three central concerns.

1. Such papers as my Presidential Address to the Aristotelian Society in London and those on the impact on theological controversy of the debate between realists and idealists in its modern form, and on the proper 'system of projection' for theological statements, bear witness to my concern for areas in which theological issues and quite technical philosophical issues play upon one another. The Rome paper on 'Parable and Sacrament' might be understood as a bridge between those papers and others which may be regarded as more definitely theological.

2. Yet where the theological papers are concerned, there is a similar preoccupation with the question of the extent to which theological perception can itself be enlarged by serious engagement with the issues raised by Marxist–Leninism, and it is no accident that these papers are in some respects among the most definitely theological in the volume. Certainly they contribute to the author's eagerness to criticize various fashionable sorts of subjectivism in contemporary theology. Finally, the paper on the concept of witness as a form of evidence for the reality of God raises the problem of the manner of God's presence in and to the world and (possibly) suggests the extent to which theologians should go to school with poets, and that not in disdain for facts, but the better to recognize those facts with which they are concerned. Again the paper on 'Parable and Sacrament' is highly relevant.

3. Finally there are those papers whose primary concern is ethical, including the address on 'The Future of Man' (given in 1967 and subsequently published in *Theology* for April 1969) and that on the problems raised by the posthumous revelations concerning Paul Tillich's personal life. These are concluded with a paper which in a measure rejoins the issues raised in those treating of Marxist–Leninism; but its attempt at a serious political realism in its treatment of the concept of *raison d'état* may remind some

readers of Reinhold Niebuhr's last major work, *Nations and Empires* (1959). To this group of papers the lecture on 'Ethics and Tragedy' may be thought to offer some concluding general reflections. Yet the reflections cannot be regarded as conclusive except in the way in which they bring out more clearly the underlying hostility to subjectivism in theology. There is need, certainly, for a further essay to complement and to some extent to correct emphases discernible in the paper on *raison d'état*, within the context provided by the general reflections suggested in the lecture on 'Ethics and Tragedy'. It is my hope to attempt this task in the Martin Wight Memorial Lecture which I am to deliver at the London School of Economics early in 1979. For the reader who wishes to learn something of the sort of dogmatic theology to which such considerations might impel the student, I would refer to the paper on the irreversibility of time, and to the many references to christological issues scattered throughout the collection. Yet it is no accident that part of this paper is devoted to fairly technical philosophical discussion and part to some comments on a remarkable modern novel, William Styron's *Lie Down in Darkness*.

If the materials collected together in this volume have any lesson to teach, it is that of the many-sidedness involved in serious theological work. There are very many escape routes proposed for the avoidance of this discipline; if this strangely assorted gathering of papers succeeds in closing even one of them its publication will have in a measure been justified.

1

The Future of Man

The subject of the future of man may well seem one on which it is
foolish to speak. One wonders how many members of the University of Cambridge in the first five years of this century were
even remotely aware of the bitter quarrels between the Bolsheviks and Mensheviks which divided the ranks of the left-wing
Russian political emigration; the events of 'Bloody Sunday' in
1905 no doubt left their mark. But the disputes to which such men
as Lenin and Kamenev, Martov and Plekhanov were parties must
surely have gone almost unnoticed; or if rumour reached Combination Rooms of their bitter quarrels, they were no doubt sometimes at least dismissed with a superior smile. Yet out of those
quarrels there was born that revolutionary force which proved
capable, by ruthless exploitation of the chaos in the Russia of
autumn 1917, of 'casting the kingdoms old into another mould'. It
is perhaps significant that few of those self-consciously *avant-
garde* Christian thinkers who proclaim what they call 'the gospel
of Christian atheism' are willing or eager to engage seriously with
the work of the man who has surely the right to be regarded as the
greatest atheist of the twentieth century, Vladimir Lenin, or
Ulyanov. It is always easier to argue with a man of straw than to
confront sombre and commanding reality; but recollection of
these events should warn anyone claiming to prophesy concerning the future of mankind.

Yet in August 1945 the present writer heard one prophecy
which was fulfilled in a period of time even briefer than the
prophet mentioned. Not long after the end of the Japanese War
I heard the late Dr Friedrich Waismann (the man among the
'Vienna Circle' whom Wittgenstein had most deeply influenced)
say that with the technological advances revealed in the perfection of the first atomic bomb amazing possibilities were opening
before mankind. Only someone, he added, who understood at
least as much modern physics as he did could decipher the signs

of the times; but he assured me that cosmic voyages would be possible within twenty years, always provided that humanity could survive during the interval. It was in April 1961, less than sixteen whole years after Waismann spoke, that Yuri Gagarin's space flight was made.

Here is an example of a prophecy, made by a man whose philosophical formation was certainly logical empiricist, which has been abundantly fulfilled. At least from this fulfilment we may generalize to the extent of being quite sure that we stand on the threshold, indeed that we have already advanced over the threshold, of an unprecedented extension of human power over our natural environment. And here we have to reckon with a twofold extension: there is one aspect leading us to an ever greater understanding of the ways in which things are, and another leading to a seemingly ever-increasing capacity to exploit the resources of our natural environment. The two cannot of course be separated; but we can to some extent properly distinguish the kind of changes brought into our view of the way things are by, for example, the advances of empirical cosmology, and the expectation of increased longevity already opening before us, thanks to advances in the field of medicine, in transplantation surgery, as well as in the use of antibiotics. No one who knows Scotland, and particularly its rural areas, can fail to be continually aware of the extent to which the life of those societies has been materially changed by the advent in streptomycin of a powerful, hardly resistible agent in the struggle against tuberculosis. The closing of sanatoria or their conversion to other use is significant evidence that with modern antibiotics TB is becoming a scourge of the past. It is a commonplace to point out that these great advances in control of our environment have themselves intensified and are continuing to intensify towards flashpoint the terrible problem of population. At a more intimate level, pneumonia is no longer at hand to be the 'old man's friend', and the beds in our geriatric hospitals are full to overflowing with those who have, in some sense, lived too long and been overtaken by the sad diminution (and worse) of senility, and its extreme manifestation in senile dementia.

Where the future of man is concerned, we have to reckon with the changes in his outlook, in his understanding of his own human situations, and in the changes in that situation itself. If I have begun by stressing the latter, it is because the kind of work done for instance at the Mullard Radio Astronomical Laboratory at Lord's Bridge is itself dependent upon high technological achievement in the devising of observational tools. Or, to take another example, the discoveries made possible through electron microscopy go far beyond those hitherto possible in their range, and the precision of attendant observational confirmation and information. That latter truth might indeed be judged analytic! Since the beginnings of the experimental method we have been familiar with the process of putting nature to the question, of approaching our natural environment not as passive observers but as examining magistrates in a court of law. In the last hundred years we have seen unexampled developments in our capacity for framing questions and for finding the answers to them; and although some of the most important developments in question relate to the construction of new and more and more powerful branches of mathematics, many others concern tools put at our disposal by an unexampled technological progress.

From the foregoing there emerges an image of the human situation which some writers of conservative temper too easily write off as Promethean. Yet the distinguished French Jesuit theologian (and close friend of Teilhard de Chardin), Henri de Lubac,[1] has pointed out that the God whose secrets Prometheus sought to wrest from him in his theft of fire for benefit of the human race was the Olympian Zeus; whereas Christian devotion is given to the God of Abraham, Isaac and Jacob, God the living and the true. Indeed de Lubac has powerfully argued that where the Christian mission to the modern world is concerned, one of its most significant and most searching tasks is that of the baptism of the archetype of Prometheus. We can no longer, if we are honest, think of our environment as something altogether opaque to our understanding; no more can we treat natural forces as if they were the instruments whereby a providence achieves ends in our respect which we are powerless either to avert or to scrutinize. This mortal life is still hemmed in by chances and by changes that we cannot foresee; but the life that is so circumscribed is the life of men and women who more and more are fashioning out of the natural world an environment after the form of their own choice.

It is true that the circumstances dictating the detail of this choice may include their own manifest inability to resolve the fundamental problem of living peaceably one with another. We need do no more than recall, where our own country is concerned, the contrast between the millions immediately available for Polaris submarines and the obvious shortage of the money required for the increased availability of kidney machines to serve the needs of those suffering from incurable renal disease. The very course of technological development is, to a greater extent than we realize, shaped and distorted by the demands for more and more effective types of military 'hardware', for anti-ballistic missiles to counter intermediate and inter-continental ballistic missiles which constitute the foundation of the weapon systems of the super-powers. We try to lull ourselves into security by reference to a 'balance of terror', forgetting until we are suddenly reminded how precarious a thing this balance is, and how easily and quickly it is replaced by a frightening instability. These simple facts should serve to remind us that if we do see in our future the promise of an increased mastery over our environment, the problems not only of the consequences of that increased mastery, but of its form and manner, are very grave. De Lubac is right to speak of the claim of the archetype of Prometheus to a Christian baptism; but baptism is traditionally the sacramental re-enactment in the baptized of the redemptive mystery of Christ's death and resurrection. We must, if we are Christian, pursue de Lubac's insight to the extent of insisting that, if Prometheus is to go down into the waters, in these waters there is for him, as for all of us, an 'old man' which needs to be put away. If such a working out of the metaphor in detail impresses on us the gravity of our human situation, reminding us that our greatest achievements bear within them the seeds of tragic disorder as well as the promise of a new heaven and a new earth, the elaboration will have served us well.

Where fundamental changes in intellectual outlook are concerned, the course to which this address belongs has been principally concerned with evolution. In one of his greatest works, *Le Milieu Divin*,[2] Teilhard has offered his readers a searching meditation in a style reminiscent both of Descartes and Pascal, in which he invites his readers to take stock of their situation in a universe both temporally and spatially immense. He is uniquely alive to the problem raised for the imagination by the sheer scale of the world, and the infinitesimally small area in its vastness occupied by the human individual, even by the indefinitely large multitude of such individuals, which taken together constitute the human race. His essay is an invitation to self-interrogation to which we should respond, a work of spirituality more relevant to our present needs than to those of the men and women of 1927, for whom it was first written. In his last years the late Dr C. E. Raven enthusiastically welcomed the dissemination of Teilhard's writings because with his overwhelming awareness of the vastness of the universe, in time as well as in space, and of the continuous processes whereby life as we know it has evolved from its primaeval origins, he revealed himself the powerful theological antagonist of any religious view which treated the created universe as the mere stage-set for the drama of human redemption and treated Christ as a *deus ex machina*. His sensitivity to the vastness of the world and his vision of the detailed manner of its creation, as well as his overtly religious teleology, preserved him against the little-minded spiritual provincialism of the devout; in his greatest work, in my judgment, this awareness elicited from him as much interrogation as affirmation, enabling him to frame in the language of spirituality questionings concerning matters absolutely fundamental to Christian faith.

Where Teilhard's writings on the prospects before human societies and groupings, national and international alike, are concerned, we may accuse him of an excessive optimism, of a failure to take stock of the realities of human conflict, and of the inescapable problems raised by the exercise and containment of power and coercive force. At least, however, he reminds his readers that the technological revolutions through which we are living are matters of promise as well as of threat, sources of opportunity as well as possible occasions of mutual annihiliation. The kind of bewildered despair sometimes encouraged by ecclesiastics (I speak of what I have encountered in speech and in writing), who tell us that we know by faith that our world must end some day, and that it may after all be the divine will that it should end in nuclear conflagration, is, for Teilhard, blasphemy at once against creature and Creator; it is a practical denial of the doctrine of creation, of the sovereignty of Creator over creation affirmed and made effective in the work of Christ. And Christ (as we shall see) is for Teilhard the Christ who has passed through death to resurrection. 'Christ being raised from the dead, dieth no more; death hath no more dominion over him.' Over him, as he is now, unlike human beings, whose life runs from the cradle through growth to maturity, and then through decline to the grave, death has no sovereign rights, no last word to speak, as speak in our case it surely will, whether soon or late, whether sud 'enly or foreseen. Christ's risen life is life untrammelled, unfettered, *absolute*; it is life *beyond* death, in which he subdues all things to his Father's rule. It is characteristic of Teilhard to fuse this theological vision with quite concrete and definite hopes for the perceptible human future, and to find in a tired scepticism in respect of that latter the repudiation of the former faith.

We may well question the detail, even the logic, of his optimism; we may well find ourselves driven to a more tragic
appraisal of the human scene, but let us be sure that the appraisal
is tragic – something very different from the mood of tired
impatience which finds nothing new under the sun, which thinks
quite wrongly that one only grasps *la misère de l'homme* by depre-
ciating *la grandeur*; whereas it is only against the background of a
true estimate of human creativity and genius that we see human
weakness, frailty and sin for what they are. It is the magnitude of
human technological achievement that enhances the quality of
outrage we feel at the extent to which that achievement is harnessed to the purposes of a hardly controllable race to perfect
means of mutual destruction. The ecclesiastical exploitation of an
anthropomorphically conceived eschatology in the supposed
interests of faith repels the imagination as a belittling of the
genuinely tragic texture of the human condition. It is fundamentally philistine in the sense in which we so characterize the
crudities of the utilitarian doctrine at its most unsophisticated; it
diminishes the rich and terrifying complexity of the human reality in accordance with the demands of an abstract dogmatic
formula. One might add that it not only rejects the Christian
understanding of the created world, but disregards the profound
explorations of the human condition we can find, for instance, in
the tragedies of Sophocles and of Shakespeare.

There is much else that requires at least a mention in an attempted appraisal of the human future. For instance 15 August 1947,
when India and Pakistan obtained their freedom, is surely one of
the watersheds of history, I have mentioned the 'ten days which
shook the world, in October/November 1917. There is a sense in
which those events and their consequences, both terrible and
magnificent, shocking, horrifying, yet still, in spite of even the
dark years of the Stalinist tyranny, not finally discontinuous with
the promise of their birth, have part of their import in significance
for the so-called developing nations. How far it is true that the
Leninist conception of the state, with its key-centres of power
concentrated in the hands of a carefully trained and selected élite
and regarded as itself the supremely effective agent of industrial
as well as social revolution, has lessons to teach those countries
which they cannot in the same way learn from the study of the
pluralist societies of the West, with their traditions of constitutional government? I do not refer to a slavish imitation; but rather
I wish simply to raise questions that must thrust themselves on
the attention of anyone for whom in government the effective

subordination of power to law, and the accountability of those who exercise power to those in whose name it is exercised, are principles of ethical significance as well as of executive and administrative utility.

Again, we must not forget the heart and centre of human life, the forces associated with sexuality, with whose power and significance in all fields of human concern we are increasingly aware. If Marx is one of the authentic makers of the modern mind and designers of the shape of the future, Freud (for all his occasional, even frequent, extravagance) is another. What will happen to our society when we have deeply assimilated his profound insights concerning the potentially and frequently mutually destructive character of mother's devotion to son and son's devotion to mother? Again, what of the consequences of the ever-widening dissemination of simpler and more effective methods of contraception? It would be a great mistake for Christians to dismiss out of hand the suggestion that the postponement of sexual initiation till marriage may not be of itself by any means the sole necessary, sufficient condition of a mature, mutual sexual experience within marriage. This is very delicate and controversial ground; but the general acceptance of the deep significance of sexual union and the moral validity of the joy it brings, apart altogether from its outcome in procreation, together with the growing practical possibility of the total dissociation of sexual activity from procreation, raises very serious problems. At all costs Christians are right to set their face against the trivialization of these most intimate and searching of all human relations; to insist on their dignity and on their transcendent significance. (This indeed is precisely the lesson which Freud in one way and – in his greater novels – D. H. Lawrence in another tried to teach.) But the vindication will only be effective if it takes stock of the changed human situation in which these values must today be formed.

Are there then no constants in human life? Most certainly there are, and their proper delineation, both in the realm of human knowledge and in the wider, less tractable world of human existence, is a central intellectual task. It is in some ways inevitably a technical philosophical enterprise. Thus where human experience of the world is concerned Kant, who gave himself to this problem with an unexampled concentration of intellectual energy, may well be right in insisting that such experience is only possible under certain conditions, and that these conditions relate at once to the world we take stock of (e.g. its character as a unitary, spatio-temporal system, the conformity of changes affecting the items of its furniture to laws in principle discoverable, etc.) and to the manner in which we take stock of it (e.g. the unity of our consciousness, the manner in which we distinguish the order of events in our autobiography from the order of events in the world in which we live, etc.) I repeat that these are technical problems which quite obviously cannot be dealt with towards the end of a paper of this kind; yet their relevance to its concerns demands that they be mentioned.

Further there are assuredly moral constants: among them I would include the inadmissibility of treating any human individual as if his or her significance rested exclusively in the role for which he or she might be cast in some individual or group purpose, whether privately or collectively self-regarding, of our own devising. There has never been an age when the role of the conscientious objector is more significant than in our own, where the imperative which he regards as bidding him revolt is more demanding, and I would insist that the scope of this imperative goes far beyond the question of participation in or support for the American enterprise in Vietnam, though I must say that in my view it should include a personal refusal to endorse that undertaking.

So we come finally to a very few remarks on the future of Christian belief. Towards the end of his lengthy study of the theological inheritance of Dietrich Bonhoeffer, entitled *Wirklichkeit und Glaube*,[3] Professor Heinrich Ott of the University of Basel has included a fascinating and profound comparison of the Christologies, that is the doctrines of the Person of Christ, in the writings of the German theologian and martyr and in those of Teilhard. For both men, vastly different though their formation and experience undoubtedly were, at the centre of their faith lay an overwhelming sense of the presence of *God-in-Christ* in the ordinary ways of the world; according to Ott (and I do not quite agree with him here) Teilhard learned this lesson in the deserts of Central Asia, when engaged in palaeontological research; while Bonhoeffer made this vision his own in the prison cells in which he spent the last years of his life before his execution.

Moreover, this universal Christ on whom Teilhard's faith was set was the Christ of Easter Day, the day on which he always hoped himself to die, and on which indeed in 1955 in New York he did die. Whereas for Bonhoeffer the Christ whom he saw present everywhere in the midst of the world was the Christ of Good Friday, calling on men to take their share in the suffering of

God in the midst of his creation. The contrast is very illuminating and extends much further than a mere difference of theological emphasis between two remarkable Christian spirits. Thus many students of Teilhard's writings (and I am thinking of such writers as Père Henri de Lubac) have tried to defend him against the charge of too lightly esteeming the reality of physical and moral evil, especially the latter. Few writers have been able to speak with greater insight than he on the problems of spiritual life raised for those overtaken by the slow diminishment of their own strength, seeming to progress almost inevitably towards the final indignities of a senile condition; but in my judgment he is far less successful where the kind of moral evil that found expression in Dachau and Auschwitz is concerned. Dr Ulrich Simon, Reader in Theology in the University of London, whose parents died in Auschwitz, has recently published a remarkable essay entitled *A Theology of Auschwitz*,[4] in which he seeks to develop a conception of objective atonement adequate to a divine engagement with evil on the scale and of the peculiar horror for ever associated with that name. It would be an oversimplification to say that his Christ is the Christ of Good Friday in the sense in which Bonhoeffer's *may* perhaps be so regarded; but his Christ is one whose significance and whose work are alike only understood in relation to the depths of evil of which in this century we have continually known the human race to be capable.

Often it seems likely enough that Christian faith as we know it will not survive; that, as Hegel and indeed Marx in different ways suggested, the Christian episode is only a short, although an extremely important, episode in the long history of the world. Yet I suspect that as long as Christianity continues to provide the terms in which men and women here and elsewhere engage with the fundamental problems of their existence, the kind of tension to which I have just referred between those who emphasize the Christ of Easter Day and those who emphasize the Christ of Good Friday will be profoundly significant. To say this is not to beg any questions concerning the precise content of the Easter faith, and the historical problems it raises – questions which I must admit that I regard as of first order importance. Rather it is to advertise an ancient tension that may well be a growing point in an enlarged Christian understanding, a Christian understanding, that is, which seeks to illuminate things as they are and to find in Christ crucified and risen, that which is profoundly relevant to our deepest needs, individual and collective, moral and intellectual and indeed aesthetic. (It is my gravest omission in this paper to have said nothing on the subject of art, except indirectly of literature.)

If Christianity survives it will be in part at least because the lonely figure, dying in agony upon the cross, crying out in dereliction to the Father, whom he believes to have forsaken him, remains ceaselessly interrogating men and women, outside as much as within the Christian churches, concerning his significance and that of his supreme hour. 'What think you of this man?' It is sometimes suggested by learned theological scholars that this figure who so haunts even now the consciousness of secular mankind is in the end little more than the projection of an ultimately parochial churchly experience and concern with his cultic import. If this be true, then the future of Christian faith is seen as inescapably bound up with the life and the future of an institution or set of institutions whose perceptible history has repeatedly in the eyes of ordinary men and women more effectively than anything else hidden from them the features of the Christ in whom they might believe. Yet obstinately we can still claim that Christ is greater than any institution claiming monopoly of his secrets, and that it may in the end be made plain that in his faithfulness unto death is the healing of our human hurt, and in his mystery the secret of our ways.

2

Lenin and Theology

The centenary of Lenin's birth is not at first sight an obvious topic for celebration in a theological periodical.[1] Yet at a time when the phrase 'God is dead' has become something of a theological catchword and in which studies of the 'gospel of Christian atheism' are written and widely discussed, it is surely salutary to turn one's attention to a man who may well be judged the greatest atheist of the twentieth century, who was a serious, passionately convinced atheist, who must also, for good and ill, be certainly numbered among those who 'cast the kingdoms old into another mould'. Again, at a time when a great deal is written and said on the allegedly morally liberating effect of violent revolutionary activity, there is every reason for pondering the formation, life and achievement of the greatest revolutionary of the twentieth century. The exercise is certainly not one that edifies; yet it is profoundly illuminating. There may indeed be, there almost certainly are, situations in which revolutionary action is made inevitable by the impossibility or near-impossibility of gaining redress of grievances by constitutional means, and by the gradual, or it may be sudden disintegration of existing forms of social organization and discipline. But these are of necessity very terrible situations; while certainly they provide the resolute with their supreme opportunity, they are also occasions of hardly calculable suffering for the innocent. They are deeply tragic in that the architect of liberation, who seeks to realize the possibilities of a new life out of the disintegration of an apparently irreformable social and political system, may prove the designer of a still more terrible bondage. 'Lenin in October' is a figure of nearly archetypal significance; we certainly do not (in spite of the excellent works of George Lukacs, David Shub, Louis Fischer and Adam Ulam)[2] possess a biography in any way adequate to its tremendous theme. It is utterly regrettable that Isaac Deutscher died before fulfilling the achievement of his words on Stalin and

Trotsky with the work that would surely have proved his masterpiece on the greatest of the three.[3] In what follows all I venture to
do is to present certain aspects of Lenin's significance for the
contemporary theologian, even – to use a word I greatly dislike –
to characterize features of the challenge his history represents.

1. It was in 1966, when I read Dr J. P. Nettl's excellent two-
volume study of *Rosa Luxemburg*[4] (one of Lenin's most perceptive
and respected critics), that suddenly I said to myself that in the
world of German Marxism, the world in which Kautsky and
Bernstein[5] argued the rights and wrongs of 'revisionism', into
which this remarkably gifted Polish Jewess plunged (she was to
perish in the suppression of the Spartakusbund in post-war
Germany in 1919 at the hands of a member[6] of one of those
sinister Freikorps, in whose service some of Hitler's bravoes
enjoyed their apprenticeship in violence), there was a fine example of the kind of intellectual atheistic world to which the
Christian, even the self-consciously radical Christian, finds himself a total stranger. There is, of course a cosy atheism that the
man of the *avant-garde* welcomes as a dialectical moment on the
road to faith; but with the conscious, deliberate and deeply convinced rejection of the reality of God as a *prius* of informed debate
and action concerning the fundamentals of human life and society, it is otherwise. In this world there is no room for the
theologian.

The efforts to establish dialogue can only expect the sort of
rebuff that Lenin administered to the early brave essays in Christian socialism of Dr Nicholas Berdyaev and Father Serge Bulgakov
in the last years before the storms of 1914 broke upon the crumb-
ling Tsarist empire. The debates into which Rosa Luxemburg
plunged were, of course, continued during the first years of the
1914–18 war, when the failure of the 'Second International', especially but not only in Germany, endowed them with a greater
bitterness and no doubt made them the context in which Lenin's
famous strategy of 'revolutionary defeatism' was hammered out.
Yet, as one reads the record, one is in a world far removed from
that of the Christian ethical writing of the time. Granted that in
the latter there was often a comparable abdication of independent
judgment before the values of embattled nationalism, there was a
complete absence of the note sounded by Lenin and his associ-
ates, of a radicalism at once free of scruple of any sort, yet instinct
with a sort of ruthless optimism that sought to bend the devastating emergency of Europe to the service of the future. Lenin was

no pacifist; yet in his passionate refusal to admit the validity of the cause either of the Entente or of the Central Powers, he was quick not only to break finally with one of his intellectual masters, the great Russian Marxist, George Plekhanov, but also to find a welcome ally in his erstwhile Menshevik antagonist, the pacifist, humanly attractive Martov.

2. To speak of these wartime controversies is to risk a certain lack of proper arrangement in the design of this article. For where Lenin's personal history is concerned, the attitude he took up in their respect was continuous with the outlook he had developed during the first decade of the twentieth century, during the period in which the issues dividing Menshevik from Bolshevik were first hammered out, and in which Lenin incorporated into the growing tradition of Marxism the characteristic insights of Leninism. If it was in the second decade that the intellectual and moral ascendancy of German social democracy in the Marxist world was decisively lost, it was in the first decade of the century that Lenin achieved his concept of the party as the thoroughly schooled, revolutionary élite through whose agency the dictatorship of the proletariat would be lifted out of the realms of near-chiliastic prediction and made effective on the plane of human history. The work *What is to be done?* – of the first years of the new century – remains one of the key works in Lenin's massive *oeuvre* and it is fascinating and instructive to compare and contrast its teaching with that of the well-known pamphlet *The State and Revolution*, written on the eve of his supreme hour and informed by a more generous admission of the revolutionary potential of the industrial masses, of their fitness themselves to prove wholly competent executants of social transformation.[7]

The roots of Lenin's concept of the party have been variously defined. There are those who emphasize the continuity of his ideas here with certain elements in the thought of Karl Kautsky; but others point to the continuing influence on them of the Narodnik tradition. (It was as a Narodnik that his elder brother had been executed, following an unsuccessful attempt to assassinate the Tsar: an episode of crucial significance in Lenin's personal development.) Between the underlying social ideas of the Narodniks and the Marxism Lenin had learnt from Plekhanov as well as from Marx himself (one must not forget his confessed admiration for Hegel's *Logic*), there was a great gulf fixed. But it may well have been part of Lenin's sombre genius to incorporate into the Marxist scheme of historical development the Narodnik conception of an élitist revolutionary organization, whose members were schooled by an intense personal discipline, collectively imposed, to serve the cause of social transformation by any or every means. It would be the greatest mistake to treat the Leninist party as an organized school of political terrorism. The history of Russian revolutionary activity was an eloquent argument against the thesis that there was any value in terrorism or violence for its own sake. Sorel's mystique of violent action, of the allegedly morally liberating experience of *la grève nationale*, was a form of romanticism quite alien to Lenin's harshly disciplined, always ruthless but never wilfully extravagant, quest for the means most effectively geared to seizure of the reins of political power. What made Lenin a revolutionary of genius was his extraordinary capacity for combining an unflinching and unyielding commitment to a particular doctrine of the concrete, historical actualities of human society, national and international alike, with a sense of possibilities that could be exploited in ways that might be thought to defy every rational prediction grounded on his fundamental analysis, provided the cadres were there trained to seize these possibilities and exploit them to the full. He was at once intellectual and man of action; he wrote with eager, angry violence new chapters in Marxist theory, with the aid of the economic analysis of early twentieth-century imperialism sketched at the London School of Economics by J. A. Hobson and developed, with an academic rigour beyond Lenin's reach, by Rosa Luxemburg. It was enough that he showed a vivid awareness that the industrial proletariat did not simply comprise one of Disraeli's 'two nations' in the advanced industrial societies of Western Europe, but included for example the indentured Chinese coolie labour, brought to South Africa after the end of the South African War to supply the necessary labour force for the mining industry, which such men as Lord Milner rightly saw as fundamental to the country's economy and as therefore demanding the use of expedients hardly distinguishable from slavery to restore its working. Because Lenin was man of action rather than social scientist, he threw his ideas together in forms that are easily vulnerable; but his ideas were to him matters of life and death.

It was typical of the man that he arraigned Bogdanov for daring to suggest that the positivistic sensationalism of, for instance, the brilliant Viennese philosopher of science, Ernst Mach, might serve as an alternative creed to his own thorough-going materialism. The argument of his work on this subject – *Materialism and Empirio-Criticism*[8] – strikes a professional philosopher as laughable; but what Lenin dreaded was the suggestion, and after all Mach had learnt much from the Irish George Berkeley, that the cutting edge of materialist dialectics could be emasculated, that naturalistic theories of the world's origin could be construed as relatively harmless devices for describing and predicting the order of one's personal experience. That way lay a kind of futility about the issues that were tearing the world in pieces, that enabled men to exploit men and to justify their merciless indifference (the issue of the indentured Chinese labour is a *locus classicus*)[9] in the name of an allegedly superior culture and civilization. Was it for nothing that Marx had urged philosophers to turn from seeking to understand the world to the urgent task of changing it, to lay aside the intellectual self-indulgence of spiritualistic theodicy and to seek rather to excise from a world that need no longer be opaque to comprehension the cancer that perverted its very substance?

3. Marxism is in a very special sense a form of historical determinism: in a very special sense, for the dialectical quality of historical materialism transforms the simplicity of the concept of historical causality with which it operates. But we are not in this study concerned with Marxism as such; rather with Lenin, who in himself existentially (to use a fashionable adverb) reconciled the claims of determinism and freedom. He was a rigorous objectivist, convinced that there were laws of historical development. Yet he was also supremely executant as well as architect of most drastic historical change. The background history of the 'ten days that shook the world' in October 1917 is murky in the extreme. One need go no further than the works of Leonard Schapiro and George Katkov to realize that, for instance, the classical presentation of Trotsky's tremendous *History of the Russian Revolution* belongs as much to its interpretation as to its description. One has to remember that a very few weeks before the often mythologized storming of the Winter Palace Lenin had been in hiding; one can also argue that things might have gone otherwise, that Kerensky might not have found himself assailed from the Right as well as from the Left, by Kornilov's threatened mutiny, etc. Always in recording the past one must allow that events might not have happened as they did. Yet the fact remains that Lenin, however great his debt to German desire to immobilize the Russian armies, if necessary by helping to promote a revolution in Russia, was ready to act, to bend events to the pattern he believed they must exemplify, to ride to power on the way of proletarian revolutionary *élan*, and to achieve, in a country only relatively recently embarked on the paths of radical industrialization, a

revolution that, if Marxist in inspiration, might well be judged by the most conservative Marxist theoreticians to defy the established laws of social evolution.

Of course the events of October 1917 were only the beginning; the end is not yet; and Rosa Luxemburg, as well as Karl Kautsky, were quick to read the signs of the future in Lenin's disregard of the claims of a promised 'constituent assembly' to define the political structure of the new Russia. The revolution of October/November 1917 brought into being a 'one party' state, and its party's grip on power was necessarily made more inflexible and more comprehensive by the bloody civil war that followed quickly upon a revolution that had indeed been made possible in the first instance not least by an exhausted people's longing for peace, for an end to their involvement in the terrible international war which was continuing to lay waste Europe. Lenin had not scrupled to exploit this war-weariness, to contrast his own readiness to withdraw Russia from the war (even at the cost of the kind of price paid at Brest-Litovsk)[11] with Kerensky's continued commitment to the Allied cause. A Plutarch of the future may remark that the autumn of 1917 was pre-eminently the season of two men, deeply schooled in the teachings of Clausewitz: one the Lenin of October, who had studied the German master in the very strange environment of the Russian political emigration; the other Sir Douglas Haig, who had learnt his lessons in the very different setting of the staff college at Camberley. One cannot understand fully Haig's commitment to 'third Ypres', to the battle of Passchendaele, except one remembers that for him as for Clausewitz war was a conflict of wills in which the stronger will must prevail. So for Lenin in the struggle for power, the man who was armed at once by deep understanding of social forces and by effective revolutionary strategic conceptions was likely by that equipment to prove of stronger will than his opponent. For Lenin the end justified the means; but when, for instance, with one's imagination quickened by the poetry of Wilfrid Owen, one turns to contemplate the horrors of Passchendaele, can one pretend that Haig and his defenders were animated by any other ethic? Their cause was more traditional. *Dulce et decorum est pro patria mori*. But it may be that some will find in Lenin's unquestioned standing as a revolutionary innovator an element that makes him at least a more profoundly tragic figure than Britain's commander in the field.

What lessons, if any, may Christian theologians learn from

Lenin's history? We are concerned here with something different from the Christian-Marxist dialogue; we are concerned with a particular individual whose name is necessarily linked with a particular series of events. Plekhanov wrote a valuable study of the role of the individual in history; he could well have included Lenin among his illustrations. For Lenin was uniquely the man of his hour; the events in which he was involved shaped him; yet he left his imprint upon them. When I read, for instance, in Theodore Dan's Menshevik account of the origins of Bolshevism, or in Donald Treadgold's study of Lenin and his adversaries, or in the recent biography of Martov,[12] the history of the neo-scholastic arguments that rent the Russian political emigration in the first decade of this century, I am made vividly aware that these debates among obscure men and women, living on the periphery of Edwardian society, meeting in dingy halls[13] to argue issues that must have seemed meaningless to those who saw themselves securely placed at the very centre of English life, who very naturally identified their own concerns with the very substance of civilized existence, must have seemed eccentric and scandalous, the vapourings of wild men who yet need not be feared by reason of their drab obscurity, which somehow cut them down to size. We do well, however, to remember that it was in the arguments of such men as these that the future of the world was shaped. One measures something of the shock their victory gave to the men, for instance, of 'Milner's Kindergarten', even after the horrors of the Western Front from 1914–18, if one reads between the lines of a memorable 'thriller' of the early twenties, John Buchan's fourth adventure of Richard Hannay, *The Three Hostages*. The cachet its impressive villain, Dominic Medina, gained from his record of service in the armies of Kolchak and Denikin in the Russian Civil War, the implicit equation of Bolshevism with a vast, subterranean tide of evil, flowing over the post-war world, the suggestion that the Fascist revolution in Italy is a prototype of the sort of national revival which may help to halt it: all these avowals, conscious or unconscious, on the part of the author are typical of a general mood of shock. There is also in *The Three Hostages* an inescapable note of anti-Semitism; Bolshevism is implicitly a Jewish phenomenon, its exponents déracinés Jews. Of course a part of this shock is accounted for by the inescapable reality of terrorism used as a weapon of defence; by such events as the murder of the Russian royal family, by religious persecution, etc. There was much, very much from the beginning in the Bolshevik régime to outrage the humane; one

can trace from Lenin's beginnings the road that ran through
Stalin's methods in the 'solution' of the problem of the peasantry
in 1929,[14] when he embarked on his policy of remorseless industrialization, through the unspeakable horrors of the purges in the
late '30s, right to the invasion of Czechoslovakia in the late
summer of 1968. Yet it is not simply moral shock that one discerns
in such early reactions; it is rather the dawning of a hidden
suspicion that the assumptions on which the old world rested
were insecure, that new forms of human association could be
fashioned to replace an old that had not been made new quick
enough to meet legitimate criticism. True, the revolution had
happened in a society where a theologically defended autocracy
had resisted to a most bitter end any plea that it should give place
to a constitutional order. One absolutism might have been
thought to have replaced another. But what had assumed power
was (to borrow Burke's phrase used of the Jacobins) an 'armed
doctrine'. And although Lenin's hope that revolutionary infection would spread throughout Europe had not been fulfilled, in
Germany it had needed the sinister agency of the Freikorps to
win the day against the Spartakusbund.

'Can any *great* thing come out of Nazareth?' Certainly one must
not romanticize the Russian revolutionary emigration. Joseph
Conrad in his great novel *Under Western Eyes* has given us a
profound study of its ethos, and one that penetrates its sombre
depths. Yet out of the debates I have mentioned there was
fashioned the concept of the state as an organ of effective social
transformation under the controlling direction of the party élite:
an immensely powerful concept, giving definitive shape to the
idea of revolution *by* the state as distinct from revolution *against*
the state.[15] It is fascinating, if horrifying, to compare Soviet
apologetic for the human cost of state-planned industrialization
with the nineteenth-century English utilitarian defence of
extreme *laissez-faire* as justified by the benefits of the industrial
transformation it allegedly made possible. (As Maurice
Merleau-Ponty well brought out in his definitive analysis of the
ethics of Stalinism – *Humanisme et Terreur* – the principles on
which Stalin's monstrous policies were defended by his devotees
constituted an extraordinary fusion of Benthamite *Erfolgsethik*
with radical dialectics.)[16] But the intellectually sophisticated
defender of the Leninist enterprise is quick to point out that in so
far as only through such industrialization can human living standards be raised, human opportunities of life and experience
enlarged, provided that the work is set in hand self-consciously,

it must be regarded as the way humanity must take if it is to assume control of its own destiny. It is as the necessary condition for the realization of the authentic Promethean vision of human advance that Leninist revolution, understood in terms of Marxian dialectics, which at once inspire and interpret it, is presented as in fact the concrete answer to the perennial question *peri hontina tropon chrē zēn*.[17] It is an answer given in terms of a way of life that is essentially collective, not individual, but one that is truly capable of realization through the utmost self-dedication of the individual person. And such a person was Vladimir Ulyanov. His claim to have decisively enlarged the scope of Marxist revolutionary theory is based on his actual achievement. In his biography theory and practice achieve a new unity, and if the desperate evils his revolutionary practice brought seemingly inevitably in its train set a question-mark against the validity of his doctrine, it is open to his apologists to argue that tragedy is of the very substance of human history, and that at least such a man as Lenin showed himself willing not to suffer blindly as the plaything of an inevitable destiny, but rather to pay the price, if necessary, of the guilt he incurred, that seemed demanded, if human kind, and in the first instance the war-weary people of Russia, its peasants as well as its industrial workers, were to be brought some way towards a promised land.

It is on the relative insignificance of the beginnings of this tremendous, world-shaking enterprise that we do well first to ponder. Contrast the scruffy, ill-lit halls in which Bolshevik and Menshevik met to argue with, for instance, the contemporary setting of Archbishop Randall Davidson's busy comings and goings. No one can read Bell's great life of that most considerable of twentieth-century primates, without being made aware that here was a man of great wisdom and unquestionable goodness, who saw his role in part at least as that of being the very effective instrument of an informed Christian presence at the heart and centre of British life in the very heyday of Britain's imperial power. He called himself the disciple of Westcott and Lightfoot, and clearly the former's hope that the kingdoms of this world might become the kingdom of God and of his Christ was vitally real to Davidson in the obviously self-confident early years of his primacy. But what does a reader of his biography today say of the world to which with such strenuous self-discipline he sought to make himself present? It is the world which began to crumble on the August Bank Holiday of 1914, which lost the first flower of its young manhood in the seemingly purposeless shambles of the

Somme and Passchendaele, whose assumptions received an overwhelming blow, thanks to the remorselessly resolute action of a small group of intellectually and morally ruthless men in October-November 1917. Had Davidson ever heard of any of them, at least before the February revolution of Lenin's year of destiny? Or if he had, did he take them seriously?[18] We are often told by those who defend the seemingly ludicrous anachronism of an ecclesiastical establishment in a pluralist society that it makes possible an informed Christian presence in places of key importance in the determination of the development of human society. While negatively it acts as a prophylactic against the virus of an introverted clericalism (one recalls the words of the Labour MP, the late Jack Jones, during the bitter Prayer Book debates of 1927–28: 'The book we are interested in down our way is the rent book'), positively it assures that a Christian voice is heard in the places where great decisions are made. *But what places are these?*

One could certainly say (and here Valentinov's *Encounters with Lenin* is important evidence) that in Russia itself such men as Bulgakov and Berdyaev essayed a very costly Christian-Marxist dialogue; but it was in a setting where decisively atheist counsels made sure it was stifled on the one side, while a supposedly secure ecclesiastical, liturgical and theological tradition on the other showed itself obstinately unwilling to allow its spiritual resources to be brought into play in such hazardous and unfamiliar argument. But this dialogue (if we may use the word, and I think we should) was something very far away from the worlds which Davidson and his fellows rated humanly significant, far from the Houses of Parliament (scene of the bitter arguments that followed Lloyd George's pioneering social legislation, that marked the protracted struggle over the powers of the House of Lords, spanning the end of Edward VII's reign and the beginning of George V's, and that accompanied the penultimate phase of the sad tale of Anglo-Irish relations), far from Grillions and the Athenaeum. In so far as the participants on one side were found in Britain, they were found in meeting places where those at home in Lambeth and Downing Street, in Whitehall and Carlton Gardens never penetrated. It was in places into which those who were self-consciously at ease in our Zion hardly deigned to glance, that the tools which were to shake the world's foundations were being hammered out. It was in fact in the very humdrum outposts of a consciously godless world.

And what of course must be said of the Church of England of Davidson's vision must also be said of such deeply self-conscious later ventures in Christian penetration as, for instance, the Christian Frontier. Could one imagine Lenin eating and talking with J. H. Oldham in the Athenaeum?[19] The conceit is comic enough. And yet one has to ask which of the two matters most in the history of the world. If there is a lesson to be learnt here, it is perhaps only an old one to be received in a new and harsher way: the lesson that we have yet to begin to learn – what it is that Christ has done in overcoming the world that his work, which his Father has given him to do in love for that world, might be perfected. 'Not as the world giveth, give I unto you.'

And this last consideration brings me to what is perhaps the most crucially important point of all. We have to reckon with the appeal to the young today of the revolutionary image, and when, for instance, one contemplates the apparent self-confidence with which, for instance, the present Prime Minister and Foreign Secretary, Sir Alec Douglas-Home, have defended the resumption of arms sales to South Africa,[20] one can understand the powerful attraction of Che Guevara for the prematurely disillusioned. Yet as I have tried to argue, Lenin is the veritable paradigm of revolutionary dedication, and study of his history continuously reminds us of the dark side of such commitment. But at the same time he presents the student of his life with a classical realization of the unity of theory and practice, a realization whose fruits abide to this present. In his life and work the Marxist idea of social transformation became terrifyingly incarnate, and we live in the shadow of the impact of that incarnation; for the weight of that incarnation lies abundantly over the world of the bitter Sino-Soviet dispute. Dare we find here a parable of the fundamental Christian reality, the Incarnation of the Word of God, the *kenōsis* of the eternal Son? Certainly for myself I find in the study of Lenin's concrete definition of the revolutionary idea, in his achievement, the source of a continual impulse to engage anew with the doctrine of the Incarnation, with the fundamental realities of Christology and soteriology. The kind of theological escape-route followed, for instance, by Professor John Knox,[21] for whom theology has rotted away into the mere articulation of the presuppositions of a narrowly ecclesiastical piety, is shown for what it is: a road that leads nowhere except to the enclosed valley of self-indulgent, spiritual illusion. If the Christian faith is true (and unless its truth-claims can be sustained we had better have done with it for ever), its truth is constituted by the correspondence of its credenda with harsh, human reality, and with the divine reality that met that human reality and was broken by it, only in that breaking to achieve its healing. At the foundation of the faith there lies a deed done, an incarnating of the eternal in the stuff of human history. It is not the delicate subtlety of our imaginative interpretations that is constitutive of this penetration of our human lot; what these interpretations seek to represent is the *act* that sets our every essay in conceptualization in restless vibration. For by that deed the very foundations of our human world were laid. What was it, what is it, this revolutionary act? At least let us be sure that it is act; for unless it is act, if it be no more than satisfying spiritual idea, it is vacuous and the world remains unshaken. Dare we convert it into spiritual idea and suppose that we remain Christ's true disciples? Rather, for good or ill, we are thralled to the conviction that as Peter Taylor Forsyth remarked, we have no other final weal apart from our share in that glorifying of the Father by the Son and the corresponding glorification of the Son by the Father.

To some it may seem strange that a comment on the greatest revolutionary of the twentieth century should end by a sharp reference to contemporary theological controversies. It is hard to conceive what a Christian/Leninist dialogue would be like; one recalls Lenin's brusque rejection of its brave initiation by his former friends, Berdyaev and Bulgakov (the last arguably the greatest Russian Orthodox theologian of the twentieth century and certainly the author of one of the profoundest studies we have of the *kenōsis* of the Incarnation). Yet as one allows oneself to be interrogated by this formidable man in the greatness of his achievement, in his decisive continuation of the Marxist tradition into the twentieth century, one is made aware that the temptation to which Christian theology is continually subject, of withdrawing into the securities of metaphysical idealism, is a temptation which would render that theology once and for all empty of significance in a world on which Lenin has sharply set his mark. It is not through new dimensions of the life of the spirit that we are redeemed, but by an act that was as much and more a matter of concrete flesh and blood reality as Lenin's in October. It was an act whose agent knew what he was doing; this though the route of his endurance and its cost was inevitably hidden from him. But Christ in the hour of his passion was no 'sleep-walker', as Hitler was in the autumn of Stalingrad. We can find in Lenin in October a parable whereby to renew our understanding of the decisive discontinuity of Christian reality and metaphysical idealism. It may be that it is only if we are prepared for such a theological discipline that we shall find a significant word to speak at a time when violence is assuming in the eyes of many of the young a quasi-mystical, humanly liberating significance which it most certainly did not have for the greatest revolutionary of the twentieth century, Vladimir Ulyanov.[22]

POSTSCRIPT

1978

It is now nearly eight years since this paper (based on a lecture given in 1970 in the Divinity School at Cambridge to mark the centenary of Lenin's birth, delivered on the most convenient day nearest to the actual centenary, which happened to be St George's Day, that attracted an encouragingly large number of students of sorts not usually seen in theological faculties) was written. Some notes have been added, notably one on Kautsky and Bernstein, and one recording an interesting statement included in a Cambridge sermon by Bishop Huddleston during his period in Stepney; I have also made one correction.

Although some of the issues of which this paper treats are taken further in the next two essays in this volume, namely 'Law, Change and Revolution: the Concept of *Raison d'État*' and 'Absolute and Relative in History', a postscript seemed to me for various reasons to be called for. At the risk of seeming to wish to advertise myself, I may be allowed to say that behind this paper, there lies a course of lectures, first given in Cambridge in 1967, on Christianity and Marxism, and behind that course the work I did (including the long, final essay) in preparing, at the invitation of G. K. A. Bell, then Bishop of Chichester, a volume of essays, entitled *Christian Faith and Communist Faith*.[23] Bishop Bell's experience and interests (extending to areas far removed from the revision of the Canon Law to which in the fifties so much official Anglican energy, at least in England, was devoted) had made him the obvious convener of a small Committee set up in 1949 to consider whether there was a specifically Anglican 'word' to be spoken in the world of the 'Cold War', the world of the 1948 Communist seizure of power in Czechoslovakia, and of the Berlin blockade and air-lift, that was compelled to accept Mao's victory in China, that was soon to see the invasion of South Korea by North Korea, and the crisis that led to Attlee's flight to see Truman in the autumn of 1950 to dissuade him (if possible) from allowing MacArthur the use of nuclear weapons, to MacArthur's eventual dismissal, and thence inevitably to the period of Senator Joseph McCarthy's hardly challengeable dominance of the American political scene. (The Alger Hiss affair was already a matter of history, and its significance had been pondered in Lionel Trilling's novel, *The Middle of the Journey*, first available in this country in the autumn of 1948.) An Anglican 'word'? Dr Bell persuaded the fellow-members of his Committee that what was needed was a book, and I was invited to edit it. The essayists included Professor H. A. Hodges, Denys L. Munby, M. B. Foster, Arnold Toynbee, Professor Christopher Evans, R. V. Larmour, Father Martin Jarrett-Kerr, CR, and myself. In the *Bishoprick* (the diocesan monthly magazine of the diocese of Durham) in February 1954, Dr Michael Ramsey wrote of the volume with rare perception of the editor's conception of its significance. That is: he saw that the editor had done his work and written his essay under the conviction that any effective Christian *riposte* to Marxist Communism must take the shape of a profound vision of God in Christ articulated in a worship, I might have said, a liturgical spirituality that effectively realized its import in the lives of men and women of the second half of the twentieth-century. In my essay I insisted that Christians shared with Marxists an ultimate hostility to any form of idealism, using the term to indicate a view of spiritual activity as autonomous, as in fact creating its own objects: this because for the Christian the *locus stantis vel cadentis fidei* was the Father's raising of his Son from the tomb 'on the third day', this to be understood as his Amen to the work of human salvation that the Son had achieved in human flesh and blood. 'In the beginning was the Work.' For the Christian who read the fourth gospel aright, the subtle metaphysics of its preface was only a prolegomenon to a narrative that sought to bear witness to the fact that at the foundation lay the deed done in human flesh and blood into which the very fullness of the Word was (if I may so speak) poured out and its deepest, most arcane sense disclosed.

The paper on 'Lenin and Theology' suggests much more than a change of emphasis (though its sequel, 'Absolute and Relative in History', recaptures some of the mood of the earlier essay). The references to the concrete realities of historical event and controversy are much more frequent, indicative *maybe* of a greater responsiveness to 'the unity of theory and practice', or just possibly of a very tentative move towards the realization of a 'religionless Christianity'. Yet its concluding paragraphs (although there is no reference to the world of Christian worship) insist that where Christian theology is concerned, or I might say, where very many Christians' understanding of their own faith is concerned, it may be that it is through serious engagement with the claims of Marxist-Leninism, that those vocationally committed to the progress of theology will find their way to a re-creation of the doctrine of Christ's person and work, and of the doctrine of God as Trinity in Unity, that is bound up with it, which neither seeks to ignore the reality of the very difficult intellectual problems that these conceptions raise, nor to admit them only to pretend that a greater theological wisdom would never have allowed the doctrinal development with which they seem inextricably bound up. To say this is most certainly not to claim that such engagement is the only means whereby, for instance, the sense of the notion of divine self-limitation, focused in the person of the Incarnate, may be plumbed. It is only that to submit to interrogation by exponents of a most rigorous atheism – (one whose unity of theory and practice certainly justifies the student in using of it Edmund Burke's characterization of the Jacobins, 'an armed doctrine') – is to say farewell to the more leisurely and gentlemanly styles of apologetic, whose end, Whitehead once said, might be described as 'seeking to furnish us with new reasons for continuing to go to church in the old way'.

Dr Bastiaan Wielenga's most valuable book *Lenins Weg zur Revolution* appeared in 1973,[24] and was not therefore in my hands when this paper was written, or the lecture on which it was based was delivered. (Indeed inasmuch as the former was published in March 1971, I could claim against Professor Helmuth Gollwitzer, who supervised Dr Wielenga's researches, and who introduces his book, that that book was not in fact the first attempt to assess Lenin's significance for the theologian!) The scale of Dr Wielenga's book makes it one of the greatest importance, and the account he gives of Lenin's arguments with Peter Struve and more particularly with Serge Bulgakov is utterly absorbing. The Lenin-Bulgakov debate has a paradigmatic quality, all the more so when one remembers that Bulgakov remained a layman until the very period of the Russian Revolution, professing economics, involved *inter alia* in important discussion concerning imperialism and the accumulation of capital, so that one is not surprised to find his writing quoted, discussed and criticized in arguments on these topics between Rosa Luxemburg and Nikolai Bukharin.[25]

Certainly Bulgakov's philosophical formation through which he first emancipated himself from a dogmatic Marxist commitment was in a sense idealist; but his idealism was of an idiosyncratic character, inspired (as was the case also with his associate Nicholas Berdyaev) by what, in his study, he read into the extraordinarily wide-ranging work of Immanuel Kant, who if his place in the history of German philosophy as defined for instance by Professor Richard Kröner in his influential study *Von Kant bis Hegel*,[26] or indeed by Josiah Royce in his very readable account of the development of modern idealism,[27] makes it inevitable that he should be classified as an idealist, yet was the exponent of views vastly different from those who followed him, whether one thinks of Fichte, Schelling or Hegel, and who (a much more important fact) included in the massive *oeuvre* of his 'critical period' treatment of absolutely fundamental philosophical issues (e.g. the relations of sense-awareness, understanding, imagination and reason, substance and causality, self-knowledge, space and time, the nature of geometry, moral goodness, human freedom, the relations of teleological and mechanical schemes of explanation, the enterprise of the transcendent metaphysician, evil) that demand the closest attention of any serious student of philosophy. Anyone who found his way out of a doctrinaire materialist commitment by 'going to school' with Kant, was bound by his choice of master to philosophize and not simply to exchange one *Weltanschauung* for another.

Thus Bulgakov equipped himself to argue with Lenin, and if a pervasive inability either to say Yes or No to revolution hobbles his dialectical skill, one could say that he prepared himself for the work he did later as a theologian, and not least for the signal contribution he makes to Christology in his very bold essay – *Du Verbe Incarné*[28] – in which, inspired in part by the image of the humiliated Christ in Russian religious thought and literature, he presents an understanding of Christ's person, totally free of the taint so often infecting treatises *de Verbo Incarnato* from contemplation of the various representations of the Christos Pantokrator.

The last report produced by the recently dissolved Doctrinal Commission of the Church of England (of which Professor Maurice Wiles was chairman) treated of the subject of *Christian Believing*.[29] The differences of view among the members of the Commission were made plain by the excellent device of including in the volume containing the report a number of essays on a variety of issues related to the central topic of *Christian Believing* by individual members of the Commission. With this clear indication of the differences between the members, it was (quite reasonably) felt that the authority of a report, which all of them were prepared to sign, was impressively enhanced. No one would question that the report is on the whole excellently written; and though there are passages, e.g. the sentences on the highly technical doctrine of analogical predication, where clarity and (in my opinion) accuracy has been sacrificed to brevity, the Commission has offered to the church at large an essay which is certainly a valuable *point de départ* for serious discussion. Thus even one as deeply critical of its approach as the present writer found it an excellent text to use in lecturing on the epistemological problems of faith. But it merits mention in this postscript for two reasons.

1. Its bias is undoubtedly subjectivist in the sense that it obstinately treats Christian believing (whether what is in mind is belief in the occurrent or in the dispositional sense, i.e. in the sense of an identifiable act of faith or in that of a settled habit of mind, or commitment,) as if it could be scrutinized in virtually complete aversion from what it is that is believed. Yet belief is surely intentional, and if we are to make clearer to ourselves what it is to believe something to be the case, we cannot disregard the sort of thing it is which we are said to be justified to believe to be the case. If this language seems to ignore the distinction often stressed (with more passion that precision of analysis) between 'believing in' and 'believing that', I would point out that if I say that I 'believe in' something, the 'believing' to which I refer has surely a determinate direction. The verb 'believe' is in fact a transitive verb.

Most certainly any discussion of Christian believing in the world today must take very seriously what I might call the hesitating *tâtonnements* of the still agnostic enquirer. In the first and (still) the only volume of his powerful impressive *Christologie*,[30] the German theologian, Dr Heinrich Vogel, whose theology was in part hammered out in the setting of the German Confessional Church's opposition to Hitler, and developed in the harsh, yet arguably invigorating climate of East Germany, points out that the question: 'What think you of Christ?' is Jesus' own question, and that the beginnings of a Christology may well be found in his continuing interrogation of those brought in some sense into contact with him, whether through the records of scripture, the witness of believing men and women or otherwise. (In the last

section of my address on 'The Future of Man', the preceding
essay in this volume, I have briefly referred to the way in which
'the lonely figure, dying in agony upon the cross, crying out in
dereliction to the Father, whom he believes to have forsaken him,
remains ceaselessly interrogating men and women outside as
well as within the Christian churches, concerning his significance, and that of his supreme hour. "What think you of this
man?" '.) Certainly no one can without blasphemy of a far greater
sort than that detected by Mrs Mary Whitehouse, and her like, for
instance in stories woven around the imagined aftermath of
Jesus' crucifixion, set limits or frontiers to the forms of that
interrogation. Whatever criticism may be made of contemporary
liturgical changes, no praise can be too high for the way in which
in the revised Roman Catholic 'Solemn Commemoration of the
Passion and Death of the Lord', prayers carefully worded (even if
the peculiar literary genius of Thomas Cranmer is lacking) first for
those who do not believe in Christ and then for those who do not
believe in God immediately precede the unveiling and adoration
of the cross, thus wonderfully conveying the fact that, lifted up
on a Roman cross, Jesus of Nazareth would draw all men unto
himself. (I might add that the revised prayer for the 'people of the
old covenant' is in my judgment, also impeccably worded.) If it is
part of the purpose of liturgy to enable men and women to realize
there and then in the action of common prayer, in themselves,
the gospel out of which that liturgy is born and which it seeks to
make contemporary, the order I have mentioned seems most
excellently to fulfil it.

But it is a Christ-orientated generosity, of which I speak, and in the
end, it is impossible to acquit the statement on *Christian Believing*
of treating the certainly complex universe of Christian faith as if it
were a universe of human activity that could be scrutinized as
something self-contained, even as a kind of awareness that in a
measure created its own objects. Thus study of such very important issues as doctrinal development and indeed doctrinal criticism is presented as if they were concerned simply with phases in
the historical evolution of an important area of human subjec-
tivity.

Certainly the sort of criticism I am here making of the pervasive
bias of this Report could be made, indeed has been made, by very
able writers who can hardly be regarded as sympathetic with
Marxism. Thus in *New Blackfriars* for February 1977, Michael
Dummett (the Wykeham Professor-designate of Logic at Oxford)
contributed an article to a discussion of the problem of Christ's

Resurrection (to which Father Fergus Kerr, OP, also made an interesting contribution)[31] that was like a breath of fresh air, for all the author's ignorance of recent study of the relevant New Testament material. This because suddenly into an argument that much rehearsal had made tired, we had an intrusion by an absolutely first-class philosophical and formal logician, to whom vague generalization concerning the 'sudden or gradual birth of the conviction that Jesus was alive' is no substitute for precise and rigorous conceptual analysis. It is as if a detachment of the Welsh Guards had engaged with 'Dad's Army'!

2. But it is more than its strong realistic bias that makes Marxist interrogation cathartic for the theological 'life-style' of the Report on *Christian Believing*: more too than its uncompromising atheism (in the single sense of denial that the concept of God has any application *in re*). It is that in Marxism we have a form of atheistic humanism that is profoundly historical in its underlying perspective. It is scarcely credible that in a report which makes considerable play with the notion of 'culture gap' there is no reference to the work of Karl Marx, especially in view of the renewed interest in his work on the part of many who are not, in the first instance, seeking a relevant form of political commitment. One could mention the serious academic attention paid to his Paris MSS and to his early Critique of Hegel's *Philosophie des Rechts*; or indeed (and the report on *Christian Believing* is in some sense, an Anglican document) the imperative to rethink the whole history of the seventeenth-century conflict of Anglican and Puritan imposed by the voluminous writings of Christopher Hill, from his early study of the economic problems of the English Church from Whitgift to Laud to his fascinating revaluation of the life and work of John Milton (the last admittedly only published in 1977). No contemporary English theologian is more obviously aware of the significance of the 'culture gap' for exegesis and theological foundations than D. E. Nineham; yet unlike R. G. Collingwood, to whom he properly acknowledges a great debt, even while one who, like myself, had the advantage of hearing three courses of lectures by that remarkable philosopher (and indeed his Inaugural Lecture as Professor, not to mention two remarkable isolated lectures on Bradley's *Appearance and Reality*) is compelled to think that he seriously over-simplifies the complexity of Collingwood's thought, Nineham totally ignores Marx.

3

Law, Change and Revolution:
Some Reflections on the Concept
of Raison d'État[1]

The topic of *raison d'état* is one that has recently received very little attention at the hands of political theorists in the United Kingdom. Thus, when in 1941 Rohan Butler published in England a book entitled *The Roots of National Socialism*,[2] he was able to present the complex tradition of German political thinking as little more than an elaborate prolegomenon to Hitler's *Mein Kampf*, and Rosenberg's *Myth of the 20th Century*.[3] Butler's book received, the following year, an admirably searching and discriminating analysis by Franz Borkenau (in the now defunct monthly *Horizon*). Borkenau, who had already won a high reputation for his study of the Communist International, had no difficulty in convicting Butler of a substantial number of serious over-simplifications, and also a failure altogether to reckon with the dimension of historical self-consciousness, inevitable in serious political thinking, since the monumental work of Hegel and Marx.

I mention this book which was, as both title and date make plain, a scholarly essay in propaganda, because it illustrates very clearly the resistance of those schooled in characteristically British styles of political thinking, to engaging seriously with the sorts of consideration which continental European experience has compelled, however distasteful the results of their reflections, continental thinkers to tackle. Here, of course, I may be reminded of Bernard Bosanquet's *Philosophical Theory of the State* (first published in 1899), and indeed, by those familiar with the detail of its arguments, of certain sections in F. H. Bradley's *Ethical Studies*. It is well known that in the bitter years of the first world war, L. T. Hobhouse found himself so outraged by Bosanquet's defence of the conception of the state as a supra-individual, spiritual whole, in whose order alone the individual must find concrete expression of his authentic will, that he felt bound to write a brilliant reply to parts of its central argument in his essay *The Metaphysical Theory of the State*. For Hobhouse, behind Bosanquet there lurked Hegel, and for him Hegel embodied in his sonorous, turgid and obscure prose, the ideas that Wilhelmine Germany was putting into practice. Yet a study of Bosanquet's work in its historical context reveals that it is less a translation of Hegel's ideas into contemporary English philosophical prose, than one of a number of treatises on political theory, in which a group of thinkers, all of them in different degree indebted to the contributions made to political philosophy by Rousseau and his successors, sought to establish alternative foundations for political attitudes, which veered between mildly radical liberalism and definitely socialist commitment, than seemed to be offered by exponents of the powerful utilitarian tradition, and especially by John Stuart Mill. It is significant to note that Bosanquet's correspondence reveals him as pro-Boer, during the second Boer War. In writing in these terms, I do no more than summarize the appraisal of the political thought of these men to be extracted from the works of Professors Klaus Dockhorn, Adam Ulam, and indeed R. G. Collingwood. Bradley, who was the most deeply original metaphysical thinker belonging to this school (although he was notoriously a solitary, even in a measure a recluse), displays a markedly different emphasis; he was profoundly conservative, and his ethical and political attitudes were suffused with a pessimism notably absent from other writers, who are loosely and inaccurately classified as British Hegelians, or British Idealists. It is a remarkable and important fact of intellectual history that although various histories of British philosophy in the last hundred years make play with a myth of Hegelian dominance in the schools, the men traditionally associated with that ascendancy failed to produce any study of Hegel himself, of lasting value, excepting only a short monograph by Edward Caird, contributed in 1883 to a series of such monographs on great philosophers, published by the Scottish publishers, Blackwood. This book, which is hardly obtainable today except in libraries and through search in second-hand bookshops, has value as an introduction to Hegel himself, far greater than the more pretentious treatises of Bosanquet and the rest. It must, of course, be remembered that access to Hegel's actual work by members of this school (including Caird himself) was crippled by the fact that it was only a few years before the first world war that his crucially important *Jugend-schriften* were made available in Nohl's edition, although Dilthey, in his book on the young Hegel, had already indicated the importance of their contents.[4]

To read Hegel's actual political writings, after acquiring a measure of familiarity with the British tradition that claimed his inspiration, is to be made aware that they come out of a vastly different political experience. If, indeed, he shares with his English and Scottish readers a common schooling in Greek and Roman history, and also in the Jewish and Christian scriptures (although a familiarity gained in a Lutheran environment, as distinct from one shaped by Anglican, Scottish Presbyterian, or English Nonconformist traditions), he is using the fruits of this education in reflection upon a political history and development to which the English situation, before and after the Whig revolution of 1688, offers no parallel. It is true that in his earlier political writings, in some sense preparatory to the *Philosophy of Right*, he offers many indications of the sorts of actual problem of political organization that engaged him. Yet the kind of sympathetic historical insight demanded, if we are to make sense, for instance, of his distinction between 'civil society' and 'the state' calls for a fusion of detailed historical knowledge with precise philosophical judgment, not often at the disposal of the professional philosopher.

It may seem that too much space has been devoted to a summary essay on an episode in the history of academic British political philosophy. But as the historian who has pondered Gerhard Ritter's recent exhaustive study of the role of the army and of military power in German political history[5] is inevitably made aware, it is in Hegel's writings (obscure and contradictory as they often are), that the issues raised by the opposition of those elements in political organization signified by the terms *Rechtstaat* and *Machtstaat* receive unmistakable expression.

It would be a mistake to ignore the presence of just this tension in the context of very different forms of historical experience. Thus, in his very interesting lectures, *Thoughts on the Constitution*,[6] L. S. Amery stresses the supreme significance in British Government of the principle: 'The King's Government must be carried on', against the traditional liberalism of Dicey's emphasis on the sovereignty of 'the King in Parliament', and, by implication, the supremacy in theory of the legislative over any competing source of public authority, even against the sharp modifications of that doctrine made by Walter Bagehot in his widely

influential study of *The English Constitution*. Amery insists that, in
the British Constitution, it is government that is affirmed as the
first and paramount reality. In terms of a distinction worked out
with great scholarly precision by Professor C. H. McIlwain in his
book *Constitutionalism: Ancient and Modern*,[7] Amery insists on the
primacy of *gubernaculum* over *jurisdictio*. Thus he insists that
government must, by its very nature, be free to act drastically to
ensure, for instance, that hardly foreseeable menaces to society's
well-being, whether by way of threat from without, of violence
from within, or sudden economic emergency, shall be met with
the appropriate action. Certainly such response should be
scrutinized and duly ratified by Parliament; but the latter's role is
subordinate to the initiative that may need to be taken in the first
instance by ministers of state, using to the full the resources of
professional advice at their disposal, but still, in the end, accepting the responsibility of decision. Amery does not ignore the
tremendous importance of the rule of law and of constitutional
safeguard, constraining ministers, in certain circumstances, to
bow before strongly voiced criticism, and in others to acknowledge obstacles in established law likely, if not certain, to be
upheld in due course by an independent judiciary to changes and
actions they may think, in principle, desirable. Thirty years have
passed since Amery wrote his lectures, and it might be claimed
that in the interval, in practice, the power of the executive at
least to impose its will on Parliament has been considerably
strengthened, even (in the opinion of R. H. S. Crossman and
others) extended in the direction of a presidential system. Yet it
would be a mistake, in emphasizing the element of drastic action
which McIlwain refers to as *gubernaculum*, to ignore the fact that
what he refers to by that term, emphasizing as he does the
element of decisive response to the unforeseen, of drastic and
far-reaching action, of decision by the man who might say, in
Truman's phrase 'The buck stops here', is still government. *Quod
Caesar imperat legis habet vigorem*. Even if prime ministerial decision has the force, not of law but of choice to be implemented,
it remains decision taken by Prime Minister (or President), in
his official capacity. What may be justified as necessary on
grounds of security which, in the nature of the case, cannot
be communicated except to a very small number of people, cannot be justified in the name of the pursuit of continued power
for the Prime Minister (or President) as individuals. It is arguable (to refer to a recent example),[8] that what is most deeply
distressing in the Watergate affair, is the apparent readiness

of President Nixon to invoke the prerogatives of 'first executive' to conceal and thereby to connive at actions taken, not in the name of American security, but in the interests of his own political campaign for re-election.[9]

In government the use of power is inevitable, and the forms of that use remain as varied as the sorts of task with which government is confronted. In Great Britain our insularity, combined with our sometimes precariously maintained naval supremacy, has enabled us to concentrate our critical attention on the exercise and control of power *within* our society. Here again we are facing a very complex situation at the present time, compelled as we are to reckon with an increasing demand for effective representation at the level of central government of national and regional groups, remote from Westminster, and with the rapid and clearly discernible emergence of a syndicalist pattern in relations between government and governed, in the sphere of industrial relations. Again where other sorts of pressure group make themselves felt, they exercise a measure of considerable influence on party policy, both at the national and local level, etc. Yet we still take for granted the stability and security of the framework within which we are enabled to come to terms with the sorts of changes I have mentioned, assuming the constancy of a particular sort of political tradition. We turn aside from the sorts of reality of which we are immediately aware when we see that *gubernaculum* must sometimes explicitly and also implicitly extend to defence of the context, within which the sorts of issue I have mentioned may be faced. It is only in such moments of supreme crisis as July 1940 that we are made sharply aware of the sombre and yet impressive reality of *raison d'état*. I mention that month; for it was in that month, when, to avert the possible undermining of that naval supremacy which, partly perhaps as a result of German naval losses in the Norwegian campaign of April of that year, for all its frightening success in extending the Nazi grip on Europe, we had been able to maintain, was suddenly threatened by the possible accession of the French fleet to our enemies. Hence the action of Mers-el-Kebir, to which I wish briefly to turn. At the outset however I might mention that it is often claimed that, tragic and terrible though the consequences of that action were, it was only the readiness of the British Government to authorize it and to see it carried through, which convinced Roosevelt that Britain was now determined to resist Hitler to the bitter end. I refer to this effect of the action in question as illustrative of the strange dignity with which action, possibly justified only by reference to *raison d'état*, can be invested, giving to such action a dangerous attraction to the imagination of those fascinated by the exercise of power for its own sake.[10]

It may seem a mistake to use as an example an episode taken from the extreme circumstances of the high summer of 1940. Yet the action against the French fleet, involving as it did the use of armed force against those who, a very few weeks previously, had been allies of the United Kingdom, and jeopardizing for the immediate future the whole Free French movement, was taken because the adherence of even a section of the French fleet to Germany threatened Britian's surviving maritime security. 'Liberty', wrote Montesquieu, 'not being the fruit of all climates, is not within the reach of all peoples.' If it was Britain's insular separation from the mainland of Europe which was a *necessary* condition of her survival, that survival demanded, as a further condition, the affirmation and defence of her continuing naval supremacy.

In conversation in 1951 with a French philosopher of my own age, Jacques Havet,[11] on the marked differences in style between contemporary post-war British and French philosophy, it was suggested to me that the British had not lived, as the French had done, in 1940, through the disintegration of a society. *Note*: he spoke of the disintegration of a society, clearly referring to something more profound than a great military disaster. Yet this disintegration, accelerated as it had been by the skill of German propaganda in the 1930s, exploiting for instance to the full the divisive effect on French public opinion of such events as the Civil War in Spain, showed itself in an almost total rejection, whether active or passive, of the political institutions of the Third Republic, that is of the French state. These institutions were clearly, in 1940, felt by a great many to be in no sense expressive of any sort of 'general will', and only among easily identifiable groups and individuals evocative of any sort of common loyalty. The claim of the Vichy régime to embody some sort of genuine re-creation of the quality of French public life was a masquerade, as very early in the history of Pétain's régime discerning spirits were quick to notice and affirm publicly, calling attention, for instance, to the almost immediate anti-Semitism of its social policies,[12] and to its built-in subservience to a conqueror whose aims France had thought it necessary to resist the previous autumn, and which, after her failure to prevent their achievement, were revealed to the world as far exceeding in their compass even the purposes she had felt compelled to try to circumvent.

Yet the Vichy masquerade would not have deceived so many, or rather there would not have been, on the part of so many, a willingness to be deceived by its pretences, had there remained a vestigial confidence in, or even attachment to, the institutions which it had replaced. Certainly there were those (one thinks, for instance, of Charles Maurras and his followers) for whom the Marshal's access to power was 'the revenge of the anti-Dreyfusards' and for whom, indeed, the anti-Semitic legislation embodied a purification of French life of the infection of '*les métèques*'. There were many more for whom the Marshal was a father-figure, even today reverenced in memory as an ultimately venerable Noah-figure, his administration seen as an ark in whose shelter men and women had hoped to ride out the flood till somehow the waters subsided.

Thus Havet's words to me pinpoint the clear relation between the disintegration of a society, with the inevitable disappearance of familiar landmarks whereby men and women may orientate their choices, and the collapse of a set of political institutions. If we speak of the disintegration of a society, we refer to a situation in which men and women are no longer able effectively to communicate one with another, in which differences between them reach a point at which there is, in some circumstances, no remedy but the terrible arbitrament of civil war, and in others a kind of stumbling uncertainty in which a shared aphasia is a kind of substitute for a common objective, testifying to the admission that all are involved in the same enveloping obscurity and confusion. In such a situation the Vichy régime seemed at once a kind of surrogate for a commonly accepted political order, while yet being itself a powerful contributing factor to the breakdown of which Havet spoke.

There are no simple answers to the questions raised by an attempt to define the relations between the political institutions under which a society lives, and the life of the society in question. The temptation to suppose that all the relevant queries can be resolved in terms of a utilitarian model fails to do justice to the extent to which the collapse of the state, as a focus of loyalty, issues in the sort of breakdown in common life of which I have spoken. Yet the collapse itself may find its causes partly in existing schisms in that common life which previously and presently existing political institutions have proved powerless to heal, or, if not to heal, at least to render less than sheerly destructive. The history of French society between the wars is, in part, the history of a society whose interior contradictions provided Hitler with every sort of opportunity, by skilfully playing upon them, to undermine any effective will to resist the extension of his power. These factors, for instance, the impact of the outbreak of the Spanish Civil War, were by no means always of his own creation. His genius later, particularly in his exploitation of the chances which came his way in the crisis of 1939–40, when his opponents almost totally failed to grasp and to respond to the possibility of the strategy of the *Blitzkrieg*,[13] while labouring under the prolonged effect of the terrible ordeal of 1914–18, provided a setting in which these divisions at once of interest and of culture worked themselves out, and in which the state was powerless to assert itself against them. But *what* was it that was thus powerless to assert itself? It was arguably that which was able to assert itself in the action of Mers-el-Kebir, that *état* of which we speak when we use the phrase *raison d'état*.

We are referring to a situation of conflict when we invoke that phrase, whether actual or potential. We suppose threats that must be resisted or negatived before they assume a positive shape. What in the last analysis is seen as threatened is a set of political institutions, a way in which, by consent within a territory whose geographical area permits their effective continuance, the public business of a given society is carried on. To say this is not to invest such institutions with any implied constancy, or to indulge in any wilful forgetfulness of their historical relativity or of the extent to which they may prove powerless in certain circumstances for instance to control effectively or even to neutralize in respect of potential disastrous consequences, economic or other transformations of the society they serve. Still less is it to adopt a morally agnostic stance which refuses to rate, for instance, a society in which change is achievable by use of persuasion as in that respect superior to one in which conflicts rooted in the denial of elementary rights in matters of distributive justice must be settled by force. 'A state without the means of change is without the means of its preservation.' Yet a state remains a state.

In such an episode as Mers-el-Kebir, the sort of organization of the common life at once exercised under law, and invested with both authority and power to sustain itself, to which we refer when we speak of the state, is revealed as a positive force, as something not easily resolvable into terms of the elements into which, in a calmer setting, we should think ourselves justified in analysing it, finding in such analyses a prophylactic against the superstition of treating the state as an organism, or even as a person. In the history of the idea of *raison d'état*, as traced by Dr

Friedrich Meinecke,[14] we are made aware of the variety of political commentary that has fastened on this deeply significant factor in the field of political ideas. We are never allowed to forget either its importance or its moral ambivalence, or indeed its dangerous attraction. This last must be distinguished from the national tradition that invokes the patriot's response: rather it is the attraction of an acknowledged, irrational intractable reality, a surd element in human affairs that lies on the very circumference of that which may be submitted to the disciplines of reason. Indeed, in the end, it eludes that discipline; but for that very reason it must most strenuously be brought as nearly as possible under its sway. Certainly in Fascist thought one can trace, (for instance, in Mussolini's essay in the Italian Encyclopaedia) what one can only call a mystique of *raison d'état*, a mystique which one can indeed find also present in, for instance, the idiosyncratic English essayist, T. E. Hulme,[15] who shared with the Duce a common indebtedness to Sorel; but to reject the mystique of *raison d'état* should not blind one to its reality, nor indeed to the fact that states have historically received part of their characteristic shape from action taken in crisis aimed at affirming their autonomy as embodied organizations of the common life of a people. These actions receive their justification in part, at least, as effective assertions of the will to maintain and defend such organization. The question of the quality of the common life whose organized expression is thus at stake remains an open one.

To pass beyond this relatively restricted example demands the equipment of the professional historian, which is in no sense at my disposal; yet the wealth of illustrative material marshalled by Friedrich Meinecke in his classical study of the concept of *raison d'état* suggests that as a concept invoked in justification of a policy, it is itself frequently discernible in arguments sometimes hardly consciously formulated, used to justify ruthless action taken to safeguard the unity of a relatively precarious national society, threatened or seemingly threatened by enemies from without and/or disintegration from within. Inevitably one thinks of such examples as Richelieu's calculated intolerance towards the Huguenots of La Rochelle. In his fascinating study of Father Joseph,[16] Aldous Huxley treated of the religious inspiration of Richelieu's mentor, and this especially in respect of his master's role in the Thirty Years' War. Yet where Richelieu's action towards the Protestants in France itself was concerned, we have to reckon with an admittedly ruthless exercise of coercive force, very nearly entirely innocent in its motivation of any religious fanaticism. One is even tempted to say that its impulses were more clearly akin to those which animated the harrying of dissident Catholics in the reign of Elizabeth, than to those which had inspired the Smithfield burnings of the previous reign. The uncertain loyalty of some of the priests sent from Europe to minister to recusant Catholics after 1570, when Pope Pius V's bull, *Regnans in excelsis,* authorized on religious grounds the assassination of the Queen, seemed to constitute them a source of national danger, especially in the context of the recurrent and growing threat from Spain. To say this is certainly not to impugn the spiritual integrity of victims of the atrocious cruelties to which such agents of the English government as Topcliffe submitted men and women of the quality of Edmund Campion and Margaret Clitherow. It is simply to suggest a possible analogy between the treatment of two different religious minorities in different countries within a relatively short distance in time, one from the other.

In the first decade of the present century, Cardinal Merry del Val, Secretary of State to Pope Pius X, displayed towards those thought to be tainted by the theological ideas articulated and condemned in the encyclical *Pascendi gregis* (1907) on the one hand, and towards the French anti-clericals of the Combes government at the time of the expulsion of the religious orders from France on the other, a totally intransigent and uncompromising ruthlessness. One might treat it as an example of *intégrisme* that would accept nothing from opponent or critic except a total religious and cultural submission. But in the case of Merry del Val, this disastrous, indeed cruel, fanaticism was one side of the coin whose obverse was constituted by his passionate religious self-dedication – reflected in his long involvement in devoted pastoral ministry to the youth of the Trastevere in Rome. One might say that it was his tragedy that he had assimilated principles of government and administration only too closely akin to those which such men as Richelieu had used, but used for ends that were primarily political, rather than religious. After all, where Richelieu's involvement with the tangled skein of religious and political loyalties of the period of the Thirty Years' War was concerned, it was the threat of seemingly perilously centrifugal tendencies in French society that he feared, and fought by the methods he used at La Rochelle. He was concerned to preserve, or indeed to establish, the unity of a people largely linked one to another by community of language, by geographical proximity, and by a common cultural heritage. Moreover, when one remembers no more than the fact that this same seventeenth-century in France was the century of Corneille and Racine, of Descartes and Pascal, and indeed in the history of Counter-Reformation spirituality, the setting of one of its richest, most varied, and profoundest flowerings, one must acknowledge that that culture was very far indeed from something to be preserved, as it were, in a museum, from a past that was irretrievably gone. The foci of the dangers that Richelieu feared were various. The readiness of the great families (as notoriously the House of Guise at the time of the 'St Bartholomew'), to use their wealth and resources virtually to emancipate themselves from effective submission to a central authority, is one obvious and grave example. Such great nobles tended to behave as if the decisive authority in France were something distributed in continually changing proportions among themselves and their equals, rather than focused in a clearly recognizable, effectual central authority, endowed with the unquestioned right to a last word in matters of dispute, and equipped with power to enforce that word when it had been spoken. It was only in such an intelligibly centralized state that there would be security for the individual, and the conditions established for effective and sustained economic growth, whether through the initiative of individuals or of public authority, or of a combination of the two.[17] Furthermore only a society constrained thus to be at one with itself could confront its neighbours without recurrent choice between ultimately submissive absorption as a virtual satellite in the system of another and more powerful, national or imperial society, or potentially destructive resistance by force of arms; enjoying a measure of self-determination made possible through interior strength, supplemented by wise alliances entered into less on grounds of a community of religious commitment, let alone sentimental recollection of some past shared experience, than of common interest, provided of course that the same sort of ultimately ruthless energy displayed in coldly analytical reason and calculated flexibility of response, was continually devoted to its protection. It is in terms of such principles as these that we should evaluate the ends and methods of the statecraft of such a man as Richelieu.

I repeat that I am not an historian (that, indeed, will be obvious to the reader of this paper). But as I wrote this section, I found myself recalling the remarkable study of Philip II of Spain by Reinhold Schneider,[18] that strangely isolated German Catholic intellectual, whose writings show a perpetual brooding on the relations of personal and political morality, who was closely

linked with many of those who participated in the actions leading
to the attempt on Hitler's life on 20 July 1944, but himself repudiated the action on grounds of deep conviction of the immorality
of assassination. In his study of Philip II, he wrote neither as an
historian nor (indeed still less) as a propagandist; rather he was
concerned to throw into the clearest possible relief contradictions
in the character of that most sombre ruler. He does not attempt to
disguise Philip's ruthlessness, and his cruelty; but he does comment on the curious detachment of which he was sometimes
capable, when his policies, through his own ineptitude, or that of
those charged with their execution, went badly astray. Inevitably, he also dwells on his austerity, and on that extraordinary
courage acknowledged even by Motley (to which the late Professor David Knowles called attention in a striking passage in an
inaugural lecture at Cambridge). With Philip, in the end, we deal
with a man undoubtedly responsible for the infliction of appalling sufferings on his fellow men; but we are also dealing with a
man whose motivations can only be explored in depth by a
student who acknowledges, as Schneider does, that his Catholic-
ism was, for him, supremely significant. Certainly his faith and
his sense of the country over which he bore rule, were closely
woven together; but to understand the evil that he did, it is with
his faith that we must reckon, and with the manner in which he
used the position he occupied to promote and define it. With
Richelieu and his life, we seem to enter a different world.[19]

It may seem an indulgence in paradox for paradox' sake to pass
from Richelieu to Abraham Lincoln. Yet if Richelieu was concerned with the establishment and preservation of the unity of
France in the first half of the seventeenth century, it was the
unity of the United States of America that was at stake in the
beginnings of the the Civil War in 1862. In that war we find a
situation in which a society drawing its inspiration from a written
constitution formed in part along lines traceable back to the
second of John Locke's two *Treatises on Civil Government*, and his
related *Letters on Toleration*, found itself impelled by circumstance, in order to preserve and to perpetuate its own defining
idea, and to ensure that idea's effective embodiment, to embark
on a civil war inflicting wounds upon itself that arguably, at
certain levels, have not yet healed. The refusal by force of arms to
allow the right of the Confederate States to withdraw from the
Union may, on occasion, be justified by the *simplificateur* as, in
fact, indirect expression of the determination of the Northern
States, which remained loyal to the Federal Government, to

ensure the abolition throughout the United States of America of
the institution of slavery. No one who has read, for instance, the
novels of William Faulkner, and in particular his masterpiece
Absalom, Absalom!, will deny for a moment that the acceptance for
many years of that institution, and the endorsement of the sort of
relation to their flesh and blood human beings, in which it
involved those who benefited by it, imposed on the emotional life
and imagination of those beneficiaries the burden of continual
flight from a corrupt reality that none the less they continued to
accept. It is inevitably to a great work of imaginative literature
that I refer in order to suggest the depth of the spiritual evil to
which the South seemed prepared to continue to assent. But it
was not as a crusade that the war was initiated; it was undertaken
to preserve the Union, and its justification lay in the fact that the
society which had sought, in its beginnings, formally to define its
own significance, could not survive the withdrawal of Virginia,
Georgia, and the other states which wished to secede.

It was by a terrible exercise of force on the part of the Federal
Government that the continued existence of the Union was sec-
ured. When one recalls the details of Sherman's march through
Georgia, one finds oneself in a very different world from that
evoked by the embarrassing lines of the 'Battle Hymn of the
Republic'. I referred to the indebtedness of the 'Founding
Fathers' to Locke's second *Treatise*, a work which, in his definitive
edition,[20] Peter Laslett has shown to have been written not as a
retrospective comment on the settlement that following the
'Glorious Revolution' of 1688, but during the Exclusion Bill crisis
in the last years of the reign of Charles the Second. One can say,
therefore, that this second Treatise, with Filmer's arguments in
favour of 'divine right' disposed of by the author in its prede-
cessor, had something of the character of a blueprint. The sources
of its inspiration are various and its interpretation frequently
much more difficult than the deceptive simplicity of its style
suggests. There are deep contradictions in the argument. But if
the student reads it over against Hobbes' *Leviathan*, he is aware
that while its author lacks the classical culture which Hobbes, for
all his attachment to the new learning, shared with Machiavelli,
he shows a greater freedom from prejudice than the earlier writer, in his readiness to draw on Hooker and even on the latter's
mediaeval sources of inspiration. This emerges most clearly in
the importance of *one* (though *only one*), strain of his thought,
namely the importance he attaches to the rule of law. While he
insists on the supremacy of the legislative over the executive,

anticipating the principle of the revolutionary settlement, whereby the latter was made dependent upon the former for the voting of moneys to carry on work of government, he is careful to differentiate this supremacy from the unlimited, absolute sovereignty defended by Hobbes as alone providing an effective dyke against the anarchy that must follow the relapse of a society into the state of 'incipient war'. Thus, although the legislative is the supreme law-making body, it must not delegate to any other body its power of making laws. But who or what is to prevent it? Locke is on edge immediately his thought is moved to embrace the notion of an arbitrary power, that is a power which theoretically is independent of any limitations, except those it may impose upon itself, and that only for as long as it thinks fit. The logic of this part of his argument inclines him towards the defence of a fixed or written, as against a flexible or unwritten, constitution, with some body charged under that constitution with the duty of deciding whether the constitution in question is violated by any act of government, especially by any legislation. It was, of course, to the Supreme Court that, under the American Constitution, this task was assigned in laying upon it the duty of judicial review, concerned to decide in matters of dispute whether the constitution is violated, or not, by any particular legislation. It was also the Supreme Court's duty, in the characteristically federal constitution of the United States, to decide whether legislative action on the part of the central government showed due respect for the rights of the individual states that constituted the Union. It is a commonplace to point out that in the Civil War the constitutional issue at the deepest level concerned the relative status within that constitution of the Federal Government on the one side, charged with the promotion and defence of the Union, and the individual states on the other. There is a sombre paradox in the fact that the sort of national existence that was thought by those who, in 1862, had recourse to arms, to be at stake, was one in which the authority of law was written into its very foundations as a fundamental principle of its life. It was the conviction that that very order which had received its initial definition in the work of the 'Founding Fathers' could only be preserved and maintained by a bloody act of collective self-assertion against those who sought to modify it by their actions, that made the Federal Government's recourse to arms inevitable. Thus a classical essay in establishing the constitution itself as sovereign, and assigning to that constitution a profoundly formative role in the creation of a society, was only preserved by recourse to armed force, and that in a civil war. One recalls Churchill's words, spoken during the Civil War in Spain from 1936 to 1939: 'The more merciful will win this war. Grass grows on battlefields; it never grows on the site of scaffolds.' And here one must remember that Lincoln perished at Booth's hands too soon to prevent the 'carpet-baggers' ' descent upon the South, too soon also to play the part that arguably he could have played in binding up some of the wounds that had been inflicted. It was the Duke of Wellington who is said to have replied to a gushing woman who cried shrilly that surely a victory must be the most exhilarating experience in the world: 'Madam, a victory is the most tragic thing in the world, only excepting a defeat.'

In his excellent study of the literature produced by the American Civil War, *Patriotic Gore*, Edmund Wilson devotes one of his very best chapters to a long study of the work of Alexander N. Stephens, the former Vice-President of the Confederacy.[21] No writer of the South receives more sympathetic treatment at Wilson's hands, and it is as a stubborn, often incisive son of the French Englightenment, surviving into the late nineteenth-century, that Stephens insists on grounds of constitutional reality on the primacy within the American system of the claims made by the individual state on a man's life, over against those exercised on him by that which is effectively embodied in the policy of the Federal Government. It is as a constitutionalist (though one who has deeply suffered), that he argues. Wilson is right to insist that his writings deserve to be pondered, as they present a very serious challenge to the interpretation of the constitution which provided the ultimate justification, in relation to the fabric of American society, of the Federal Government's action in having recourse to war. But the Confederacy to which Stephens adhered was defeated, and the very character of the United States, as formed by her constitutional origin, decisively affected by the way in which, in that time of supreme crisis, the Federal Government affirmed its interpretation, and made it prevail. It is true, of course, that the United States came into being by a revolutionary act, involving indeed armed resistance to Britain's attempt to reassert her superiority. But this initial act was quickly followed by something which can be seen partly as an attempt to use a constitutional instrument as a means to conjure the uglier realities of human society and of politics out of sight. (This paper is written in a period when we have been suddenly made aware again of the ruthlessness with which the indigenous Indian population was treated in the North American sub-continent.)

The illusion that the way of life, which the constitution sought both to articulate and to secure by indicating a protective framework congruous with its principles, could be safeguarded and brought to incorporate within itself, and do justice to, insights that were inevitably, because of historical circumstance, obscure or unnoticed at the beginning, without recourse to force of arms, without the use of power, and the bitter cost of conflict, was shattered in 1862. Lincoln and Richelieu make strange bedfellows; but reflection on the two together may suggest that both alike understood, however imperfectly they could formulate the concept, the claims of *raison d'état*.

The example chosen of the American Civil War is particularly significant in view of the use made at the outset of this paper of McIlwain's distinction between *gubernaculum* and *jurisdictio*. The very role assigned to the Supreme Court under the American Constitution is clear evidence of desire to establish a form of government in which law should be supreme, and to chase the will o' the wisp of a near complete impersonality at the level of political institutions, seeking by the device of the division of powers to prevent undue preponderance in control of coercive force from accruing to one particular organ of government, and ensuring that the verdict of impartial judicial authority should be readily available to check any legislative activity likely to imperil the fundamental principles of the system. One can smile at the immense self-confidence of such an enterprise and the assurance that a scheme drafted in the light of the insights of a particular epoch, even as the result of a particular historical experience (although as I pointed out in my remarks on Locke's second *Treatise*, drawing on the resources of considerable traditions of political thinking), should be of perennial validity. What, for our purposes, is supremely significant is the fact that in the concrete the society whose formative principles were contained in this instrument had to fight for its continuance. In that crisis of its existence we have to reckon with the primacy of *gubernaculum*, and that *gubernaculum* was something much more than the originating initiative of executive action, seeking to alter the law or to change circumstances so that what might have been judged illegal shall be, in a particular case, permissible in the interests of public policy. It is the demand that one part of a particular human collectivity commit itself to war upon the rest, accepting the discipline and the bitter suffering of the conflict, as well the hard task of reconciliation, in order that the conditions under which alone the political experiment of the United States may hope to survive, shall not be in danger. The sanction of the conflict lies only in *raison d'état*, in as much as on the conflict's outcome the survival of the political reality depends. To turn aside from the struggle would be abdication from the task of preserving, and indeed expanding the state's existence.

From the crisis of the American Civil War, we may turn to the early years of the Russian Revolution. In Adam Ulam's long study of Soviet foreign policy, *Expansion and Co-existence*,[22] the reader is made familiar with a central paradox in the evaluation of post-revolutionary Russian foreign policy, namely the parallel presence and participation of accredited Soviet representatives in the conventional world of diplomatic exchange, and all that belongs with it, and the perpetuation (mainly through the activities of the Communist International) of the near-messianic 'revolutionary' impulse characteristic of the first days of the revolution. To use such language is not to ignore the tangled historical realities of the months between February and October 1917, nor to forget the sheer ruthlessness that marked the Bolshevik seizure of power. Again, if one allows oneself to speak of the October Revolution as Marxist, thereby finding its central intellectual inspiration in a set of ideas that were Western European and not indigenously Russian in origin (although it would be a serious mistake to underrate Plekhanov as a radical Marxist philosopher), one has to realize how much its initial form owed to the peculiar history of the Russian autocracy and the circumstances of the Russian revolutionary emigration, in which the schism between Bolshevik and Menshevik took place. Lenin's own fusion of Marxist insistence on the unity of theory and practice, and the dialectical analysis of social and economic development with the Narodnik tradition of desperate conspiratorial activity as a measure of revolutionary commitment, is something hardly exportable to societies with very different social and political traditions. Yet, in the context of the history of international socialism, the success of the October Revolution was an astonishing vindication of the strategy of 'revolutionary defeatism' which Lenin had advocated on the outbreak of the 1914–18 war, and which had been rejected by the majority of the leaders of the 'Second International', in the German 'Social Democratic Party' by Karl Kautsky, as well as by Eduard Bernstein. In J. P. Nettl's life of *Rosa Luxemburg*,[23] it is made plain that the young Polish woman intellectual, who had embraced Marxism, travelled to Germany, as to the Rome where the ideas she professed had achieved, and were continuing to receive, decisive articulation as the formative doctrine of a great political party. It was the German Social Democratic Party that was the 'pace-setting' member-party of the 'Second International'. Luxemburg found this party rent by the 'revisionist' controversy. Moreover on the outbreak of the 'Kaiser's War', that party made that monarchist cause its own. During the years that followed, the 'Second International' had its meetings, and Kautsky, for instance, showed a readiness to go back on his initial agreement that his party should not vote in the Reichstag against the credits required for the prosecution of the war. But further, on the far left, including Rosa Luxemburg and Karl Liebknecht, the author-ity of German social democracy was forfeited by this capitulation before the claims of embattled nationalism.

It was Lenin's hope that the Bolshevik victory in October 1917 would release the latent revolutionary potential of the European nations which, over three years of war without issue (he supposed and hoped) had been robbed of faith in the societies that had com-mitted them to the struggle. After all, it was the Bolsheviks' readiness to withdraw Russia from the war (even at the cost of Brest-Litovsk) that had substantially contributed to strengthen-ing their popular appeal *vis-à-vis* the Kerensky government. Was there not good reason to believe that in the more advanced societies of Western Europe, the revolutionary impulse would spread, and in fact by spreading help to secure the advance of the nascent Soviet society.

It is a commonplace to emphasize the contradiction at the very beginnings of the October Revolution between the appeal to the elements of mass support available, and Lenin's brutal disregard, for instance, of the claims of the Constituent Assembly and his steady accentuation of the monolithic quality of the Bolshevik dictatorship expressed in a completely intransigent ruthlessness towards opponents of the Bolshevik claim from within and from without. This cannot be regarded simply as the working out of what was implicit in his concept of the Party, as the concept was articulated in the controversies of the first decade of the century. (This though that aspect of the matter was stressed by Luxem-burg in her very remarkable pamphlet on the October Revolu-tion.) Rather, Lenin was acting as head of a government that sought, in the end, to impose on a vastly complex society a new style of political institutions whereby, indeed, the very texture of its life might be transformed. One could say that we have to do here with government interpreted in terms akin to those in which Plato's 'philosopher kings' understood their task, that is, as a work of total cultural transformation, rather than as one of disciplined reform, orderly administration, etc. One must never forget that the initial formulation of the principles, by reference to which such a revolutionary dictatorship was justified, were formulated in the Menshevik–Bolshevik controversies of the emigration. One could even say that in those controversies a new concept of *raison d'état* was formulated, wherein the state in question was understood as the effective and indispensable instrument of revolutionary transformation. *It was, however, a concept that received further and more terrible definition in the actual circumstances of the first years that followed the October Revolution.*

The paradox goes very deep. If the struggles of the Civil War made inevitable a perpetuation of the sheerly dictatorial structure of government which Lenin had set up, and on which he came to rely, the failure of the revolutionary infection to spread thrust that same dictatorship into the world of international relations, and compelled its champions to undertake the task of identifying, for example, its diplomatic victories with a profounder dissemination of its principles in the minds of men. Ulam traces this history in bold outline; but one can see a crucial facet of it in microscopic detail in Richard Ullman's study of intervention in the Russian Civil War, and especially in the most recently published third volume – *The Anglo-Soviet Accord*[24]. In his exceptionally well-documented account of the trade negotiations of 1920, in which the chief roles on the Soviet side were played by the very different figures of Krassin and Kamenev, and which coincided in time with the crisis of the Russo-Polish struggle, Ullman traces the extent to which Kamenev, in particular, played a dual game. At one level he was involved in trade negotiations, in another he was seeking to ensure that, if necessary, any renewed British intervention, whether in support of Wrangel or of Pilsudski, should be nullified by drastic industrial action. Indeed, the diaries of Field-Marshal Sir Henry Wilson, on which Ullman draws, make it plain that Kamenev's presence in the United Kingdom was construed as an effective incitement to mass revolutionary action, which might call for a counter-revolutionary use of force.

One could say that such behaviour is continuous with the messianic hope of the early months of the Revolution, which suffered its first major defeat in the confused struggles in which the Weimar Republic was born, with the victory of Ebert and Noske over Luxemburg and Liebknecht. But it is over-shadowed by a recognition that *raison d'état* of a relatively conventional sort demands the postponing of revolutionary fervour to the security of the Russian bastion against the future. The process is a complex one, and to trace its history would take one deep into the sombre story of the evolution of Soviet society; but one is perhaps justified in saying that what reached an appalling climax in one aspect of Stalin's policies, might be characterized as a victory of *raison d'état* over revolutionary messianism. It must never be thought, it was certainly never thought by Trotsky, that the latter was something that should be identified with a relatively genial anarchism; the element of ruthlessness, of unchallengeable dictatorial concentration of power, was never eliminated; but it was a ruthlessness that could in part be disguised as an essay in 'revolution by the state', under which the society's resources of coercive power are bent to the services of the universal idea, striving in the end to bend the whole course of history to its effective incarnation. Where Stalin's policies were concerned, as Maurice Merleau-Ponty makes clear in his excellent analysis of their ethical structure, *Humanisme et Terreur*, we have to reckon with choices ultimately justified by a perverse utilitarianism. But this latter can also be presented with a more brutal simplicity in terms of *raison d'état*, in terms of a survival and a prevalence on the plane of power. It is indeed in these terms that the swing from the 'popular front' policies of the mid-thirties to the preparations for the Ribbentrop–Molotov pact of August 1939 may be partly interpreted.

In the concluding example, the intrusion upon ideological politics of considerations of *raison d'état* may be interpreted almost in utilitarian terms, and this must inevitably strike readers of this paper as extremely paradoxical in view of the hostility between the utilitarian and the *étatiste* traditions of political thinking suggested at the beginning of the argument. The former tradition is in the broad sense aggressively rationalistic, usually optimistic, always impatient with unanalysable elements treated as somehow irreducible constants in the human scene, which seem to bar the way to a more or less complete subordination of traditional structures to the pursuit of human happiness. But as Merleau-Ponty excellently brings out in his study of Stalinist ethics, it is in terms of a merger between Benthamite objectivism and revolutionary dialectics that the enormities of the ethical creed of Stalinism can be made intelligible. So, too, the developing conception of the state in Soviet international relations must be understood in terms of a tactical fusion of the concept of *raison d'état* with that of the state as an organ of revolutionary transformation, and in this fusion both understandings of the state are affected one by the other.

What lessons are to be drawn from this already over-long paper? I am not quite clear, except that one of them may be a renewed insight into the flexibility of the concept of the state, and that even without going beyond its use in the relatively restricted context, provided by discussion of the concept of *raison d'état*, which might be thought to impose precise limits on variations in its sense. Yet if these examples of invocation of the principles of *raison d'état* have shown anything, they have surely suggested that the differences are as important as the similarities. But the use of a single concept under which these vastly different historical situations and responses may be subsumed, serves not only to advance the analysis of the concept in question (a secondary intellectual operation), but to advertise unsuspected analogies, giving to the student a stronger purchasehold on the elusive realities of political existence.

There is (as I have said) no doubt whatsoever that in the central tradition of political thought in the English-speaking world the concept of *raison d'état* has been profoundly suspect. J. L. Stocks, writing in 1932 of Locke's second *Treatise on Civil Government*,[25] said of the philosopher that he had thought 'to convert a beast of prey into a beast of burden'. Even in the far more complex political thought of Edmund Burke, government is characterized as a 'device of human wisdom for satisfying human wants'. The language is not far removed from Godwin's definition of morality as 'a system of public advantage'. It was with great insight that Halévy exhibited the essentially paradoxical character of Burke's thought by speaking of it as 'a half-empirical, half-mystical doctrine, founded on the principle of utility'. If reverence for the past is an important dimension of Burke's whole attitude to history and government, it is a reverence subtly and decisively different from that awakened in Hegel's breast by recollection of those institutions, (e.g. the system of Prussian public administration) in which he saw at least in germ the kind of institutionally embodied identification of individual and social whole, in which the opposition between the individual and society, characteristic of 'civil society', would be overcome.

In his recent study of the political thought of Thomas Hill Green,[26] Melvin Richter suggests that in his *Principles of Political Obligation* (the most considerable work of British idealist political theory) Green sought to integrate the insights embodied in the essentially continental tradition of *raison d'état* with elements much more characteristic of the British liberal tradition. It is well known that Green saw the state's role as one of overcoming 'hindrances to the good life'. He was a pioneer of donnish involvement in Oxford local government, and he attached the greatest possible importance to Rousseau's much criticized insistence that men may sometimes 'have to be forced to be free'. In political thought Rousseau was his master and the concept of the 'general will' his *idée maîtrise*. Yet he was before all else a teacher, who sought to train men for the work of government, by providing them with a vision of its significance and of that common good, which was its end and by which their efforts, whether in political life or in public administration, they might help to promote. The Cambridge historian G. Kitson Clark in his book, *Churchmen and the Condition of England 1832–1885*,[27] is justified in his suggestion that Green's state is a kind of secular counterpart of the church as the Body of Christ, and Richter is similarly perceptive in entitling his study of Green *The Politics of Conscience*. Moreover it is always Rousseau who is Green's intellectual master, and although Rousseau in the very obscure sections of *The Social Contract* which he devotes to the figure of 'the legislator' shows himself sharply aware of the problem how the state shall be called into being and sustained, it is characteristic of him that he casts the Lawgiver and not the Warrior for this profoundly significant, creative role.[28] One wonders on what side Green would have stood in the Governor Eyre case, that mini-Dreyfus affair of late nineteenth-century England. Although passages in his work in which he extols the achievement of Napoleon, without any apparent perception of the cost at which it was achieved, show an unattractive kinship with the brutal romanticism of Thomas Carlyle, one may hope that on this issue conscience would have ranged Green with John Stuart Mill and not with Carlyle, and (one adds with regret) Charles Dickens.

Yet the problem remains, which Thucydides makes Pericles state in his last speech:

> You cannot drop the Empire now, not though loss of nerve in the crisis drive some to make a virtue of inaction. For what you have now is like a tyranny, which (so it seems) it is wrong to take but unsafe to let go. Men of the sort I mean quickly ruin a city, if anyone listens to them, or if anywhere they are their own masters: since the inactive cannot survive except by the support of the active; and the safety of submission may do for a subject city, but not for leading Power.[29]

There are circumstances in which the survival of a way of life depends upon the maintenance and effective reaffirmation of a

set of political institutions, and the maintenance and reaffirmation of those institutions is in turn only possible through the
exploitation of every resource that historical contingency, geography and the like have put at the disposal of the defenders.
'Liberty, not being the fruit of all climates, is not within the reach
of all peoples.' It was the Channel that helped in 1940 to make
British survival possible. So too did the still continuing resources
of Britain's imperial strength. Yet one might say that though most
certainly not a sufficient necessary condition, still a necessary one
was acceptance of the political institutions under which the management of the affairs of the United Kingdom were carried on.
While in France men and women were heard to say, 'Better Hitler
than a repetition of the Blum experiment', in Britain, however
deep the largely justified social discontent, there was agreement
that our institutions (however much in need of overhaul) provided the setting and the means whereby acceptable change
might be achieved, and that what Hitler would allow in their
place would fail altogether to provide a framework for a tolerable
human existence. And here inevitably the argument which might
be restated in terms of that aspect of the doctrine of the 'general
will', which regards that will as basically the 'will for a state',
rejoins earlier references in the substantive paper to the Mers-
el-Kebir episode of July 1940. To do justice to the notion of *raison
d'état* without plunging into the deadly moral and spiritual fal-
lacies characteristic in one way of Thomas Carlyle and in another
of Charles Maurras – that is the central problem.

One might say that the problem arises not only when one
considers action taken in fact to establish a set of political institutions, in the sort of context which invites men to speak of 'imposing a solution' on intractable social conflict. I am not thinking of
the sort of situation in which it is claimed that, for example, the
replacement of Allende's experiment in Chile by a brutal military
despotism, which is provoking the Roman Catholic Church in
that country to stronger and stronger protest, is justified by
bien-pensants in the name of public order or on the shallow
utilitarian ground that tyranny is preferable to anarchy. It might
be said that we heard such specious argument too often in the
thirties, to begin to believe it in the seventies. I am referring rather
to the sort of situation that confronted General de Gaulle over the
Algerian situation, after 13 May, 1958. His double entendre, 'Je
vous ai compris', remains classical and the statesmanship involved in the solution of a very complex controversy that was
clearly dragging France to the very brink of civil war, an astonish-

ing, even paradigmatic essay in the 'imposition of a solution'. It is arguable (I write as a fool) that an important element in the authority of the Fifth Republic, in so far as it may be the object of a 'general will' (again in the sense of a 'will for a state'), derives from the way in which its initial realization conveyed the solution of the Algerian question. In that crucially decisive assertion of its authority, it achieved a legitimacy that has survived (precariously enough) the barricades in the 'Boulemiche' in the summer of 1968.

In the two contrasted models of the development of political institutions, offered by Plato in the second book of his *Republic* and Aristotle in the first book of his *Politics*, the latter's construction of the emergence of the *polis* (embodying as it does, historical recollection of, for instance, the phenomenon of *synoecismus*) into the pattern of his 'four causes' analysis of growth, reveals his usual readiness to extrapolate biological patterns. But Plato (if one returns to him after a study of the contrasted politico-metaphysical mythology of his greatest critic) is shown as locating the achievement of characteristically political institutions in the need of human societies to maintain themselves against internal and external dangers. It is not as a dyke against anarchy only to be found through the concentration of all legislative and executive power in the hands of an unchallengeable central authority that Plato introduces his governing class, but as professionally trained, responsible champions of the society's continuing unity. (Aristotle rightly criticized Plato's obsession with unity as such.) Of course such action is only possible in the context of some underlying agreement (however vestigial) of the sort of way of life that those men and women want, whether informed by uniformity of assumption, or by admission of an acceptable plurality of fundamental commitments which are expected to fall within the jurisdiction of the authority in question when established. In a moment of great emergency (as in France during the Algerian crisis) issues are sharply clarified, the dangers are great enough to provide the statesman with the basis on which to act. Yet inevitably in such a situation his action has to be drastic, creative, even ruthless.

Historical analogies are always dangerous, and the author of this paper is no historian. Yet it is fascinating to compare de Gaulle's concept of the state which he sought at once to establish and to secure through his resistance to the OAS with that of Catherine de Medici in the years leading up to the 'St Bartholomew'. In her fascinating recent book on those years,[30] N. M.

Sutherland suggests with an impressive mustering of evidence that we have here to reckon fundamentally with a final catastrophic failure of Catherine's careful statecraft when the escalating tension in Paris in the latter half of August in 1572 ceased to yield to any sort of rational control, and when in a mood of dull despair she abandoned, in the last hours before the massacre, her long-drawn-out attempt to impose a kind of crude harmony and order through assertion of the state's distinctive authority.[31] Her failure stands over against de Gaulle's success, and both are surely illuminating for the analysis of the notion with which we are concerned.

The whole argument of this paper demands a sequel on the topic of conscientious objection and a remarkably effective starting-point might be provided by General de Bollardière's *Bataille d'Alger, bataille de l'homme.*[32] It is to that subject I hope later to turn, finding my starting-point in the unconditional moral inadmissibility of torture as a method of interrogation. But it is because I am convinced that such an essay *must* presuppose some recognition of power-political realities that I have felt bound to devote such space to prolegomena. My debt to Reinhold Niebuhr (and not least to his relatively late work – *Nations and Empires*[33]) will be obvious; but I would neither regard him as necessarily agreeing with what I have written, nor with the sequel.[34]

4

Absolute and Relative in History

A theological reflection on the
centenary of Lenin's birth

I

When we discuss questions relating to history, we have to distinguish two sorts of question, the one ontological and the other epistemological or logical. The two sorts of question overlap, intertwine, impinge, one upon the other. Thus, to take a familiar example, Marxism includes an answer to the question what is really happening in history, and an answer to the question to what aspect of the study of human society the historian should assign fundamental significance. Thus, very many who would not regard themselves as Marxists would admit that where, for instance, the study of the English Revolution of the seventeenth century is concerned, Marxist historians, notably Christopher Hill, have, by their insistence on the prime significance of the economic factor in the development of human societies greatly deepened our understanding of what happened. But as professional historians, they are primarily interested in the deepening of understanding achieved through an alteration of perspective, or a changed distribution of emphasis. They are not servants of a revolutionary purpose, whose fulfilment at one and the same time they suppose to be historically inevitable, and to contain in its fulfilment justification of the long and bitter sufferings of human-kind, which have gone to its preparation. The Marxist is concerned less to understand than to change; his concern with understanding is the concern of a servant of change, a servant who seeks to grasp the interior dialectical movement of historical events, in order that he may work upon the opportunity which they provide to the effective mastery of their deepest tragedy.

Here we are made immediately aware of the extent to which what I called, at the outset of this paper, ontological and epistemological issues, inter-penetrate. To speak of Marxism as an ontology is not to forget its fundamentally dialectical character. The Marxist is concerned less with being than with becoming, or rather as one who is in some sense a disciple of Hegel, with becoming as the way in which being is realized. But he is a realist in so far as he insists that theory must be fashioned, not in accordance with our aspirations, but in accordance with the way in which things are, and with the manner in which human societies are changing, in accordance with laws which must never be conceived mechanically, but which are none the less expressive of the way in which things are. He is a revolutionary, but one whose concept of revolution is not expressive of any romantic vision of the morally therapeutic potential of violence, but of a deep-seated, extremely subtle understanding of the way in which things are, issuing in a moral dedication at once unreserved and flexible. A world of difference separates the Leninist revolutionary from the academic philosopher debating questions concerning historical method, questions concerning, for instance, the role and nature of historical imagination, the analysis of the concept of interpretation etc. The element of dogged realism, of insistence that truth consists in correspondence of belief with fact, persists obstinately in Marxism, even when Marxist revolutionary commitment urges a complementary emphasis on the creative individual, who, by his initiative taken always in a tightly organized group, transforms a given situation by drastic realization of its revolutionary possibilities. The breach with idealism, and with the kind of comfortable relativism that is often its handmaid, is fundamental. Of course, Marxism stresses the relativity of perspective to social situation, the relativity of cultural tradition to economic ascendancy. But it is a relativity that we must recognize in order to press urgently forward to a point of view from which we can see things as they are, a point of view from which relativity is transcended and issues in a sense of presence to the way in which human history is at once actually moving, and through which it can be brought to itself. Such insight is precarious, hardly won and hardly maintained. The cost of gaining it is great; so, too, the cost of holding to it properly. The present crisis in the Marxist world is in part at least a crisis in the understanding of the Party as the context within which alone this insight can be achieved and made effective. But deep and hard of resolution though this crisis must surely be judged to be, there is still no going back on Lenin's achievement of imposing by action, taken in accord with strong intellectual conviction concerning the way in which things are, a pattern upon a particular stretch of human history, after which nothing can ever be the same again. There was no hint of indulgent contemplation of intriguing alternative possibilities in Lenin's seizure of power. His action was tortuous, at times unexpectedly hesitant, always devoid of scruple, always harnessed to the revolutionary potentialities of the situation confronting him. But it was the action of a man of philosophically crude, but passionately committed intellectual conviction. It was again profoundly, even uniquely expressive of a fiercely defended vision of the way in which things are.

The suggestion that all history is somehow contemporary history, that there are as many valid conceptions of human history as there are historians (each one of which is more or less in bondage to the assumptions and priorities of his age), seems to the Marxist something very near blasphemy. It is anyhow expressive of a fundamentally frivolous attitude towards existence, tainted by what Kierkegaard called the aesthetic. Only those who have leisure, detachment, irresponsible freedom enabling them to indulge their fancy and follow it where they will, can speak in such terms. The stuff of human existence is altogether harsher, its built-in evil something inviting the intervention of the surgeon's knife, rather than the detached comment of the fastidious dilettante. The Marxist is whole-heartedly committed to a particular conception of historical causality, and is at once completely out of sympathy with any conception of historical understanding which suggests that the historian's role is to re-enact the past imaginatively in his own situation, and abstain not only from judgment of value, but from attribution of cause.

There are deep lessons to be learnt by the contemporary theologian from serious engagement with the Marxist rejection of idealism; for it is a profound and an informed rejection (one recalls Lenin's admitted deep admiration for Hegel's *Logic*!). For there is a sense in which idealism remains a besetting temptation of the theological understanding. Indeed, one can recognize a deeply rooted tradition concerning the method and subject-matter of theology, which would suggest that the theologian is, before all else, concerned with a complex tradition of spirituality, admitting of historical understanding, both in respect of its successive phases and of its development. Its beginnings are hidden from us; the purposes of the creative individual who set the impress of his life upon Christianity remain opaque, inscrutable in themselves, altogether hidden from us. What in a measure we can understand is the spiritual tradition, which his action set in motion. We can enter into its phases, although, of course, in our doing so we are in bondage to our own historical situation, our own inheritance, our own experience. The alleged wisdom of one age will be replaced by the transformed understanding of another. There is no continuing city of the mind, only a series of essays in the imaginative comprehension of the experience of those who have gone before, by those who must always remember that their own essays in understanding will supply subject matter of sympathetic penetration to those who come after. The category of the decisively significant is banished. Or, rather, it is replaced by the vague concept of a developing spiritual tradition which somehow plays down the heights and depths of human existence, mutes the cry of Jesus in Gethsemane, turning his agony into a kind of charade. The unity of theory and practice, an idea invoked in ways at once significantly resemblant and significantly different, by Marxism on the one hand and Christianity on the other, is obliterated. For practice is greeted as something only significant in so far as it helps to trigger off a system of ideas, attractive enough for those who have time and opportunity to indulge themselves in tracing their development, but leaving the depths of human existence untouched, the substance of the human situation unexplored. There is a sense in which one might claim that no one today has the right to comment upon the theological problem of the historical Jesus, who has not first sought to measure up to the reality of 'Lenin in October'. The mention of Lenin at this point may seem an unwarranted indulgence in paradox for its own sake. Yet I find in the study of Lenin's concrete re-definition of the Marxist revolutionary idea in his achievement, a continued impulse to engage anew with the doctrine of the Incarnation, with the fundamental realities of Christology and soteriology. It is the extraordinary interpenetration of idea and deed with which we are there confronted, that supplies a kind of parable of the embodiment in concrete human action of the very Word of God. In his recent study of the theology of the incarnation, *Menschwerdung Gottes*,[1] Hans Küng, after his elaborate and fascinating exploration of Hegel's understanding of the doctrine of the person of Christ, begins the development of his own restatement of the fundamental theology of these matters by a chapter significantly entitled 'The Historicity of God'. It may be legitimate for me at this point in my argument to convert at least the title of Küng's chapter to my own use. Yet, while Küng finds the sources and inspiration for his highly significant restatement of the traditional theology of divine impassibility in Hegel's massive philosophical work, for me there is a comparable inspiration in the recollection of Lenin's achievement, when the target of criticism is less the metaphysical assumptions of the Fathers than the besetting temper of contemporary idealism. We have to resist the illusion of supposing that in history nothing ever really *is* done, that to speak of the causal import of human action, to employ the categories of necessary condition, sufficient condition, necessary sufficient condition, etc., is to be guilty of a fundamental mistake. We have, I repeat, to resist the drift into a state of mind which regards all that passes before it as a kind of play, run for its interpretation, empty in itself of deep and drastic significance, except that significance be one which, in the mood of our generation, we impose upon it. For we are told that, if historical events have significance in themselves, the significance is beyond our reach; what matters is their resonance in the present, not what they were in the hour of their accomplishment.

Of course, where Lenin's work is concerned, we are utterly foolish if we forget its continuance in the medium of human memory, interpretation and bitter debate. But what supremely gives it significance is what it is in itself, or rather what it was in the fusion of complexity and simplicity, which characterized its tremendous accomplishment. And here, unless I am utterly mistaken, there is discernible a highly significant analogy with the work of Christ.

We live in a period in which all traditional theological categories are in the melting pot, when, indeed, to speak of finality is to invite derision for the ideas one seeks to clothe with that supposed dignity. Yet it is very hard to see how anything which we can continue significantly to call Christianity can survive the withdrawal of the predicate *final* from the work of Christ. Certainly, our understanding of that work requires continual correction, modification, radical revision. But to suggest that what we seek to understand is something which in itself can assume whatever form the historical imaginations of successive ages wish to bestow upon it, is to evacuate it of the kind of finality that must be said to belong to it. It is at this point that we touch what is absolute in history, what is absolute, that is, in an ontological sense. For the Marxist, Lenin's achievement in October, that paradigmatic union of theory and practice, likewise possesses an absolute character. Nothing can ever be the same again. Here is a deed that is more than a deed, one that transforms the very texture of world history. And so it is for the Christian theologian, where Christ's work is concerned. It is not a matter for edifying meditation, a story around which imagination can play and discern within it fresh layers of significance relevant to the supposed needs of successive ages. It is an action that is complete in itself, that brings about in the very substance of the world irrevocable change. Indeed, as Küng argues in his extraordinarily impressive book (if I understand it), it is by reference to this action that the very ways of God himself are to be understood.

To some, at least, the argument of this paper so far must seem rhetorical, and repetitious. Yet it is aimed at impressing upon the reader the significance of the opposition between idealism and realism in the understanding of history and the cruciality of this opposition for Christian theology. The references to Lenin are not arbitrary insertions, but integral to the whole movement of its thought. They are not introduced simply to suggest that the category of revolution is one that can be bent to the service of Christian theology, without proper criticism and discrimination. Rather, Lenin's achievement is mentioned in order to set a question mark against the quick rejection of finality as an historical category, against a facile dismissal of the treatment of individual historical actions as in themselves supremely significant. It is, after all, at the level of action that men and women engage themselves, suffer and make others to suffer. It is where informed choices serve carefully conceived policies of individual or collective conception that men and women achieve what they do achieve, break others and themselves are broken in pieces. It is at the level of raw human existence, where we make play, not with ideas but with the substance of our lives, that for good or ill we make our mark upon the sands of time. We cannot trivialize such achievement and such suffering by suggesting that, for the historian, it is nothing apart from the significance which he himself gives it. There is an element of creativity to be reckoned with in the human situation, – creativity for good and for ill. Of course, memory is a vitally important medium for the perpetuation of both the good and the evil that men do. Of course, in growth to spiritual maturity a vitally important part is played by coming to terms with the inheritance of memory, both personal and collective; but in the background there lies the actual work of men, and it is this that gives significance to what we recollect, and to our efforts as disciplined historians, to reshape the raw material of our recollection, more in accordance with actuality.

But what can we say of the work of God in Christ that at once receives a measure of very varied historical comment, and that is, at the same time, *in itself* relevant to the needs of men and women? It was Lenin's stupendous and, one may say, gravely mistaken claim that the action which he took in October 1917 was potentially of universal significance, that the way of revolution which he pioneered was a way on which others would be inspired by his example, and aided by his achievement, to follow in their turn. But what of Christ's claim to be *the* Way? In what sense, if any, can such a claim, if we suppose it historically justified to say that it was in some sense made and wrought out in history, be sustained? Are there any needs, at once so fundamental and so universal, that we can suppose them met for all time in a single place, and by a single action? It is with this crucial question that the second half of this paper will be concerned.

II

Where the flight from 'the historical Jesus' is concerned, we have to distinguish two positions.

1. According to this view we have to accept that, as a matter of fact, the actual lineaments of Jesus' ministry and teaching are irrecoverable. Such a view allows that it is possible (although highly improbable) that evidence will be discovered permitting a reconstruction not at present possible. A parallel to this possibility might be found in the way in which, where seventh-century ancient Greek history is concerned, archaeological discovery has enabled us reconstruct trade routes and vastly enlarge our knowledge, for instance, of the Lelantine war. It is not self-contradictory, it is even empirically possible, that we may one day learn enough, for instance, concerning what Jesus was doing in exorcizing the demons to advance our present tendency only to define the role of the *belief* that he was so active in the structure of the gospel according to St Mark.

2. There is a much more extreme view which insists, that the whole striving after the historical Jesus is expressive of a theological *ignoratio elenchi*. What we have are classical documents of the church's faith. It is for us to enter into that faith, to make our own, if we can, the obvious contradictions between the theological outlooks of Matthew, Mark, Luke and John, to realize within ourselves (and this involves, inevitably, a kind of translation; for our outlook is not that of any of the four) the experience that

achieves definition through the contradiction and the com-
plementarity of their witness. We cannot go beyond the experience of the community; it is for us to enter into it, in our own
terms.

Now it is with this latter view that I am concerned to argue. In
my judgment, it is idealistic in that it attributes an ultimacy to
ecclesiastical experience, to that experience whereby, within the
church, men and women come to themselves through coming to
terms with an inherited faith. Indeed, by this spiritual activity,
they are alleged to make themselves. Questions of truth and
falsity are dismissed almost out of hand: the validity of traditional
ecclesiastical existence is taken for granted. Whereas a normative
action, a creative Incarnation of the divine Word in a human
history, Incarnation, – as in the faulty but deeply significant
theologies of Nicaea and Chalcedon, the Fathers invoked the
subtle apparatus of substance and related categories to affirm it, – a
work of redemption, an event which excused the extravagance of
the popular English novelist, Dorothy Sayers (so praised by Karl
Barth), in calling it 'the only thing that ever really happened': all
these are at worst fantasies, at best abstractions from the continuing, ultimately non-referential language of spiritual experience,
of piety collective and personal. But what if it is only in terms of
such an action that we can understand, for instance, the tense,
complex history of the concept of resurrection in Christian theology, itself deriving from the more or less general language of
apocalyptic hope and transformed through attachment to the
vindication of a particular, distinguishable, identifiable individual, so that its use of the resurrection of Christ becomes (in
Aristotelian terms) its 'focal sense'? Thus all other resurrections
are seen as relative to the raising of Jesus from the dead, whose
raising becomes a *summum analogatum resurrectionum*. Indeed, it
might be said that what we have done by speaking in these terms
is to do little more than express, in Aristotelian idiom, what is
said by the fourth evangelist in his crucially significant, but historically and theologically very difficult, tale of the raising of
Lazarus. When, in the course of that episode, Jesus is represented as saying that he is the resurrection and the life, the
proposition which he affirms is synthetic. He is saying something
about himself that could be denied without self-contradiction,
that is, indeed, precarious in that his glorification depends upon
the consummation of his obedience, which is still future, still
contingent. But once after his passion and death Jesus is constituted in himself resurrection and life, he is become resurrection,

and where else we speak of resurrection, we speak relative to him. Yet we do not do so in such a way as to obliterate the peculiarities of other raisings, their vastly variant content. So Paul rules out literalist speculation. We do not know the eventual comprehension of the concept of resurrection, while learning from Jesus at once that flesh and blood, human existence as we know it in ourselves, and in our neighbours, cannot inherit eternal life, and at the same time that it is as an entity identifiably one with the corpse laid in Joseph's tomb that Jesus by insufflation bestows holy spirit, and proclaims the possibility of an apostolic absolution, deriving from his own achieved absolution of the world.

What sort of action do I have in mind? In his book, *The Death of Christ*,[2] the American theologian, Professor John Knox, argues that great men do not know what they are about, that they move *pedetentim*. He does not, I suppose, mean that they are 'sleep-walkers' as Hitler supposed himself to be in the winter of 1942–43, when Paulus was overwhelmed at Stalingrad, and in the Third Reich men and women heard clearly the rumble of the wrath soon to overtake their acquiescent acceptance, if not their actual support, of the criminal aggression of their leaders. According to some Roman historians, after Munda, when Julius Caesar found himself master of the Roman world he did not know what to do, but eagerly embraced the project of avenging Crassus' defeat at Carrhae by a Parthian campaign which would enable him to postpone the day of decision. The judgment is disputed, and the evidence against it is strong. Thus historians of equal competence claim that at the time of his murder he was indeed more or less committed to inaugurating in Rome an oriental-style despotism, perhaps with Cleopatra as his queen. Yet it *is* arguable that he did not know what to do with the power that was his; great men do sometimes hesitate, are sometimes uncertain, and the uncertainty may touch the very foundations of their policy of action. *But not always*. Of course, they will allow for the lessons which changing circumstances will teach them, the opportunities that alteration in the balance of human forces will put in their way. But it is a sheer mistake to treat them as (I will not say) continually bowed in prayer for guidance, but as creatures of a fluctuating inspiration, their purposes not knit together by some policy of action to which they are committed, and with which they have identified themselves. If I may revert here to the first part of this paper, it will be clear to any who have read it that I do not regard Lenin as any sort of 'sleep-walker' (in the midst of the rapidly changing situation which followed the first revolution of February 1917). Certainly his fortune fluctuated; for a time he was indeed in hiding ('his hour had not yet come'); but with Kornilov's mutiny, the threat to Kerensky from the Right now poised to endanger the whole revolution of the spring, the moment of truth had come. Lenin knew where he was going. Are we to say less of Jesus?

Of course, for him the Father's words are sovereign. In his flesh we are to see the Father's mercy on mankind. Of course he hesitates, more than hesitates. His approach to a death (horrible in the Roman manner) lacks the Socratic calm (yet drinking hemlock is one thing, the methods of Roman executioners another). And again the way of the cross was one of utter failure; his whole ministry ended – where? Thus Luke, who softens the bitterness of Mark's passion narrative, includes the strange *rencontre* with the women of Jerusalem: 'Weep not for me but for yourselves'. One is reminded of the reproach to the sentimental woman who cried on an earlier occasion (again according to Luke) 'Blessed is the woman that bare thee' etc. Only here the crushing of an emotional, even a perilous devotion is more astringent. There is nothing any longer that Jesus can do towards averting catastrophe; the cross wrote *finis* to any possibility of his counsels of patience availing through his apparent periodic influence on the men and women to whom he spoke, to deflect them from the folly of attempted extremist remedies for the griefs of Roman rule. The arch of Titus was erected in Rome in spite of the sombre heroism of such men and women as the defenders of Masada and of the temple – 'There was not left one stone upon another.'

Yet, if we have to write of such events '*et voilà tout*', must we not attend also to the plea of faith, to gloss such seeming pessimism with a parallel *tetelestai* or *consummatum est*? But we must not forget, if we do accept such a gloss, that in the ending of the 'day of preparation' (or the first day of passover, according to the other chronology), Jesus became humanly (to borrow a memorable phrase of Barth's) 'pure pastness', living only in the memory of those who mourned him as, in the bitter moment of bereavement, the dead are suddenly almost overwhelmingly present in the circumstantial detail of their lives to the bereft. Jesus' short human career was over, his role as an individual who played a certain small part in history was finished and done with.

Certainly, if the career of Jesus is thus over and done with, we have to reckon with the Christian movement; and it is well known that theologians are not wanting today who reduce without remainder the resurrection of Jesus to terms of the beginnings of that movement. Yet one could say, if one regards that movement as the only positive sequel to Jesus' strange fidelity unto death, in the words with which, in Shakespeare's *Julius Caesar*, Antonius whips the mob to fury, thereby eliciting an instance of the regularity the words affirm:

> The evil that men do lives after them;
> The good is oft interred with their bones.

To Christian faith, Jesus is without sin; yet from his life, as a matter of historical fact, there flows a dark inheritance of evil as well as good. One has only to think, for instance, of the infection of anti-Semitism present in the Christian church from the earliest years, and reflected in the New Testament documents themselves, to be made aware of this fact.

If we take Jesus seriously, we do so if and only if in the light, certainly, of his resurrection, we are able to face the reality of his historical failure, and to confess that for him acceptance of that failure could significantly be regarded as purposive and intentional, at least in the simple sense that he knew what he was doing, that here, and not elsewhere, he supposed the way appointed by his Father to lie. This though in the agony and dereliction of Gethsemane and Calvary, in the unfathomable silence of the holy Sabbath, in the complete accomplishment of *kenōsis*, he passed whither he knew not. A man is come to a country where aphasia is, for the most part, his only speech, where silence is punctuated only by broken words; where the loudest utterance is one of dereliction when, using the traditional language of his people's piety, he cried *loudly*. Here was no interior meditation movingly expressed.

'Hitherto, philosophers have sought to understand the world; our task is rather to change it.' This comment by Marx on his Hegelian inheritance is often quoted; but those who refer to it today, and who stand in the Marxist tradition, have to reckon with the fact that the world has been changed, that for good and ill decisive action has been taken. It is certainly true that here we have no continuing city. Thus Rosa Luxemburg, brilliant socialist analyst and Spartacist victim of the Freikorps (grim heralds of the Nazi storm-troopers of a short decade later), was quick to criticize the dark, tyrannical threat implicit in the immediately monolithic character of the Bolshevik dictatorship. Already, in the first hours of the 'ten days that shook the world', one can glimpse, a long way off admittedly, the coming horrors; the events of 1929, when Stalin finally adopted Trotsky's insistence that all must be sacrificed to heavy industrial development in the USSR and identified that 'all' with the peasants he made his victims, the great terror of the thirties and the rest of the sombre tale, up to and including the crushing of the recent Czechoslovak attempt to realize a Marxist socialism 'with a human face'. Lenin could not foresee all that was to come; yet the limits of his prescience do not obliterate his claim to know what he is about. Because a man cannot foresee all the consequences of his actions, he may be allowed to grasp some of them, and thus to be able to identify those actions as what they are. As with Lenin, so with Jesus.

At this point this paper seems to invite a study of the character of the gospel documents, an attempted answer to the question – What is a gospel? – treated as an epistemological question. But to introduce such consideration here would inevitably extend the argument to quite unacceptable length. We will continue, therefore, discussion of the narrower issues to which attention has been directed so far: the problem of the extent to which, and the sense in which, the ministry of Jesus can be regarded as ultimately decisive action, the problem of what remains of the Christian heritage if that ministry is evacuated of any such import. And here, in the context of the Christian-Marxist dialogue, insistent questions are posed to Christian theologians. Are Christians not, in fact, being encouraged to adopt an attitude sometimes regarded as progressive, according to which nothing ultimately significant happened *within the frontiers of the ministry of Jesus*. Thus that ministry is little more than the historical starting-point of the Christian experience, a vastly profounder and more inclusive whole, which it is alleged we can only begin to conceive when we avert from any conception of awareness that analyses that awareness in terms of subject and object. In the end such views lead to a depreciation of the concept of the Incarnation, to the assumption of a kind of intellectual and spiritual superiority towards those who argue that, in the end, the renewal of Christian theology demands a refashioning of that concept, indeed a reconstruction of the corpus of theology on the basis of its radical renewal.

In his very considerable study of the doctrine of the Incarnation, to which I have already referred, Hans Küng, in his concluding appendix, pays tribute to the work of Hans Urs von Balthasar, in attempting to combine a profound, though critical, loyalty to the theological tradition of the Greek fathers, with a ceaseless emphasis on the notion of *kenōsis*. Küng could have added that it is a *kenōsis* that is always to be understood in close connection with a *theologia crucis*, and this by a theologian whose masterpiece is significantly enough entitled: *Herrlichkeit*. It is possible that von Balthasar has already achieved that great work on *kenōsis* which we need. It may be that he has only done indispensable work towards its completion. What I would suggest in the conclusion of this paper is that its argument demands, as a next step, that we seek to comprehend the relation to eternity of the historical action which it has stressed, the resonance within the being of God which is implied by its unremitting stress on a historical action. What sort of God is it that so engages with his creatures in a work that is at once one of remorseless judgment and utterly compassionate redemption, whose ways are declared in this work, the very *ratio* of his creative purpose discernible in this endurance and agony, this defeat and destruction, this always enigmatic victory?

We have to reckon as the *summum analogatum* of the presence of God to his creation this engagement with the extremities of its plight, this acceptance of the schism that tears men and women asunder in their self-consciousness, rather this realization of the conflict that splits human beings in two, compelling them to serve truth and justice, or forbearance and pity, but always forbidding them the very possibility of reconciling these obligations, thereby estranging them from the very substance of themselves. It is Christ who accepts the human situation as it is, and who, by his acceptance, not only defines that situation, but provides the expression within the limits of concrete human existence of the very inwardness of God himself. So this acceptance, which is always presented as an act of obedience to the Father, that is indeed a very parable of the Son's eternal response to the Father in the unity of the Holy Ghost, ends (or so von Balthasar suggests) as a response which, in its absoluteness, seems to jeopardize the very *vinculum Deitatis* by which the Godhead is constituted. For here is a mystery of action that throws into a kind of confusion the assured constants of a traditional metaphysical theology, when we invoke their aid in the effort to represent it. I say, a mystery of action; for it is in the work of redemption that the substance of God is disclosed, that work which is the prerogative of the Word, which is of one substance, that the Father achieved in flesh and blood. To this deed there is no similar, only analogies with which we may make play, to deliver our representation of its inwardness from the bondage of a tender-mindedness which would diminish actuality to the level of human concept, which would evacuate human life of its deeply tragic element in the name of an intellectual security, which is allegedly the consequence of a radical scepticism, but shows itself more deeply to be expressive of a trivialization of existence. To convert history into a ballet-dance of ideas is to deny the tragic; to exploit the resources of idealism to avoid the cutting problems of theology is ultimately to anaesthetize one's intelligence before the demands made on it by the *mysterium Christi*.

And that mystery is of a God engaged to give sense to history by receiving from human existence the very depths of its problems. Thus in any attempt to engage with the question of the relative and the absolute in history, the theologian finds in the end his sympathy with the thesis that it is in the historian's consciousness that history takes its shape, cut short by his recognition that such a view inevitably leads to the identification of the Christian verity with a complex tradition of spiritual experience. Whereas that verity is rather to be found in the way in which human existence receives its shape, its order, its restored patterning, from the deed of Jesus. 'In the beginning was the Word'. Yet, at the foundation of human existence there lies the deed of the Word made flesh; the rational form of that existence is insinuated into it by the obedience of Christ unto death, the realization in temporal history of the ontologically ultimate response-moment in the unity of the Godhead.

Of course, in our understanding of the heights and depths of this act, there is a radical incompleteness. It is the function of the *heteros Parakletos* to show to each age the things belonging to the Christ who has received in the completion of his work the glory that was his, ere ever the world was. Is there such a thing as a final formulation of the inwardness of Christ's work? Its ultimate *ratio* is the secret of the Logos himself. But this surely we must allow, that the deeper we penetrate the ultimate conditions of human existence – the sheerly intractable that seems to defy the imposition of rational order – the nearer we approach that with which the deed of Christ seems to engage. Moreover, as we evacuate our understanding and imagination – in approaching the mysteries of that deed – of the illusion that we shall find here a metaphysically assimilable solution of the problems set by the world's existence, and allow ourselves to be measured by its rough, untidy, always concrete actuality, so the more that same understanding and imagination are alerted to refuse the solution of a humanly tidy dismissal of life's roughest edges. There are theologies which are at once the enemies of genuine intellectual honesty and fidelity to their own special subject matter. We can make the *Via Dolorosa* itself the plaything of our supposed cleverness in a specific dialectic, and congratulate ourselves for the apologetic dexterity we display in the exercise. But we convince nobody, and hide from ourselves the fact that we are concerned here, not with a system of abstract concepts with which we can play what games we will, but with human life as it has been, and is, and will be lived, and with the Incarnate Word which twists and turns its shape into the strange form of his own response to the Father. And as the Amen of that response is found in the unfathomable strangeness of Easter – where human perception touches the very frontiers of the eternal – so what is made of the ultimate sense of our history, individual and collective, remains a secret – 'Of that hour knoweth the Father only.' But it is ours to be sure that we do not in our imaginations wilfully diminish the rich and dark complexity of the human reality, or forget the corresponding and even more elusive complexity of the divine action whereby its sense is found.

So in this year, 1970, which brings the hundredth anniversary of the birth of Vladimir Ulyanov, arguably the greatest atheist of the twentieth century, one theologian has found himself moved by the memory of his sombre achievement, to treat that achievement as a veritable parable of the work of Christ, letting himself be driven by recollection of Lenin's ruthless concreteness, to represent the reality of that action by which, for Christian faith, the world is remade, and to ask the consequences for theology, and especially the obscure subject of the theology of history, of this insistence that it is in the action of Christ's pitiful flesh and blood, his very humanity that the ultimate secrets of the Godhead itself are disclosed.

5

The Problem of the 'System of Projection' appropriate to Christian Theological Statements

The problem with which this paper is concerned is that of the 'system of projection' appropriate to theological and religious matters of fact.

To say matters of fact is to commit oneself at the outset to the view that some important religious and theological expressions are descriptive and referential in intention. Thus if I say the Queen of England is at present touring South America my statement refers to the Queen and describes her present whereabouts and activity. Again if I describe in detail to a friend an experience which I have had, for instance a conference in which I have taken part, my statements are again descriptive and referential. In the former case we agree that the proposition 'the Queen of England is at present touring South America' is true if and only if the Queen is at present touring that country. It is false if she is actually attending a sale of bloodstock at Newmarket, or if although in South America she is not touring the country but staying with friends in Lima or Buenos Aires. Again my description of the conference may be faulted in innumerable ways. For instance, I may attribute a paper to Professor A which was given by Professor B, misrepresent the amount of time devoted to discussion of the present state of Set theory etc.

I

A very great deal that we say in daily life is of course neither descriptive nor referential. If I say to a friend 'I am delighted to see you', I may not be using the words to make an autobiographical statement; I may indeed find my friend's visit a vexatious interruption and by use of such a form of words I may be disciplining myself against the ejaculation of annoyance that springs to my lips. Where religious language is concerned we have to reckon with the language of confession of faith and the language of adoration; I restrict myself deliberately to two examples.

1. A man says: 'Lord, I believe; help Thou mine unbelief'; or a congregation in church sings 'Credo in unum Deum Patrem Omnipotentem'. The first expression combines confession of faith with prayer: it gains force by the element of paradox, even self-contradiction, in the juxtaposition of the two clauses. In the second case a body of people join publicly in a liturgically formal profession of a faith allegedly shared by them all, or of a faith to which, however individually its professors may differ in what they believe, they are prepared to give the shape of a common declaration.

In both cases the agents' verbal actions are significant, even in the latter case, where the formulae to which assent are given are highly sophisticated and complex. They acquire a part of their significance from their use in profession of faith. Thus the *homoousion* is an affirmation only intelligible to those who have made some study of the highly abstract discipline of ontology: yet within the context of a liturgical profession of faith, its high technicality is suffused with a different quality, viz., that of a significant element within a linguistic whole which may serve the needs of believing people seeking, however imprecisely they understand the detail of what they are doing, to orientate their thought and imagination in a particular direction. It will be noticed on such a view that in such a confession of faith the cognitive element in what is confessed is diminished but not eliminated. Thus it is implied that the direction of thought and imagination, encouraged by the act of confession, is the correct one. If the formulae are regarded as signposts these signposts are supposed to be pointing in the right direction. This way rather than another a man may find the goal which he seeks. Where the first case is concerned the verb 'I believe' is left without an accusative; the emphasis is on the believing and not what is believed, not even the one in whom the believer believes. The phrase expresses an act of belief in the sense of self-commitment and is followed immediately by a prayer that that commitment should be made more absolute (I am, of course, taking the sentence out of its context). Whereas if a man is giving an account of his beliefs and alleges that he believes a proposition we know he does not believe, e.g. that Euclid's axioms and postulates hold unconditionally of actual space, we say that he is making a false statement, either deliberately misrepresenting what he knows to be the case, or else mistaken concerning what he actually believes. Whereas if we challenge a man's personal confession of faith, we would not fault his autobiographical accuracy. Rather we might query his practical wisdom in making a commitment whose consequences he had hardly weighed up. We would not regard such a form of words as 'Lord I believe' as expressing what is true or false; yet if subsequently the confessor departed from his profession, we would judge it less than whole-hearted or vulnerable to pressures hardly foreseen at the time. Our criticism would be of the believer's sincerity, or our sympathy would be with him over the disasters that have overtaken his profession.

2. 'Sanctus, sanctus, sanctus, Dominus Deus Sabaoth; pleni sunt caeli et terra gloria tua. Hosanna in excelsis' – here the language is of adoration. Can one speak of it as true or false? In a moment of adoration we do not concern ourselves with such things. We are lost in praise. Yet if we sing that heaven and earth are full of God's glory, should we not remember the criticism of the argument of the presence of design in the universe which runs as follows: 'Sir', the protester addresses the Supreme Designer, 'you have written a very bad detective story; all the clues point in the wrong direction.'

Are heaven and earth full of the glory of God? To use a technical theological idiom – will the circumstances both natural and man-made of our world warrant our free use in the praise of God of language suggestive of a completely 'realized eschatology'? We sing that heaven and earth *are* full of God's glory, and we do not use the future tense appropriate to the expression of hope as yet unfulfilled.

So in both cases our analysis suggests that even in language in which the descriptive or referential element is reduced to a bare minimum, questions concerning truth and falsity break in. Even in (1), a deep scrutiny of the believer's self-commitment would involve us in some effort to characterize its direction. To treat commitment as an end in itself, irrespective of that to which the agent commits himself, is to flirt with the romantic illusion that 'authenticity of existence' is won by abandoning the discipline of reflection (the unquestionably valid element in the Cartesian doubt) as something morally suspect, and by enlisting in the service of any cause whatsoever which demands or seems to demand heroic self-disregard. Yet voluntary service in Hitler's legions might be regarded as providing precisely the sort of opportunity suggested and the record of their deeds remains a terrible story of the ease with which heroic self-dedication may be perverted to the service of the unquestionably and irremediably evil.

The problem of the truth or falsity of what we believe remains with us, even when our exploration of the rich complexity of religious language reveals how little much of it directly engages us with the problem of its descriptive import and reference. What then of such language when it is regarded as presenting that which is the case?

II

We need to free our minds of obsession with a *simpliste* model of correspondence. In two papers written in Oxford in 1946–47 and recently posthumously published in a volume entitled *How I See Philosophy*[1], Friedrich Waissmann (an intimate friend of the late Professor Moritz Schlick, a member of the Wiener Kreis, and a man who saw a great deal of Wittgenstein during the period between the end of the first world war and the latter's return to Cambridge in 1929) wrote of the 'open texture of the concept of truth'. One got the notion wrong if one took as one's paradigm the correspondence of the details of a photograph with its original. Certainly in a criminal investigation one needs a very accurate photographic likeness of, for example, the sexual maniac the police are seeking. When one passes from photography to portraiture, however, the matter changes dramatically. In Bishopthorpe, the residence of the Archbishops of York near that city, there is a portrait by the English portraitist Orpen of Cosmo Gordon Lang, Archbishop of York in the early part of this century and later Archbishop of Canterbury. It is an unforgettable study of prelatical arrogance, in which the artist has used the scarlet of the Archbishop's chimere and doctoral hood to emphasize the relentless pride of his subject. A Swedish ecclesiastic, seeing the portrait, said that the artist had painted him 'as the devil intended him to be; but by the grace of God he is not like that'. Yet Lang was a very ambitious man; this was part of his story, and the artist in a portrait, not a photograph, throws that fact into relief.

The portrait, we say, does not lie. But what of the truth of a scientific theory – say Newton's Inverse Square Law? One may say logically that such propositions are universal propositions of unrestricted generality. But what sort of correspondence is there between such propositions and (in this case) the actual relative accelerations *vis-à-vis* one another of moving bodies in the world? Where unrestricted generality is at issue, we have something of a quite different order from universal propositions of restricted generality, e.g. every one in this room is interested in the philosophy of religion. That proposition is a conjunctive truth-function of a set of singular propositions about each individual in the room. If one, and only one, were bored to tears by philosophical discussions of this kind, it would be falsified. Propositions formulating laws of nature (even as simple, aesthetically satisfying and conceptually comprehensive as Newton's Law) are subject to *analogous* falsification procedures, (note that I say 'analogous'); they do not enjoy the invulnerability of *a priori* propositions; yet their truth is not a matter of their comprehensiveness regarded as enumerative records, but resides in part in their significance in organizing and integrating a vast amount of theoretical material.

But what of the propositions of pure mathematics? What of the theorem that any even number is the sum of two primes? Waismann in his paper spoke of pure geometry: that is a system organized as a hypothetico-deductive scheme, where theorems are deduced from axioms and postulates. It was of such, he suggests, that Russell spoke in his famous *mot*: 'In pure mathematics we do not know what we are talking about, nor whether what we say is true.' In his *mot* Russell had in mind the correspondence model of truth; Waismann suggests that in such a case as a pure geometry, we have to accept internal coherence not as the criterion but as the nature of truth. It is what truth is in such a connection.

Again what of the truths of works of fiction? One may say that one learns more what the Battle of Waterloo was really like from Stendhal than from a military historian; or again one may say that Shakespeare's *Julius Caesar* throws a flood of light on the predicament of the German conspirators of 20 July 1944, who with such unforgettable courage attempted a great tyrannicide. Again Waismann himself insisted that what Kafka said concerning the human situation in *The Trial* or Thomas Mann in *Death in Venice* could only be said as they said it. Where fundamental moral issues are concerned which face all men or women sooner or later or some men and women some times, one learns much more from e.g. William Faulkner's great novel *Absalom, Absalom!* (on the guilt of slavery), from Tolstoi's *Anna Karenina* (on adultery), from Conrad's *Lord Jim* (on the inward self-deception of the man

who lives with a fantasy picture of himself), from Dostoevsky's
Brothers Karamazov (the problem of the use of power) than from
the writings of many moral philosophers and most (if not indeed
all) moral theologians. Yet how different they are one from
another! One has only to see Dostoevsky and Tolstoi over
against one another to be reminded of this. Yet we use the terms
truth and falsity in connection with what they write, even as we
pay tribute to the immense feats of disciplined organization that
go into their handling of their material and help to differentiate
their work from the careful newspaper report of a natural disaster, a murder, a liaison.

Again where Shakespeare's *Sonnets* are concerned, we speak of
learning new facts concerning the world of lust: learning them
through the poet's command of language as a vehicle of insight.
To speak of lust as the 'expense of spirit in a waste of shame' is to
say something that informs, that is more than a piece of phrase-
making, rather the formulation of a painful discovery. But what
sort of discovery? How is it related to an archaeologist's discovery
of a long-buried hoard of which he can offer an accurate inventory that we would not hesitate to call a true account?

Nothing is original in this section of my paper except some
of the illustrative material. Dr Waismann's conclusion is that
the notion of truth is one of which no simple account is possible; there is nothing in which truth consists anything more
than there is something in which (in Aristotle's example in the
last chapter of the *Categories*) *having* essentially consists. This I
shall dispute; but I want to suggest the great relevance of this
recognition of the analogical unity of truth to our enquiry. Why
should we not consider that religious and theological statements
may claim truth or be dismissed as false in accordance with
principles and criteria internal to their nature? As we shall see this
is no soft plea for a kind of facile tolerance; rather it is a demand
that we consider the system of projection to which they belong as
a complex whole, vulnerable to falsification in different ways, but
still in itself what it is and not something else.

III

Yet the absolutely central problem raised by religious and
theological language, if we suppose it in some sense factually
representative or referential or descriptive, remains. And that is
the problem how reference to or characterization of the transcendent is possible. If we treat theological statements, for instance,

God exists; Christ came from God and went to God; the Father raised the Son from the dead, as possessing factual import, we are at once involved in the riddle of the ontological status of that to which they refer. When we speak of the transcendent we speak of that which lies beyond the familiar world, that on which it depends with a dependence which is asymmetrical (it is not a mutual dependence), that which is at once the ground of the familiar world and altogether uninvolved in its processes, (whether we think of its natural or historical processes), that moreover to which the familiar world by its existence points and whose lineaments are supposedly faintly traceable (as in so many parables) in features of the familiar. By the description – the familiar world – I refer to much that is in obvious senses unfamiliar, including indeed those first beginnings of the cosmos which empirical cosmologists seek to trace, the state of our planet when life was as yet unknown, the monsters that roamed the earth and eventually became extinct, the denizens of the depths of the ocean, the most primitive beginnings of human life, the shape of the future in so far as we can discern it. That to which we refer as the transcendent is that which lies beyond this world, using the term 'beyond' in no crudely anthropomorphic spatial sense, but in full acceptance of the anti-anthropomorphic disciplines familiar to the historian of metaphysics from Plato's criticism of his own use of *mimesis*, *methexis* and *parousia* in the *Parmenides* onwards.

Ineluctably religious and theological language takes the transcendent for granted; and this indeed comes to conscious expression in confession of faith, hymn of adoration etc. as well as in what seems more immediately descriptive or referential in intention. In the act of adoration what we adore outsoars the limits of the world to which we belong; its self-existence owes no debt to that in which we are ourselves, in virtue of our humanity, implicated, inheritors of a long development that is the condition of our being what we are, as well as victims (if so we see ourselves) of those chances with which we have been 'thrown' into life (I echo Heidegger's *Geworfenheit*). In confession of faith we commit our ways to that which is in no way whatsoever compromised by involvement in the guilt of which we are aware in ourselves, in the ambiguity that sets a question mark against both the validity of our aspirations and the viability of our most cherished hopes. It is not a matter of casting our burdens upon some substitute mother or adopting the inspiration of a new style father; rather it is a self-submission to the verdict of a completely penetrating scrutiny, at once ultimate and intimate, beyond which we can conceive no appeal, whose omniscience is conceived by us as that which makes the very concept of such an appeal irrelevant. For where all is known, then nothing remains to be disputed. In his sight we are known as we are; this is the secret of what we are made of and of what we have made of ourselves.

Of course if we soft-pedal the referential element here, emphasizing much more that of performance in confessions of faith etc., we gain a certain advantage. We are entitled to treat the transcendent as an *als ob*, a fiction of the imagination that we project in order to give a particular direction to our essays in self-knowledge, to our search for the kind of courage that enables us neither to turn aside from what we are, nor to be overwhelmed by a sort of despair in the recognition of the sorry mess we find ourselves in fact to be. We are enabled to represent such knowledge of ourselves as something received, as the declaration of the verdict of an ultimate court, at once objective and necessarily accepted. Any boast we may be tempted to make of our supposedly brave honesty is muted at the same time as our hope is sustained by the imaginative suggestion that where we are condemned, we are also accepted. The concept of transcendence receives definition by the suggestion of its role in the process whereby a man comes to himself, takes stock of himself in a relatively novel way, which reconciles honesty with humility, courage with forbearance and self-depreciation with hope. And in this process, of course, the proximate agent is very frequently the other who stands over against him, the 'thou' who confronts the 'I', who transcends the 'I' in the elementary sense that he will not yield himself to inclusion within the world of the 'I''s self-regard. In this sense we can quite properly speak of the 'thou' as transcending the 'I'; but it is a restricted transcendence, a limited over-againstness that is at once an instrument and a parable of that supposedly absolute transcendence with which we are concerned. From the transcendence of the other person to the absolute transcendence of God, there is a movement involving a *metabasis eis allo genos*, an extrapolation of the notion that must bridge the hiatus between absolute and relative.

Yet in Christian theology the concept of the transcendent is bent to services quite incompatible with this attempted reductive analysis of its import, the terms of its role in a process of self-definition. For Jesus Christ is presented as one in whom the familiar and the strange, this world and that which lies beyond it, are united in the concrete of a single person. He is presented himself as that receptivity made flesh which men and women must receive. The riddle of his person is an ontological one; it cannot be dissolved by any method akin to that by which we evacuate the transcendent, of that which bewilders us in its content, through assigning the notion its role in a process of self-evaluation. We may indeed believe that we can dissipate the problems relating to the status of metaphysical and theological concepts by a bold revivification of idealist methods, that is methods which suppose the autobiographical uniquely transparent to the subject and therefore matter for *bold and confident* assertion, quite improper where what is otherwise the case is concerned. We are present to ourselves as we are not to the world around us; let us therefore find in the articulation of that presence, in the self-definition which belongs to its essence, the role of the notion of transcendence. The notion is an *als ob* that makes the fulfilment of the imperative *gnōthi seauton* possible. Yet the matter is altogether different if we are confronted with one whose history is presented as the veritable *parousia* of that which is ultimate, which is all-overriding in the manner of the transcendent, whose history indeed is presented as requiring the definition *in actu* of that transcendent to integrate its order and confer its sense. The career of Jesus moves from life to death to resurrection and in Christian theology it is the Father's raising him from the dead that is the very paradigm of the relation of the transcendent to the familiar. It is not that the notion of the relation of the transcendent to the familiar, as that as has been developed by classical metaphysicians, is properly dismissed by Christian theologians as vacuous. The paradox of what has been asserted in the theology of the resurrection can only be seen against the background of earlier metaphysical essays, for instance those of Plato and Aristotle, as well as the prophetic engagement with the problems of evil and suffering, both physical and moral. But in the Christian tradition the point at which previous schemata receive their transformation is an event, a deed, something indeed received by a man when, his life having become 'pure pastness' and his body entombed, he is brought again from the dead. We are not moving at the level of idea, but at that of being and becoming. We are not operating with a concept that we can domesticate by assigning to it the role of an *als ob* in a process whereby we invest the sorry stuff of our humanity with a new complex dignity; it can in Kantian terms neither be regarded as a category capable of transcendental deduction nor as an Idea to which a valuable, though dispensable, 'regulative use' can be assigned. Rather we are engaged with that whose presence to our human scene in Jesus was disclosed in the climactic reinterpretation of the quick broken movement of his human existence in the resurrection. Granted that here is the necessity of radically transforming our previous concept of the transcendent and the manner of our world's relation to it, that transformation only seems to emphasize the ontological import of the action. If God is wrongly characterized as part of the furniture of the world, yet we are not wrong to say that no inventory of what there is can be complete without mention of him; for he is that apart from whose existence there would be nothing of which to make our inventory nor any investigator to set the work of marking it in hand. For Christian theology he moreover it is whose way of dealing with this world is Jesus his Christ, at once the one who wholly depends upon him and with whom he is one, the one moreover whom he has brought again from the dead.

IV

So we return to the problem of truth.

Aristotle in his doctrine of being in the *Metaphysics* suggested that all forms of being (here including accidental being and privation) formed a unity by reference to substance: this even as health of climate, complexion, diet are relative to the health of the bodily organism. So too in *Nicomachean Ethics I. 6*, when he asks how goods are related one to another, having rejected the quasi-Platonic doctrine of a single universal good, and refused equally to regard them as *tuchē homōnuma*, entities that happen to have the same name, he asks briefly whether they may not be one in virtue of their contribution to a single all-embracing whole, presumably the good for man.

In his *Metaphysics* he affirms the classical correspondence conception of truth; but although his language is careful and guarded (he is not in bondage to the picture theory of the proposition) he does not ask himself whether in fact there may not be, in relation to this pivot or central notion of correspondence, very many ways for a proposition to be true.

In his novel *Lord Jim*, as analysts of the work have shown, Conrad drew on much that he had heard and read concerning in particular a maritime disaster and the subsequent judicial enquiry, during his Malayan period. Yet he wrote not a piece of *rapportage* but a classical study of the *miles gloriosus*. We judge his presentation true for that reason, for the subtlety with which it lays bare the spiritual make-believe in which such a man indulges, with which in its climax aided by a specific narrative device, it deliberately leaves the quality of his final action ambiguous. We suspect a further failure; but we are not quite sure, and here we are glad to have the support of the narrator Marlow's partial suspension of judgment. If we claim truth here we claim it for the results of the author's probing; we even claim it for the carefully designed ambiguity of his conclusion. Yet if we speak of truth here we are not moving to a different world from that in which we claim that *this piece of paper is white* is true. If we speak of the truth of a work of fiction, we do not suppose it *rapportage*; yet to call it true and to call the report true is not to use in respect of both a mere homonym. There is an analogy; the one has its own sort of truth that we may regard as at once logically derivative and yet more humanly significant. For truth is correspondence of proposition with fact.

What then of theological language?

1. The proposition *God exists* is true if and only if God exists, even as the proposition *snow is white*, is true if and only if snow is white. The atheist who denies that God exists is insisting that it is no more the case that God exists than that hobgoblins exist. The theologically sophisticated may say (suggesting a certain sort of logical positivist) that it is nonsense to say that God exists and nonsense to say that he does not exist. By this he claims to do justice to the fact that if we say that God exists we imply that he exists as one particular individual among many, even as when we say that the Queen of England exists we imply that there is one isolated individual satisfying the given description. But God is not an individual any more than he is *a* substance: (to speak of him as *ipsum pelagus substantiae* is to present him as substance, not as *a* substance). So we may say that he does not exist; yet to speak so aligns us with the atheist; so we prefer to proclaim the impropriety of the language of existence where God is concerned. Yet one could argue that, if one is a theist, to say that God exists is to advertise one's acceptance of the problem of God as a problem set to one by the way things are; one is in fact refusing to dismiss a whole range of problems. As a learned Thomist once suggested to me, God is 'the name of the problem the world by its existence sets', and the so-called *quinque viae* are five ways in which that problem is more sharply particularized. So if one insists on his existence as distinct from his non-existence, one is advertising one's adherence to the problem of the transcendent, allowing this as set to us by the world's existence. Moreover one is insisting

that this problem, this bewilderment, this unease is about something. One is implying that it is a real problem, not a *Scheinproblem*. To defend the validity of this conviction, to vindicate the perplexity as other than vacuous, is certainly a central problem of metaphysics. But at least it purports to be perplexity about something, intentional in its concern. And although in Christian theology it is radically disciplined and changed, its ontological bias is transformed, not annihilated. For when we confess the resurrection of Jesus from the dead as much as when we profess that God exists it is what is the case or what is not the case that confirms or nullifies our confession or profession. Is there anything to be bothered about? The question is as simple as that. Yet to make its import plain we must be sure that we know what we are talking about, that we have got our 'system of projection' right.

2. What then of such propositions as (*a*) that Christ came from God and went to God and (*b*) the Father raised the Son?

(*a*) This proposition is true if and only if Jesus of Nazareth existed, if there lived such a human being. This is not its sole truth-condition; but it is one of its necessary truth-conditions. That Jesus lived and died in precisely the same sense as Julius Caesar and Vladimir Lenin is a condition of the truth of the Christian faith. If it is unfulfilled, *cadit tota quaestio*. Of course the proposition Jesus lived may be true and the Christian religion false. Because Jesus is an historical individual, reconstructions of his life and work are conceivable and indeed defensible which would render obviously inadmissible the claim that in a unique sense he came from God and went to God. There are those who suggest that the historical probabilities concerning his doings and sayings and purposes are irrelevant to his claim to be *the* revelation of God. In Bultmann's phrase it is enough that he reveals this, namely that he is the revealer, namely that what he discloses is that what he is in the bare fact (*Dass*) of his existence is the disclosure of his Father. One may commend this theologian's theocentrism; but one must question whether he does not in fact come very near investing one who where the detail of his life is concerned is a bare individual, with a quasi-magical efficacy as God-disclosing, in total aversion from the moral quality of his life and his solution of the human conflicts (of personal and collective existence) into which he was thrown. His significance is diminished below that of other figures in human history whose behaviour had an unquestionably tragic dignity, revealing the depth of the problem of evil and the ambiguous, yet unmistakable, glory of those whose endurance makes them in a unique way the victims of its distinctive power. One can take examples almost at random and mention men as far removed in time and circumstance as Socrates, Marcus Brutus, Thomas More, Thomas Cranmer, Oliver Cromwell, Pius X, Vladimir Lenin. From the lives of all alike we learn, because something of their achievement, their failure, their virtue, their sin is known to us, and we may claim that if Jesus is to be more than any other, not simply a servant of and witness to the truth, but himself constitutively Truth itself in his historical existence, he must be more than a variable to which we can assign whatever value our devotion prompt us. And it is to this status, if I understand them aright, that the Bultmannians would largely reduce him: the Bultmannians, and supremely the American *Neutestamentler*, John Knox.

But to say that he came from God and went to God is to go beyond mere historical assertion. It is to insist that certain contingent historical facts, viz. the life and death of Jesus, are uniquely grounded in the transcendent. The language is of movement; but it is not movement through time from place to place but from the eternal to the temporal, from the temporal to the eternal. Can one speak of such a movement without seeming to be guilty of sheer mythologizing? What is central to the Christological language of the New Testament, to the Christian 'system of projection' is just this sort of juxtaposition of references to eternal and temporal. To take another example – 'Before Abraham was I am'. What Jesus avers is that what he eternally is, that which is expressed in time in his mission and work but which belongs in its origin to his eternal nature, stands over against the successive phases of human history past, present and to come.

Again, by having spoken to many, for instance the woman at the well of Samaria, the truth about themselves, he uses the word 'truth' shortly afterwards, characterizing his purpose in his life and passion as witness to that truth *which he is*, that truth which includes the secrets of men and women who become what they really are not simply through their reaction to him, but by his taking that reaction up into himself and transforming it in his work. Here Jesus shows what it is for a man to be the truth of his fellows, to be the author of what they really are, to be creative of their inmost actuality: and this not simply as the author of their being in creation, but through a creative act that is realized and fulfilled in and through a particular human history. What belongs to the creative activity of God is what is brought to full expression in time in the ministry of Jesus. 'Before Abraham was I am.' It is this history that gives content to the notion of creation, to the giving of light to the world, drink to the thirsty, food to the hungry, health to the sick, truth to the ignorant and life to the dead. But the history is a human history and therefore it moves to death. Its *telos* is a lifting up on a Roman cross, a final condemnation of Jesus to annihilation, that is of course also the last judgment of the world. In that condemnation the whole tragic potentiality of human history is actualized and comes to rest on the central figure, who experiences defeat in no make-believe sense, but in the sense that he must let all those whom the Father has not given him slip from his grasp. Judas goes out into the night. Christ's ministry ends in sheer disaster.

Such then is characteristically Christian language and the 'system of projection' demanded is a richly complex one, oscillating between the overtly mythological and the ironic with an occasional sharp intrusion of the precise idiom of formal ontology (e.g. 'I and my Father are one thing'), thus disciplining the poetry by a bold use of the seemingly inescapable concept of substance. It is indeed a system in which one form of expression complements the deficiency of another.

(b) But the focus and centre is the confession that the Father raised the Son from the dead, the confession of the resurrection. It is indeed in the light of this confession that the tale of Jesus' ministry is told, that its details are allowed to fall into place. Its profession is the *prius* of Christian construction, even if events belonging to that construction are its own necessary condition and are so presented. It is the central theme of Christian proclamation and, in conclusion of this long paper (which is too short for its purposes), I want to indicate how the disciplines of logic may enable the student more clearly to see its problems.

Already we have seen the complexity of the system of projection to which the Christian faith is committed. It is this complexity that precludes a simple answer to the question whether Christian theology is committed to the defence of metaphysics or to its radical criticism. It is clear that Christian theology has made extensive use of the investigations of ontology in the strict sense, that is of the kind of effort made by Aristotle in large tracts of his *Metaphysics* to give a comprehensive account of such concepts as thing and quality, existence, truth, causality etc., which enter into organized discourse concerning any subject matter whatsoever. It is in the assertions of the New Testament itself that such concepts are at once taken for granted and enlisted in a new service; the understanding of that new service depends upon the self-conscious mastery of the use of these concepts in more familiar contexts. Yet the climax and centre of the problems raised by the Christian system of projection is found in the statements made concerning the resurrection of Jesus. And here we encounter not only questions concerning the relation of the temporal to the eternal, questions also relating to the violation of alleged natural laws concerning the processes of human *post-mortem* decomposition, and questions concerning the causal properties (and therefore the status) of the risen Jesus in contradistinction from those properties attributed in the fourth gospel to the resuscitated Lazarus, but also questions of an epistemological order concerning the relation of seeing, hearing and touching to believing. Indeed one could describe the twentieth chapter of St John's gospel as one of the classical Christian documents concerning the relation of perceiving (and especially visual, auditory and tactile perception) to faith. The author, who has organized his exceedingly complex material in a masterly way, has more than any other of the New Testament writers (and here I include St Paul) faced the questions of the grounds, the occasion, and the objective of belief; (he does not use the noun *pistis*, only the verb *pisteuō*). For more than any other Christian writer he engages with the issues of the relation of faith to perception. Because the Word has become flesh, he has become visible, audible, tangible, even matter for smell and taste (the flesh and blood of the Son of Man are the veritable food and drink of men). Yet such perception of the incarnate is unavailing; it is spirit that gives life, spirit that remains unavailable to men and women until Jesus is glorified. But when risen and ascended he shows himself to them behind locked doors, gladdening their hearts as thus he identifies himself to them and not to the world at large, he immediately confers upon the ten whom he greets that which he had promised. After the formal greeting of *Shalom*, he tells them that as the Father has sent him, even so he sends them, and breathing on them he bids them receive holy spirit, assuring them that theirs is the power to remit and retain sins. It is through holy spirit that the ten perceive that the glory of Jesus is visibly expressed not in the transient insignia of a coronation (the work of a moment of passing enthusiasm), but in the signs now made perpetual of that cruel mortality which conformed his likeness finally to that of the sons of men. Yet the condition of their discernment was their acceptance on grounds of human perception of the identity between this sudden apparition and the dead man laid in the tomb forty-eight hours before, and (by implication) the identity of both alike with that which unseen and unheard had left the tomb in a manner utterly unlike the Lazarus who had stumbled out of his grave on the fourth day in answer to Jesus' call, and with that which refused the Magdalene's embrace, following the *noli me tangere* with the order to proclaim to his disciples the imminent consummation of his rising, in his ascension to his Father and theirs. Yet Thomas, who does not see, doubts the verbal report and demands a minute, clinical verification of the declared and visibly advertised identity. Seven days later he is offered the right to perform the examination he demands, and without delay the one who proclaimed himself ready to go with Jesus that he might die with him confesses him Lord and God. Yet Jesus' words to him in answer to his confession are a partial rebuke: 'Because thou hast seen me thou hast believed: blessed are those who have not seen and yet have believed.' Visual perception was in the end sufficient for Thomas; he did not need to touch. Yet it is implied that hearing should have been enough, viz. hearing the statements of Mary and the ten. Those who came after would hear, though not see.

So here ontological problems are raised and so are epistemological. Both benefit from being set out in relatively precise terms. Thus what of the relation of the empty tomb to the raising of the Son by the Father? If the tomb was empty, it is a matter of empirical fact that it was so, and the proposition that it was empty is a contingent proposition. How is this contingent proposition related to the proposition *the Father raised the Son*? And what sort of proposition is the latter? One is tempted to say that it also is contingent; yet at the same time one has to say that it relates to no matter of empirical observation and that one is *slightly* ill at ease in calling it contingent. Yet one is also ill at ease in calling it necessary, whether one thinks of the necessity of such a truth as that *any even number is the sum of two primes* (which if true, is necessarily true), or such a truth as *either p or not-p*. It is very hard indeed precisely to place on the logical map the proposition *the Father raised the Son*. Yet even if we avert from discussing the important question what sort of proposition it is, we can go on to discuss its relation to the proposition that the tomb was empty.

If we suppose that as a matter of empirical fact the tomb was found empty, we may think that its relation to the Father's raising the Son is best expressed in terms of the Russell-Whitehead relation between the truths of two propositions, known as material implication (in its generalized form as formal implication). If we say that p materially implies q, we mean that it is not the case that p is true and q false. Thus, if we say that *the Father raised the Son* materially implies that the tomb was empty, we mean no more than that it is not the case that *the Father raised the Son* is true, and the tomb was empty is false. We are simply asserting that the truth of the one is relevant to the truth of the other; we are doing little more than denying the truth-independence of the two propositions.

We may, on the other hand, go further than this and insist that the relationship between the two propositions is the one which Professor C. I. Lewis called 'strict implication'. If I say that p strictly implies q, I mean that it is impossible for p to be true and q false; the notion is one that introduces into the definition of the notions of implication and deducibility, regarded as that which implication makes possible, the fundamental modal concepts of possibility and impossibility. It is obvious that the relationship which Lewis calls 'strict implication' is a much more stringent one than the relationship which Russell and Whitehead called 'material implication'. The paradoxes of material implication understood as an analysis of the notion of deducibility are well known, viz. that if p materially implies q means that it is not the case that p is true and q false, then a true proposition materially implies every other true proposition and a false proposition materially implies every proposition. These paradoxes are avoided where Lewis's conception is concerned; although, as is well known, other paradoxes follow, viz. a self-contradictory proposition strictly implies any and every proposition and a necessary proposition is strictly implied by any and every proposition. But as Professor Jonathan Bennett has pointed out in a most important paper in the *Philosophical Review*,[2] these paradoxes do little more than work out in formal terms the obvious logical facts that if one feeds a self-contradiction into the premises of one's argument one can get any and every result; whereas if one treats logically necessary propositions as, for instance, Wittgenstein did in his *Tractatus* (viz. as tautologies of the two-valued propositional calculus), one exhibits them as degenerate truth-functions, that is, statements which are completely vacuous or empty of import. Thus to say that such propositions are strictly implied by any and every proposition is to do no more than point out in formal terms that one, for example, learns nothing about the weather if one is told that either it is raining or it is not raining. This digression is intended to suggest that the mere occurrence of paradoxes, even in the system of material implication, is not by itself sufficient to justify dismissing that notion out of hand; still less are we wise if we do not use the resources of the much more stringent notion of strict implication to bring out a very important point of view concerning the relation of the two propositions with which we are concerned.

Many theologians have said that the truth of the proposition *the Father raised the Son* is so related to the truth of the proposition *the tomb was empty* that it is strictly impossible for the one to be true and the other false. The latter assertion is not a part of the former in the way in which, e.g. *this surface is coloured* may be said to be part of what we assert when we say that *this surface is red*, or the sense in which we say that *this is a triangle* is part of what we say when we say that *this is a red triangle*. Yet if the two propositions are related by the relation of strict implication, then the truth of the Father's having raised the Son is so connected with the truth of the tomb's being empty that it is strictly impossible for the one proposition to be true and the other false. Such a view as this might be thought to be the view of those for whom the emptiness of the tomb is a sign pointing to the risen Lord, less a manifestation of his Father's action upon him, or of his own activity as risen, than its *prius* in the order of understanding. On such a view it would of course be the *prius* of his revelation to Paul, 'the abortion', on the Damascus Road as well as of his revelation to the eleven much nearer in time to the crucifixion. The emptiness of the tomb is a publicly visible state of affairs, a state of affairs belonging to the common world which believer and unbeliever can inspect; but it is in itself ambiguous in that it is compatible with quite other naturalistic explanations of its occurrence. Yet if we say that it is strictly impossible for the Father to have raised the Son and the tomb not to be empty, we say that the action between the two is more than the *de facto* coincidence of two states of affairs (if the Father's raising the Son may be spoken of as a state of affairs) which is supposedly enough for a material implication. Yet it is not a connexion which involves the emptying of the tomb as part of the raising of the Son. It is compatible with such a relation, but also with a slightly less stringent connexion.

The question of the identity or non-identity of strict implication and entailment has been a matter of acute controversy between logicians. (In his outstandingly able paper Professor Bennett argues powerfully for their identity.) But for our purposes it is permissible to point out that there are logicians who argue that the sort of relationship obtaining between such propositions as *this is red* and *this is coloured* is not quite adequately conveyed by the relationship of strict implication. Here what has been called 'intensional entailment' is involved, a relationship which does not allow of the relatively rigorous formal treatment that strict implication has received in Lewis's system of logic and its derivatives; we are in fact involved in the extremely difficult logical controversy concerning the ultimate validity of the distinction between analytic and synthetic propositions, and the equally difficult related issues concerning the nature of definition. If we say, however, as a *gedankens experiment*, that there is such a relation as *intensional entailment*, then we can ask what we are saying if we say that the Father's raising the Son intensionally entails the tomb's being empty. On such a view, in the resurrection of Jesus, as part of that to which the description refers, a uniquely miraculous intervention of divine power is involved, setting it apart altogether from the anticipated *resurrectio mortuorum* (however that may be conceived). Decision on such an issue raises questions soteriological, cosmological, metaphysical.

Yet centrally they touch the way in which we conceive the work of Christ, the extent to which indeed we must allow validity to the Marxist-Leninist plea that what belongs to the achievement of reconciliation, and the excision from the deepest level from human life of all that may be called alienation, must be planted in the material context of human history, and not regarded as something to be embraced as an ideal actuality. The conflict within Christian tradition of the competing *attraits* of idealist and realistic philosophical styles is significant here. It may be a gain from the somewhat tedious logical exercise which we have pursued that we are enabled to see as clearly as possible what is involved in choice between a vaguely agnostic sense of the empty tomb as somehow relevant to the resurrection faith, a conviction that it is 'a sign pointing' to the depths of that faith, and a conviction that it is an essential part of that faith and indeed of the Christian faith as a whole. It would be a mistake to suppose that decision between these conflicting points of view is a matter of logic in the sense in which that term may be used of e.g. a study of the merits of rival systems as offering formal explications of notions used in precise argument. But recourse to the assistance of logical models may have the effect of revealing as clearly as possible the precise places in which fundamentally convictions diverge.

Yet even more complex is the Johannine treatment of perception as ground or condition of believing. Do we suppose that the conjunction of A or B perceives and A or B believes is one of the bare conjunction of the truth-values of the two propositions? Or is the one's truth related to the other's truth by the relation of strict implication, so that it is impossible that A or B should believe *and* A or B should not have seen? Yet to this the final words to Thomas give the lie. But again one immediately asks whether those who do not see but believe have heard at second, third, or fourth hand from those who have seen; or whether the seeing which is implicitly rebuked is the seeing of signs and wonders (ambivalent perceptual objects) and not the seeing of Jesus with the insignia of his passion everlastingly upon him to witness to the role of his mission and work in the constitution of all men's relation to God. Thomas's fault is perhaps slightly, but decisively, to misconstrue the role of these insignia. They are evidences because of what they evidence, namely the fusion in the Son of Man of the roles of Lamb of God and Judge of the world. It is certainly possible, in some sense, to believe and not to have seen, even as the example of Peter at the sepulchre reveals that it is possible to have seen and not to believe: this presumably because the proper *Vorverständnis* (in Peter's case of the scriptures) is lacking.

Yet faith and sight (and perception) belong together. What is this belonging? Is it not an implication of the Johannine argument that the logical models of material and strict implication and intensional entailment, when applied to the relation of perceiving and believing, break down?

One must use these models; yet what one seeks to capture is unique. One's use is part of the way in which one takes hold of the system of projection involved in the Christian faith; the taking hold of a problem from which one continually retreats, preferring the *ersatz* of an allegedly formal orthodoxy, or the security of an absolutely autonomous faith, unbound by the factual, and creative of its own objects, or the greater manageability of more tractable presentations of the fusion of complexity and simplicity characteristic of the evangelists' portrayal of the central figure. Philosophy, whether metaphysics, descriptive or speculative, or logic, is never master in theology, but its indispensable servant, never however giving a service that can be construed after a formula but one that throws light, now in one direction, now in another.

6

Some Notes on the Irreversibility of Time

I

There is no metaphysical problem more demanding in the range of expertise required for its effective treatment than that of time. At the centre of this daunting complexity there lies the fact that the problems set by this most pervasive form of the world of our experience, and of our experience of that world, involve at once issues of cosmology, requiring for their treatment considerable technical mathematical skill, and at the same time facets of the human mystery that have fascinated across the centuries poets, dramatists, and novelists of the highest order. Further, the theologian is immediately compelled to engage with the status of time. A most powerful religious tradition insists that ultimate salvation involves not only emancipation from temporal succession, but achievement of a perception that dismisses time as altogether unreal. Again, it is a commonplace that Augustine insisted that time came into being with creation, and that creation itself therefore could not be represented as itself being in time. Further, the influential American theologian, Reinhold Niebuhr, remarked that he could conceive no deeper division between one cultural tradition and another than the one established by the fact that in the one a Messiah was expected, while in the other such expectation had no place. One could, indeed, say that one of the most persistent and most nearly central problems of Christian theology across the centuries has been raised by the belief that in Jesus the messianic age has come in its fullness, and yet in such a way as to leave its fulfilment inconceivable in an unknown future. 'The hour cometh and now is.' The paradox of these words bites very deep.

It is very tempting indeed for one who, like the present writer,

is very far from being even faintly at home in the world of
cosmology, to treat of the extent to which the exploration of
temporal experience in great works of literature helps formulate
the sort of question to which, in the mystery of Christ, the outline
of an answer may be found, and at the same time protects the
exploration of that mystery from the sort of trivialization that
continually threatens it at the hands of professional apologists
and theologians. For such men quickly make of that which is
offered to us as the measure of our humanity something devoid
of all depth, the counter in an argument whose issue has already
been determined. Certainly in probing the theme of time and
alienation, such an essay would be entirely relevant. In a very
remarkable American novel of the early 1950s, *Lie Down in Darkness*, by William Styron, the central figure, a young woman
named Peyton Loftis, on the threshold of suicide, in a prolonged
soliloquy, rehearses the course of her life, which has been variously presented from other points of view in earlier sections of
the novel, the whole being set in the context of the funeral
journey of her mortal remains from railway station to cemetery,
in the Virginia in which her roots were found. But in the author's
organization of his material, the soliloquy is the climax, and if the
reader is to grasp its inwardness he must bear in mind all that he
has learnt concerning the experiences which have brought
Peyton to her ultimate extremity. There are very many memorable individual passages in the book, and it is part of the author's
achievement that he does not attempt, in the soliloquy, to recap-
ture many of them in detail, but rather to catch their resonance in
Peyton's consciousness. The end is her disintegration, and her
relations with her family have been so explored that this disintegration is accepted as inevitable. There is a very brief sequel in the
account of a baptismal service that formed the first climax of a
Negro revivalist's visit to the area in which Peyton had been born,
and in which her Negro nurse, who had followed her body to the
grave, took enthusiastic part. This revivalist would seem to have
been not simply a charlatan, but a thorough-going rascal. Yet the
sincerity of those who responded to him is beyond question, and
the book ends leaving altogether unanswered the problem of the
yawning gulf between such simplicities and the desperate need
of Peyton Loftis in her last hours. I mention this work deliberately
because the author's treatment of time and his representation of
temporal succession, whereby the crucial phases of Peyton's
tragic life are intercalated into the narrative of her funeral journey, have often received comment. The revivalist meeting itself

takes place on the evening of the funeral, and it would seem to have been beyond doubt the author's intention to present that day as gathering together and imposing the terrible final comment on all that had led up to it. Therefore it is within its context, even the setting of the sometimes almost comical delays that held back the funeral journey, that Peyton's history must be presented and seen.

Certainly for Styron, as for many other writers, the past is encapsulated in the present, and therefore, if we are to understand that past aright, we must set it in the context of that present to which it has given rise, as well as hinting at that future which lies ahead. But to write in these terms is of course not to suggest that a man's or a woman's actions and choice are at the mercy of what a future, which he or she cannot be expected fully to foresee, will make of them. Still less is it to ignore the fact that what men and women must steadfastly seek to impose on their contemporaries and their successors may provoke a violent reaction, the consequence certainly of their remorselessly executed policies, but a consequence often the very opposite of that which they had foreseen and intended. Thus it is a commonplace of contemporary comment on the styles of contemporary youthful religious enthusiasm that they have been encouraged by the peculiar complacency of the sort of humanism that supposed all problems in heaven and earth quickly soluble, and the kind of dogmatic religious faith that seemed to embody a comparably Philistine disregard of the strangeness, the richness, and the complexity of human reality.

But in the more perilous and more fragile world of personal life, men and women must reap what they sow, and those who find themselves at their mercy in the way in which, for the while at any rate, a child is at its parents' mercy, are inevitably the victims of their failures and their faults. To say this is not for one moment to imply that the child who quickly grows from childhood, to adolescence, to maturity, is a passive victim, submitted to the impact upon his or her humanity of the unresolved conflicts in its parents' life as anvil to hammer, or clay to potter's tool. As the child grows, so a measure of involvement, even of complicity, conscious or self-conscious, becomes nearly universal. If the stuff of human existence is frequently tragic, and men and women estranged from what they would be by an inheritance they have not fashioned, and are powerless to control, we must eschew, in speaking of that existence, the idiom of a facile determinism. The language of reaction, of inevitable consequence, of inescapable condition, which we naturally use in such connection, suggests indeed rigid *a tergo* determinism, and most certainly we have to reckon with causality. But what we also have to recall is what human beings in their suffering make of that which has made them what they are, which indeed they themselves go on to fashion or to refashion. One would not easily use teleological language in respect of Peyton Loftis' soliloquy; she is too deranged to come to terms with herself to impose, let alone to find, any design in the terrible circumstances through which she has come to her final crisis. Her language is expressive of the desperate incoherence of suffering; she is not able to formulate the need that she would have somehow met, and therefore she destroys herself. Yet she knows that it is her past, including those elements of that past that she herself has fashioned, that has brought her to the place in which she finds herself, from which there is no deliverance.

Of course, as those who know the novel to which I have referred will not need to be reminded, at the very centre of Peyton's painful recapitulation of her life is the memory of the nearly explicitly incestuous element in her relations with her father and his with her. We could even say that the guilt of this memory is the organizing principle of her life as she sums it up on the threshold of her death. In such remembering we do organize, imposing form or shape, even a terrible design upon the items of our recollected biography. Such organization is an element in remembering, humanly a very important element, yet always subordinate to sense of the past as something given. We do not organize in order to escape, at least if our organization is to claim any measure of validity. We organize in order to bring home to ourselves what is there, even to achieve proper emphasis in the weight we distribute between the constituents of our biography.

To come to terms with human existence one must employ the concept of causality. Without that concept, memory degenerates into the haphazard recollection of the near senile, who in conversation wearies his fellows with minutely detailed records of individual happenings. The recall of one suggests another, and before the tale of the former has been told, the old man plunges into the detail of the second, all relevance, even coherence, fading away in childish self-absorption. But it is through causality that memory is disciplined, and the items of our lives assume relative significance. To suppose human beings in their history exempt from causal determination is to suppose them exempt from a most fundamental condition of their humanity. And in their lives causality is exemplified in the power of the past to affect the present. Indeed it is through the notion of causality that the notion of the past itself receives that quality of sheer inexorable givenness with which we invest it. We say that the past cannot be altered, and when we say this we refer to events remote in geological or historical time, which have nothing to do with our own individual biography. Again, we are quite familiar with sequences of events whose order cannot be changed, say the departure of a train before the giving of a lecture, that the one, as matter of objective fact, happened before the other, and that nothing can alter such order, even though there is, in the second event, nothing to which the occurrence of the first is remotely relevant. Where there is objective time order, objective before and after, there, though we can trace no element of determination between one event and its successor, we invest that order with an element of necessity borrowed from what we have learnt of the remorselessness of event sequence, when one determines another.

It was part of Kant's philosophical achievement to recognize the intimate relation between time and causality. His argument in the Second Analogy of Experience of the Critique of Pure Reason, is dauntingly difficult, and it is a commonplace to point out the extent to which he is in bondage to the physics of his day, and presenting arguments that the great changes in physical theory of the last century have outdated. Yet it could be claimed for him that he saw that it was only in a world in which we could trace the writ of a certain sort of causal order that we could come to recognize objective temporal sequences. Where there is causality, there we have to reckon with an 'Although' character in the sequence concerned. That is, although we might like it otherwise, when one event has happened (unless drastic action can be taken and is taken) certain consequences will follow. If a child has consumed Paraquat, then that child's life is at risk. More fundamentally, in the natural world we fasten on features in our universe which impose upon us sense of inevitable direction. How do we learn that time has a direction, except we find in the world 'Although' sequences on such a scale that they impose upon us sense of temporal direction, even as we bring home to ourselves the dependence of one event upon another by expressing this dependence in form of 'if . . . then'?

To write in these terms is not to defend Kant's treatment of causality, still less his treatment of time as a subjective form of inner sense. It is rather to raise the important issues focused by the so-called causal theory of time, namely its acknowledgment of the extent to which temporal consciousness is bound up with certain features in the world or rather, I should say, the universe, which are beyond question contingent, but which would seem necessary conditions of our coming to think of time as having a direction, and therefore ultimately of ourselves, as having a history in which one facet deeply affects another. The world of personal existence is irreducibly unique; yet in setting to ourselves the problems which it raises, in seeking to frame, even in the sort of extremity in which William Styron portrays Peyton Loftis, the stuff of which we are made and of which we have made ourselves, we take these notions for granted; we suppose that where our own lives are concerned the concepts of temporal direction, causality and the rest unquestionably apply. We reach beyond the sort of self-interpretation that a facile determinism might achieve, to a teleology or quasi-teleology, by way of the kind of organization of which I have written above. Yet such self-definition takes for granted that where the ultimate reaches of our being are concerned, causality has valid application. But we are coming to learn that there are realms in the universe, the so-called 'black holes', where such constants as space and time have no significance, where indeed they cease to be (whatever these words mean). Have we used cosmological conceptions of only relative import to present to ourselves the ultimate problems of our existence? And if we have, is not the validity of this supposedly ultimate self-interrogation in question?

Whether we like it or not, the world of the cosmologist impinges upon the intimate world of existential exploration, and its forms. For the human world is in a perfectly significant sense part of that larger universe, a part in which the most deeply disturbing questions that that universe poses receive formulation.

And it is at this point that I would turn to the theology of the Incarnation. Although the best texts of the third gospel do not include the verse, in many texts of St Luke's gospel Christ is portrayed as praying in the hour of his crucifixion: 'Father, forgive them; for they know not what they do' Only one totally innocent could use such words, one altogether without ultimate complicity in the complex circumstances that had brought him to the gallows. Otherwise, the very contribution that by complicity he had made in producing the circumstances that had led to his arrest, trial and execution, would have made the occasion such that in part, even in very small part, he must admit that his executioners knew that for which they were exacting penalty. As it was, they were destroying the innocent, and therefore the innocent was in a position to convert his very guiltlessness into a plea for his destroyers. For he alone knew what they were about. Yet here too, at a depth one fears to explore, one is taking for granted direction of time, causality, and the rest. A man is able to present his total innocence as the expression of a mercy that lies beyond justice. But to do so he must first have come to terms with himself, and have supposed such coming to terms to have an ultimate significance.

II

Further treatment of the problems of time with which this essay is concerned must involve transition from metaphysics to theology.

What of the maintenance of the order of the world by the Logos during the period of the Incarnation? It is often made an objection to so-called kenotic conceptions of the Incarnation that they compel us to reckon with the parallel activity of the supposedly depotentiated Logos within the decades of the life of Jesus, and of the Logos through whose agency all things come into being, and are held in being, that Logos who remains as the Father's wisdom, which can no more be withdrawn from the unity of the divine being than can its power and its love.

Within the field of the Incarnate life, we read of growth in wisdom, as well as in stature. What is it that grows? If we say that it is a child who passes into boyhood, into adolescence, and into manhood, we speak of one who, by virtue of that swift maturing, discards the thoughts of childhood for the restless, uneasy dreams of adolescence, and replaces those dreams by the more mature understanding that comes with manhood. Yet this understanding is not something won once for all, but painfully affirmed. Or rather, if there are moments of vision, their content has to be painfully transcribed in the ragged piecemeal succession of human actions, performed in circumstances not entirely foreseeable, and even when foreseen, still in the cruel impact of angry exchange, always less manageable than even the clearest foresight can make the wise man realize.

In all these remarks temporality has been taken for granted, as a form of growth, but also inevitably as a form also of estrangement. For the past gives way to the present and the present is succeeded by that which is future. In Christ's life there is estrangement from the past, but without that loss of compassion which is part-product of the bitterness which in human life so often succeeds what at least in memory seems fraught with promise, and part-working out of the seeds of corruption which, all unnoticed, were sown in days that in the harsh present seem suffused with a tenderness that at best only half belonged to them. For Christ there is the estrangement involved in abandoning his human origins, in tearing his life up by the roots to put himself at the disposal of the men and the women to whom he believed himself sent. The marks of that estrangement are upon him, reflected in the harshness of his rebuffs to his mother, and to his brothers. Mary's own sorrow is a resonance in her spirit of that bitter grief, and it is the memory of days past that makes for her son the bitterness of the act wherein he plunges home the sword of her necessary human grief.

These are but random illustrations of the manner in which acceptance of the conditions of temporality belong to the very substance of the Incarnate life. If we ask concerning its peculiar burdens, we find that we must speak of time. For if we confine ourselves to the sort of human perspective criticized in other places in this paper, we find that freedom from temporal limitations is something that presents itself to us as a kind of peace, a kind of immediate wholeness without the cost of letting go, but with the possibility of the vanishing in totality of the bitterness of those parts which in their individuality seem cruel, at least in recollection. We strain after a transcendence of time that is humanly conceived, a timelessness that is before all else an absence of those elements in human time that disturb us. But timelessness, the eternity of God, is otherwise.

In Christ that eternity is conjoined with the particularity of a human career. It is a supremely creative conjunction. But if its creative quality is not to be lost, its paradox must first be affirmed. So, too, the deepest perplexities concerning the status of time, with which the earlier part of this paper has been concerned, must receive as clear a definition as possible. This not because these perplexities, which belong to the very stuff of reflective human existence, receive any sort of direct answer at the distinctively theological level, but because at that level they can be reformulated and refashioned.

How does the historically achieved innocence of Jesus make effectively present in temporal terms the very creativity of God, that creativity which in traditional theology is supposedly exercise unbroken by Logos? The Word of God proceeds into the world, yet leaves not his Father's side. How is the everlasting channelled through that which is temporary, even when that which is temporary is able to be given enduring reality by the resurrection? What is it that is raised and what can we say of the raising? To end this paper by a series of questions is not simply perhaps to show that it is incomplete, but that in reflection concerning time every sort of problem is raised. As in a kaleidoscope, fundamental questions of cosmology, ethics, metaphysics, dogmatic theology, seem to pass one into the other. The paradox of the union in Christ's person of God and man becomes more tormenting than ever, and at the same time the relativity of the form of human beings' self-interrogation raises anew the issue of their standing. Almost we reach for heights and at the same time discern depths that call for the genius of a new Pascal to face them, to find the idiom by which they may be conveyed.

7

Finality in Metaphysics, Ethics and Theology

It is impossible in discussion of these issues to avoid being controversial. Is there finality in metaphysics, ethics, theology? Is there that which admits of no revision, that can be formulated once for all?

I

Let us take metaphysics first.

1. Do we suppose that in *metaphysica generalis* there are certain truths which we know beyond shadow of question? There are contingent truths which we so know, for example, that Julius Caesar was murdered on the Ides of March, 44 BC; that there was a very severe storm in the west of Scotland on 14/15 January 1968; that we are at present in Rome. But these truths, although we would say that they are incorrigible, are not metaphysical truths; they relate to particular matters of fact, that are as they are and are not otherwise. Certainly we know that they are so. We do not believe them in the sense in which we believe, for example, that there is now a fast train running on its journey between Rome and Naples, that General de Gaulle is at present in Colombey des deux Églises, that there are at least a dozen cats to be found in the buildings of Rome University. Our evidence for these propositions varies and our grounds for believing them are not equally strong. We admit that evidence may be adduced to strengthen or weaken our belief in any one of them. But what we claim to know (unless, of course, we are compelled to reject our claim and say that we were wrong to speak of ourselves as knowing one or other of the facts) is not thus subject to modification. I may say significantly: 'I believe that there are at least a dozen cats in the University buildings; but I may be wrong'; but it is nonsense to

say that I know that Caesar was murdered on 15 March 44 BC, but that I may be wrong.

Are there any metaphysical truths of comparable certainty? But firstly, what is a metaphysical truth?

(*a*) Clearly it is not enough to say that it is non-empirical. Mathematical truths, for example, that any number is the sum of two primes, are non-empirical. Such a truth is subject to rigorous proof; it is immune to observational confirmation or verification. If I say that as my sample approaches infinity, so the ratio of heavy smokers to contract carcinoma of the lung tends to come to rest in the ratio 6:10, observational results may confirm or falsify my findings. The ratio may not approach, even asymptotically, the proportion given. But if I say, for example, that the square of the sum of two numbers is equal to the sum of their squares plus twice their product, what I say is immune from any observational confirmation. Numbers are not constituents of the world around us as beads and balls, telegraph poles and stinging nettles are. Moreover such arithmetical truths are universal and necessary; they cannot be other than they are. While the motley of mathematics is ever including new sorts of proof and equation, while its frontiers are open, if we suppose in mathematics we are learning and discovering, not inventing and constructing, then we are establishing universal and necessary truths concerning what lies outside empirical observation in the sense in which sticks and stones, flowers, trees, animals, sculptures, chairs, etc. lie within it. Yet although Plato supposed a very close relation between metaphysical and mathematical truths, even he recognized very significant differences between the latter and the former.

(*b*) A metaphysical truth of the kind we are now speaking of does agree with mathematical truth in claiming universality and necessity. Like them it relates to what must be the case, but to what must be the case in a way significantly different from that in which we say of mathematical truths that they must be as they are. Among candidates for the class of such truths we may include the thesis that all that happens belongs to a single time order, that nothing happens without falling along some causal line in terms of which it is explicable, that there are relatively permanent things to which events happen, and that truth itself consists fundamentally in the correspondence of a proposition and a fact.

These truths (if truths they are) are not established by the special sciences. If we speak of the second as a formulation of the law of causality, we do not suppose that law to be akin to, but more general in scope than particular causal laws, for instance Newton's inverse square law. It is in Wittgenstein's words, 'less a law than the form of a law', viz. all laws of a causal form. These truths are cetainly in some special sense necessary. We cannot conceive that they are not true. At least we do not know what we should count as evidence against some of them (causality is in a special case here). They possess the authority which comes from our obstinacy in disregarding alleged evidence against them, and in part they can be vindicated by showing their indispensable role in descriptive discourse. Yet we hesitate to regard their authority (in spite of Kant's strenuous work) as quite independent of the inveterate eagerness of our imaginations to see things so, and not otherwise. It is as if we were fettered psychologically against the kind of flexibility which would enable us discard the concepts of thing, quality, causality and the rest; or conceive truth less narrowly than in terms of correspondence. It is a commonplace to say with Whitehead that, following the work of David Hume and Immanuel Kant, the notion of substance, of that which exists of itself and of that which makes what exists to be what it is (*substantia prima* and *substantia secunda*) has been in ruins and that practitioners of *metaphysica generalis* have sought a substitute in vain. The rigour of mathematical proof is anyhow lacking. If Descartes sought to extend the competence of mathematical method to metaphysics, Kant laid his project in ruins, and as we have remarked, if Plato assigned to mathematics a uniquely close relation to metaphysics, it was as a propaedeutic study only on the road that led upwards to the vision of transcendent being. Yet the principles noted provide an *ébauche* of the subject matter of *metaphysica generalis*. We are concerned to give account of thing and quality, existence, time, causality: those notions whose principles enter into our discourse, shaping its conceptual syntax, organizing at once our enquiries and our discoveries. Can we conceive understanding without causal insight, however various our field or fields, however sophisticated the issue? In history we may say that we find the dynamics of action in a particular society or individual more easily conceivable than those of another, the mind of the humanist more accessible than that of the martyr, the mind of the conscript more accessible than that of the Crusader, at once flamboyantly devout and flamboyantly cruel. Where martyrs are concerned, we may find the temper of the hesitant martyr less obscure than that of Ignatius of Antioch, eager, as he wrote to the Christians in Rome, to feel the lions' bite upon his flesh.

Yet always we invoke the notion of causality, both to master the origins of the attitudes we find congenial or opaque and our own responsiveness to the one and recoil from the other. We find ourselves using the notion in the very effort to take stock of our relativity.

2. Of course over against *metaphysica generalis* stands *metaphysica specialis*, including natural theology, with its claim to establish the existence of God, the immortality of the soul, etc. by light of natural reason. In Roman Catholic theology the decrees of Vatican I have insisted that such truths can be demonstrated. The word 'can' is important. It is not claimed that the demonstration has in fact been carried out. Thus as it may be that a mathematician will prove rigorously one day that every even number is necessarily the sum of two primes, so in created things by light of natural reason man may one day trace (in abstraction from divine revelation) the unmistakable handiwork of the Creator in his creation. The 'five ways' of St Thomas (leaving aside the fourth way, the most Platonic of the five) are too entangled with Aristotelian physics to command easy assent, and the attempt for instance of Reginald Garrigou-Lagrange, OP, to present them in almost Leibnizian form ignores the Aristotelian inheritance of the Angelic Doctor and involves the author in the necessity of defending the principle of sufficient reason.

What do we mean by *metaphysica specialis*? A series of projects, of speculative essays, including the central books of Plato's *Republic* and Aristotle's *Metaphysics Λ*? But these are concerned with radically different enquiries – the ontological foundations of conduct, the ultimate implications of cosmogony and cosmology conceived in terms of motion, itself specially understood. One may suppose the point of departure of the one or of both significant. Yet what survives is more an interrogative temper than anything else, a sense of human conduct and the self-criticism in which it involves us as pointing beyond itself, the suggested presence to the changes and chances of this fleeting world of a ground of its processes, self-contained, perfect in itself, spiritual activity at once inexhaustible and complete. Do we have argument here or vision? In Plato's case it is vision intuitively discerned and converted into graspable principles of dialectic. It is vision that passed from guesswork to irrefragable certainty, and while remaining incommunicable provides the very foundation of systematic understanding of the world. At once conduct and understanding are systematically reconstructed. We have here a classical instance of the dynamism of the heart, restless until it rests in the Absolute, a rest achieved that is no tranquillity but a profound intellectual satisfaction.

3. Yet one cannot stop there. What of immanentist metaphysics? I think particularly of the Hegelian image of a universal reconciliation in which conflicts at once of ideas and of institutions achieve solution through a dialectical self-development, which is all-including, all-integrating. It has been widely-remarked that the roots of the Hegelian dialectic can be found more in Aeschylus' *Oresteia* than in the Socratic dialogues or in the highly self-conscious argumentation of such later works of the Corpus Platonicum as the *Sophist*. Certainly (and here we touch the opposition between Hegel and his greatest pupil, Karl Marx) the so-called 'problem of evil' lies just below the surface of the writing of his earlier and more seminal period, viz., that concluded by the achievement of the *Phenomenology of Spirit*. But for our purposes we have to ask how far his metaphysical explanations are capable of inclusion in the kind of general pattern of *metaphysica specialis* we have sketched above. Historians of logic are accustomed to regard the logic of Hegel and his successors, including here the English logicians F. A. Bradley and Bernard Bosanquet, as a kind of sport, interrupting the nineteenth- and twentieth-century renewal, through the work of such masters as Frege and Russell, of the classical tradition of logical theory established by Aristotle. Yet the revolutionary impact of Hegelian metaphysics is felt today, even increasingly. Certainly a large part of the work of the so-called British idealists (ignorant as it was of Hegel's *Jugendschriften*) is of little more than historical interest. But neither the existentialism nor the Marxism of the present day can be understood without a deep knowledge of Hegel's speculative adventures. It is arguable that there is profound innovation here: a seriousness about the reality of historical change, and an attempt to treat such change as the most significant dimension of becoming, but also a deliberate if not always conscious rejection of the most profound spiritual error of transcendent metaphysics, the relegation of evil, whether physical or moral, to the category of *steresis*, the treatment of evil as *privatio boni*. We have here an attempt to heal the schism achieved by Plato between philosophy and tragedy, even to incorporate in the texture of systematic philosophy uninterpreted Christian insights concerning the 'way of the Son of God into the far country'.

It is here perhaps that we find a paradigm case of revolution in *metaphysica specialis*. But one might look elsewhere and enquire more deeply and more rigorously the extent to which one supposes the 'five ways' of St Thomas (apart from the fourth) to be uncritically woven together with an Aristotelian system of the physical world. There is certainly much in Aristotle (I take as examples his explorations of substance, his doctrine of 'focal meaning', his conception of the method of ethics, his analysis of the concept of possession), quite independent of his cosmology; and so there is in St Thomas. But if, as a very able Dominican Thomist whom I once had the privilege of teaching put it, one regards God as 'the name of the problem which the world by its existence sets', and the 'five ways' as five ways in which that problem may be more precisely set out, must one not ask oneself whether for us the problem may not be quite differently posed? One may go further, and referring to the *arcana* of the fourth way (the doctrine of degrees of being so vulnerable to the treatment of the concept of existence in modern logic) suggest that for us the crux is much more whether we can attach any sense to the motion of the world by its existence 'setting us a problem'. Is such language intelligible, or do we not find ourselves reduced to inarticulacy, if not *aphasia*, as soon as we seek to pose such metaphysical questions? We come to understand the grounds of this *aphasia* through the certainly constant studies of *metaphysica specialis*; we become self-conscious concerning the limits of language against which we thrust in the effort to form for ourselves ultimate questions. But does such 'thrusting' in any way constitute proof as understood by Vatican I? It is perhaps a manifestation of the restless heart; but if we affirm that this restlessness must have a cause in which formally or eminently the perfection of its effect is contained, does our intellectual self-consciousness concerning the import and power of the crucial concept of causality justify such generalizations concerning the content of what we call cause? There is no setting any limit to the importance for metaphysics and theology of the critical reconstruction of the concept of causality in the philosophies of Hume and Kant, and in particular the latter's vindication of its authority as an objectivity-concept.

In the end, if we leave on one side the certainly valid, if very difficult and obscure enterprise of *metaphysica generalis*, we find constancy (if constancy may be regarded as equivalent here to finality) *only in a certain temper of interrogation*. It is a style or set of styles of questioning rather than a set of answers. We can study the latter as philosophical analysts, and as historians; we can glean a suggestion here, a hint there, catch the vague outline of an argument in one place, be fired elsewhere by the impulse to formally visionary speculation. If there is a *metaphysica perennis*, it is found more in the strange immunity to the acids of criticism of a programme rather than in a positive body of achievement. Where there is achievement it resides more in the deepened awareness of what such a programme involves, and of understanding of the conceptual tools we need for its advancement – and here of course I refer to the interplay of *metaphysica generalis* with *metaphysica specialis*: an interplay that we are immediately aware of in the classical authorities, Aristotle and Kant.

Over against this we have to reckon with the Hegelian incorporation into the body of speculative philosophy of the cry for redemption. It is through literature (which Plato so vigorously censured) that the bitterness of that cry is caught. It was through classical theology that the quality of its dereliction was somehow concealed by the supposedly comforting relegation of evil to the category of *steresis*, thus by an ontological trick reconciling the universal scope of the divine causality with the goodness of its operation. At the level of *lex orandi* the Christian church was wiser: yet fearing here to allow *lex orandi* to become *lex credendi* in an understandable fear of the consequences of an ultimate dualism, not least in the soteriological form of the near perverted styles of predestinarian doctrine. Yet if men and women cease to believe, it is, as a matter of fact, less because they find the *credenda* unintelligible than because their most poignant cries go unheard. If metaphysics has a future, it may only be through the implementation to the full of the change wrought in its structure by the inclusion within its scope not simply of human nisus towards the transcendent, but of human revolt against the burdens historical circumstances as well as nature has laid upon man. It is a commonplace that in his later and more conservative phase Hegel sought to break down, even dialectically to destroy altogether, opposition between real and rational, between what is and what ought to be, that he construed reconciliation too nearly in terms of men's acceptance of the rational necessity of their lot, a lot that was admittedly always in process of change. But Marxist criticism of this development, and the testimony against it of Hegel's own *Jugendschriften*, are evidence enough that this later development belongs to the accidents rather than the substance of his doctrine. At its heart there lies the recognition that historical self-consciousness belongs to the very stuff of human existence, that freedom in the sense of a true autonomy is at once the foundation of our every effort to make sense of our inheritance; but that it is a freedom menaced all the time by forces, many but not all of which lie outside our control, facing us by the pressure of their ugly insistence upon our purposings with a sense of overmastering futility, defeat, even besetting cruelty. The threat is of something much more profound than that of Cartesian *malin génie*, it is the menace of a backlash somehow built into the heart of things that will lay our sanity itself in ruins. We are face to face not with a grisly theodicy that allows historical greatness to provide its own moral order (there are more than hints of this in Hegel), but with a cussedness which seems totally recalcitrant to the logos of any justification of the ways of God to man. And here the last word is with the cry for redemption.

II

So we pass inevitably to ethics.

If we say that the moral philosopher is concerned with 'no light question' but with the question how we must live our lives, it seems altogether absurd to suppose that here there can be finality. For what is human life apart from the circumstances in which it is lived? It is absured to suppose that a twentieth-century Roman curial official can understand the problems of a South American guerilla in the struggle against social injustice in which he is plunged. Absurd also to suppose that the latter's response to his extreme situation can illuminate the curricular problems of the Western European University student of the 1970s. Again, one hears it said with perfect justification that it is foolish to suppose that the most intimate problems of the married can be adequately assessed by the average (I say average, advisedly) seminary-trained professional clerical celibate. The latter's rigorous self-discipline imposes obstacles in the way of understanding that are inevitable. There is gain, as well as loss; but that gain has been paid for.

But these examples, though important, are relatively circumscribed. Those who speak of moral finality and who advance beyond the relatively vacuous *omne bonum est sequendum, malum vitandum* etc. – tend to appeal to a code of precepts which may not be presented (in deontological terms) as self-justifying, but are regarded as comprising the substance of the good life. If the code lists a series of prohibitions, they are prohibitions related to virtues cultivated and achieved through the avoidance of what is prohibited: such virtues as reverence, singleness of heart, honesty, self-control, chastity, forbearance, and the rest. The detailed problems attendant on their cultivation in every life, the content for instance of personal honesty in the case of the executive of an advertising firm, or of a government servant with a special responsibility for intelligence, espionage and security generally, is left to the casuist, whether or not his work is specially orientated to the administration of the discipline of the confessional, or whether its scope is more widely conceived. Every sort of device is exploited to still the scruples of the man who seems almost estranged from the substance of himself by the commands laid upon him by public authority, to help him shelve the burden of personal responsibility and regard his inmost core as untouched by the accident of his being compelled to carry out a repulsive duty. One thinks here of the case of Bishop Defregger: but one also remembers with a reverence that the bishop's example hardly elicits the case of the brave Austrian peasant, Franz Jägerstätter, who refused any such escape routes, and by his martyr's death reminded his contemporaries that the accommodating ways of the casuist may enable a man to carry on the business of living only at the cost of a cultivated neglect of its ultimate demands.

Yet it is not with the doubtless partly compassionate absurdities of the casuist that we are here concerned: more significant for our purpose is the extent to which a moral tradition may be shaped and deformed by the unacknowledged assumptions and situation of its interpreters. This is abundantly true of ecclesiastics. It would be widely admitted today (one thinks here indeed of actual papal documents as well as of the outstanding work done by such men as Fathers Desroches and Girardi) that the appraisal of Communism in the papal encyclical of 1937 – *Divini Redemptoris* – was fatally and hopelessly inadequate to the reality. Indeed its temper can only be paralleled by the feverish preoccupation with supposed anti-constitutional conspiracy that inflicted official circles in Great Britain in the early 20s, and is reflected in the popular literature of the period. Both alike failed totally to engage with the complex and sombre reality that Leninist and Stalinist Communism undoubtedly were. There was a failure to come to terms with a terrible human reality, an escape into security provided by allegedly evident abstractions concerning truth, property, freedom and the rest. But there was no effort to enlist the imagination in service of an attempt to understand what made men and women embrace at sacrificial cost this grimly demanding way of life, what made the social order those men sought to achieve a goal of human aspiration, what indeed (as in the tragically confused circumstances of the Spanish Civil War) made men who were certainly not Communists in the Moscow sense, ready to accept the latters' alliance in resistance to the threat of a military despotism, which, if favourable to the external framework of religious observance, seemed to threaten the very possibility of a radical social justice and a significant political freedom. Here is an almost classic case of the extent to which interpreters of a moral tradition showed themselves the bond-slaves of their inheritance, the enemies less of innovation than of the effective renewal of that committed to their charge. For as the examples of Socrates and Jesus alike make plain, it is only in dialogue that moral understanding is advanced; there is a refusal of dialogue, a preference to speak *de haut en bas*, in detached authoritarian idiom, which is paradoxically the very abdication of authority itself.

What is true of the ecclesiastic is also true of the academic moral philosopher. He can create an island of delicate abstractions and name his creation the moral life; he can ignore what is actually happening to men and women, or rather what they have done and are doing. In what follows my debt is great to Henri de Lubac's profound study of 'L'Homme Nouveau' (a lecture later published in his *Affrontements mystiques*).[1] Before Bonhoeffer's *Letters and Papers from Prison* were published in 1953,[2] de Lubac enabled his readers to take stock of a central transformation in their world in respect of which they must make their moral concepts significant. Men are becoming to an ever increasing extent the masters of their environment; there is no uniform, linear progress towards betterment; it could be (in such cities as Calcutta, perhaps it already is) a road to catastrophe. Men have increased, they are increasing expectation of life; pneumonia is no longer 'the old man's friend'; the scourges of TB, of cholera, of diphtheria, are obliterated. Soon maybe cancer will yield its dreadful secrets, and the most feared of all terminal illnesses will be beaten. But all the time the rate of the 'population explosion' accelerates with no possibility of expanding productive resources or habitable space to keep pace with its demands. Rather an indisciplined use of pollutant agents may be thought to reduce even further the adequacy of natural resources to supply the needs which they must meet. Maybe we cannot avoid the disorder which threatens us; but it is a situation which touches the very substance of our lives and it remains true that it issues in part from our own achievement. If we were not so successful in reducing the incidence of disease, in raising materially the chances and duration of human survival, the problem would not face us with the same sharpness. What we have to come to terms with is the consequence of our own achievement. To speak in these terms is of course to over-simplify. There are very many other problems raised, for instance, by the imprudent ruthlessness of our exploitation of natural resources, by the repudiation of traditional pieties towards our environment, pieties whose claim to our serious regard can be justified by inductive argument as well as by appeal to tradition. But we have to realize that some of the gravest dangers that threaten us come from what we have done, and that it is indeed a significant chapter in human history in which arguably widespread use of artificial means of birth control is less a matter of hesitant permission than something which is a sheer duty. It is not that men and women *may* use such means to limit the size of their families, it is rather that it has become their duty to do so. This if the quality of human life is not to be forfeit, and human existence overtaken by the violent, angry brutality and must characterize a struggle for survival.

Yet in the Promethean age in which we live there are other questions which press upon us. In the West we are aware in a quite new way of responsibility for the so-called underdeveloped areas of the world. I say – in a quite new way; for our awareness is at present little more than a painful recognition that the paternalist self-esteem which saw Western nations charged with a civilizing mission towards 'lesser breeds without the law' is giving place to something else, something which at present hardly achieves satisfactory definition, but which we realize we must somehow find, if again destruction is not to overtake us. So far I argue on a prudential plane; yet prudence alone may bid us realize how much that we have inherited from the past, that is sentimentally dear to us perhaps as belonging to a vanished Christendom, is expressive of prejudice and folly, pride and cruelty. No one of my age in Europe today can escape a measure of responsibility for the mounting tensions between Jew and Arab in the Middle East which have followed the development of Israel. This because widespread acquiescence in the enormity of the 'final solution' on the part of allegedly civilized European men and women makes it inconceivable that Jews should ever listen to their plea for moderation, when bitter experience has taught them the need of a technically powerful *Machtstaat* to protect their own from the Eichmanns of this world, and those who couch in subtly diplomatic language their grounds for refusing to interfere with their designs.

We live in a new world, and the temptation of the academic, as of the ecclesiastic, is to reduce its novelties to terms of the comfortable and the familiar. Indeed we live in a world which by reason of the extent to which we must assume responsibility for its shape may make us let slip many burdens imposed upon us by the illusions of past ages; especially is this true of the manner of Christian presence in the world. We live in a period in which the traditional moral conception of an inviolable human norm, a natural law, is called in question, and some of us (including the author of this paper) find the issue further complicated by relatively arbitrary authoritarian reassertions of the elements in that tradition that are most seriously open to the gravest questioning. To dismiss the problem raised by the proper employment of methods of artificial contraception by an uncompromising rejection of their use in any circumstances is in fact to put the highly significant tradition of a human norm in further jeopardy: and that when its reassertion in terms significant for the age of Prometheus is a task of quite fundamental importance. There is a moral Luddism which seeks to dodge the task of the baptizing of Prometheus by the depreciation of his gifts, and by the by-passing of the problems the use of these gifts has raised.

The origins of this highly complex tradition of natural law are found, I suppose, in the sophistic severance of *nomos* from *phusis* and its criticism; but very many other elements, Stoic, Jewish, and Christian, ethical and juridical have contributed to its evolution. Its concepts have been invoked in the service of a radical critique of the claims of deeply entrenched inherited power to ride rough-shod over elementary human rights. Its concepts have also served the conservative critics of the claims of self-appointed revolutionary élites to refashion human societies after the pattern of their abstract idealism. In the field of personal morality it has helped to articulate the vague persistent sense that men and women have constantly found pressing on them that the proper order of human life is not a matter of arbitrary choice or decision, but that however the contours of human life may be changed, or its horizons enlarged, there are still constants with which men must come to terms – birth, marriage, old age, death, the claims of the other who confronts them, the limits imposed on permissible disregard of his or her claims etc. The individual's very sense of his own dignity as an autonomous subject, whose personal responsibility for what he does and is cannot ultimately be alienated to any authority, however august, is seen as bound up with his parallel sense of a human norm which he must affirm. If the International Military Tribunal at Nuremberg in 1946 was more than a device for ensuring that indiscriminate vengeance on the executants of unspeakable atrocities should not help perpetuate the evils they had brought into being, it was surely a public avowal of the deeply significant principle that obedience to superiors, or alleged involvement in the acts of a public authority, does not exculpate the authors of actions which must be regarded as an outrage against humanity. Triumphant disobedience is always a human possibility: the Jägerstätters of this world sit in judgment upon the Defreggers, though the former earn a martyr's death and the latter episcopal dignity.

The tradition of natural law has to be resurrected in forms significant for an age in which a vast number of the most searching novel problems which confront mankind, whether personal or collective, spring from his increasing technological dominion over his environment. This dominion has to a considerable extent forfeited any innocence which might have marked it. One thinks not only of the harnessing of nuclear power to the services of a globally destructive military technology, but also of the infection by the temper of a lawless acquisitiveness of our exploitation of natural resources. If one repudiates a Luddite nostalgia for alleged past simplicities, which too often prove on detailed investigation to be little more than veils cast over unimaginable crudity and cruelty, one must also reject a Utopian endorsement of the comtemporary simply because it is contemporary. We need in fact to find the means of stating to ourselves the fundamental moral question, the problem of establishing the lineaments of the human in the Promethean age. And the menace that confronts this task from the standpoint of an authoritarian traditionalism is that of seeking to impose as a solution the behaviour patterns of a previous cultural epoch. Of course they are no solution; how can they be, when the attempt to put the question is impatiently cut short. It is no doubt very hard for those who see themselves as appointed to teach all men to define to themselves their task in an age in which the form that deepest reflection must assume is almost inevitably interrogative.

Where metaphysics is concerned, we have suggested that what is final in the sense of resistant to the dissolvent force of the problem of evil on the one side, and to the authority of a logic and methodology deeply empiricist in temper on the other, is an interrogation or, to use language more fashionable on the Continent of Europe than in the United Kingdom, the way in which the problem of the sense of being presses upon us. But we need not be empiricists to reckon here with a unity of theory and practice.

For those who are most beset by a metaphysical questioning are those on whom the question of the way in which they should live most urgently presses. It was Jacques Maritain who, in the bitter thirties of this century, wrote that the very crisis of the economic order compelled us to study metaphysics. One need not subscribe to Maritain's somewhat dated neo-Thomist conception of metaphysical enquiry to admit the general validity of his suggestion. It is indeed out of the crisis of the traditional moral order as we discern it that our metaphysical questioning is born.

We have to ask what sense we give to the notion of an inviolable human norm or paradigm in an age in which we have to reckon with the hardly foreseeable extension of technical mastery over our environment on the one hand, and with the growing recognition of the moral significance of the category of revolt on the other. The sense of limitation, the sense of norms that men and women only transgress at the cost of hardly explicable *hybris*, the sense of norms built into the stuff of human reality – all these have gone to shape the tradition of natural law. Granted that they have proved of revolutionary as well as conservative significance, there is no doubt that in Christian spirituality they have been integrated with a body of teaching that counsels humility rather than protest, obedience rather than revolt. The effect of this *de facto* congruity alleged between the true road of human existence and the prescriptions of established authority has been almost entirely disastrous. It is not for nothing that it has become currently fashionable to characterize the conversion of Constantine as the greatest single historical disaster to overwhelm the Christian church. But whatever our verdict on the past, Christians today face the perils and opportunities of a post-Constantinian age, an age in which the human norm has to be sought and affirmed in a mood of radical questioning, recognized in fact as the interrogation of the changing human order in the name of a human ultimate, the last-named at once a *datum* and a *dandum*, at once a starting-point and a goal. What abides finally is the kind of interrogation that, in the complex of threat and promise under which we live, confronts us in the end with the pressure upon us of the commandment of a relevant charity. And here there is continuity with the past.

III

We come lastly to the question of finality in theology, perhaps the most controversial issue of all. For here we have to reckon not only with what may be defined as the *articulus stantis vel cadentis fidei* but with the validity of doctrinal developments which many today would do more than question. Inevitably one thinks primarily of the two Marian dogmas, the dogma of the Immaculate Conception, defined in 1854, and that of the corporal Assumption, defined in 1950. Of the two it is the latter which most immediately raises inescapable problems. Granted that the definition admits of a certain ambiguity of interpretation (thus there are those theologians who affirm that Mary never died in the sense in which, for instance, the Apostle John died, and those who, like Yves Congar, OP, invoking the Breviary office of the feast, argue that in her assumption Mary enjoyed an anticipated resurrection, the fruits of the paschal mystery in her come proleptically to fullness), it is still clear that the dogma affirms something to have happened which many people believe did not happen, and that latter on the good ground that there is no evidence which would furnish the basis for even a tentative affirmative historical judgment by a historian. It is argued that as a matter of fact the declaration of the dogma by Pius XII on the Feast of All Saints 1950 represented an authoritative response to the widely disseminated belief that the corporal Assumption happened. But is the fact that in particular milieux an alleged historical fact is widely believed to have happened evidence that it did happen? There are many beliefs which have been widely held, whose aetiology we may now trace and which we recognize to be in fact little more than superstitions. Of course there are many unverifiable beliefs that we do well, as empiricists, not to dismiss too lightly. They may embody groping intuitions of what is the case. But do these beliefs relate to matters of history? They may refer, for instance, to the world which concerns the psychical researcher, or even the physical theorist, feeling his way after a new model or a new theory that he lacks at present the mathematical resources necessary exactly to formulate. We are, for instance, familiar with historical traditions embodied in folk-memories of particular regions. But with the Assumption we are on different ground. It is an alleged event of the same order as the precariously, but still definitely, evidenced resurrection of Christ from the dead. There we lack decisive proof of the sort we have, for instance, for the death of Adolf Hitler in the bunker under Berlin in 1945; but there is *some* evidence, for example, the apparent powerlessness of the antagonists of the early Christian preaching to produce Jesus' decaying corpse to silence the claim that he was raised.

There is indeed discernible in the proclamation of this dogma the flirtation with the perilous illusion that 'believing makes it so'. Again one could offer a general rationale of dogma, to some extent legitimatizing the proclamation, by treating dogmata along the lines sketched by Le Roy, whereby they are regarded as prophetic syntheses of experience, powerful to promote and continue the experience they formulate. Yet such a view is rightly criticized as perilously subjectivistic in nuance, suggesting that faith is adequate to create its own objects, the *fides qua creditur* powerful to spin out of itself the *fides quae creditur*.

It is hard for a non-Roman Catholic to acquiesce in an oracular infallibility which, even on rare occasions, adds to the sum total of *credenda de fide* what admittedly is widely professed by the faithful, on grounds indeed consisting largely of that wide profession. It is as if authority intervenes to endorse the weavings of religious imagination; and that at a time when the central issue confronting the professors of the Christian faith and threatening not least its historical foundation is that of its claim to truth. For the crux of Christian faith is this, 'that Jesus Christ is come in the flesh'. It is the mystery of the Incarnation which supremely and centrally sets Christian religious interrogation in motion, the concrete actuality of the Rabbi of Nazareth, his teaching and ministry, his works, his strange and terrible controversy with those to whom he came, his way of sorrows, his rejection, pain, dereliction and death, the mysteries of his origin and consummation, and beyond these of the role in the created universe of the Word affirmed as manifested in him. And his Jewish mother (his special personal link with the inheritance of Israel) has her deeply significant place in his story. According to the nativity stories of Matthew and Luke, he is 'virginally conceived'. Difficulties in his relationship with 'the handmaid of the Lord' recur during his active ministry. Thus his mother's acceptance of his departure from her side, of his rootless, ambiguous existence, is hardly won; the sword of uncertainty and agonizing questioning pierces her spirit before the end. If there is indeed in the growth of Mariology the authorized deduction of seemingly inevitable conclusions from a highly questionable *a priori* theology of the *privilegia Deiparae*, a great deal that must in my judgment be rejected root and branch, it is still essential to point out that liberal Protestant and Anglican theology has largely pushed aside the problem of the role of Mary; too often through an unwillingness to face openly the complex historical problem of the 'virginal conception'. It is no accident that Karl Barth, who has faced this issue (see his *Church Dogmatics* I.2), emerges as a grave critic of Roman Catholic Mariology, but has complemented this criticism with profound affirmation of Mary's significance for the understanding of faith itself. If one rejects a particular development, even stigmatizes as the invention of a perverted religious consciousness that which is defined as *de fide*, one has to allow that rejection by itself is not enough. One must dig deeper to find in the failures of one's own tradition the causes which have helped to make a particular development historically almost inevitable.

Yet again, as the references to the presentation of Mary in the gospels have suggested, it is to the correct forming of the fundamental question that we are driven. Here the question is one of kerygmatic interrogation. If theology is *ministerium verbi divini*, we must serve proclamation not by seeking ways of making it effective, but rather by seeking ways of ensuring that its questioning shall be searching. Does Jesus Christ effectively interrogate men and women in the twentieth century? To this question one is tempted to give a completely negative answer. But that would be at once denial of one's own experience and of the empirical facts of contemporary church history. In the very present through which we live there is much that we can properly call response to Christ's interrogation, human response admittedly, marred by the egoism individual and collective that distorts all human reality. Yet *sub Deo* this response becomes part of the interrogation itself. The men and women who allow themselves to be questioned are, by the scrutiny to which they submit themselves, permitted and enabled to become part of the question set for others. Indestructible authority is found not in oracular definition, not in authoritative *magisterium*, but in the ferment that is still set in train by the *mysterium Christi*; that still has his mystery as its focus; and in it men seek the prevalence of his Spirit over human error. And here in the field of theology we touch that which is final.

It is for this reason that we have *malgré tout* the sense today of living through the birth pangs of a rebirth of faith, suddenly aware that the 'gates of hell shall not prevail against Christ's church'. If there is finality in metaphysics and ethics, it is found in different analogous and related ways in the besetting constancy of a set of questions. In the world of Christian faith, the finality is found in Jesus Christ, whose 'other Advocate' continually takes of his and shows it to us, even to ourselves. And this as we live *in statu viatorum*, yet not without foretaste of the vision we pray may be ours hereafter.[3]

8

Evidence: Preliminary Reflections

The notion of evidence is an excellent example of the sort of notion which, in different contexts, and in different disciplines, acquires significantly different senses, yet maintains an underlying unity of meaning. If one asks the completely general question, 'What is meant by saying that one thing is evidence for another?', one is made immediately aware that, as it stands, the question is incapable of an answer, while still having a certain significance in that it advertises community of import in all cases where one can significantly speak of evidence. In this paper it is my hope, by use of quite elementary, if diverse examples, to suggest the range of the concept, the variety and diversity of its application in diferent fields, and yet at the same time to argue that this wide variation in sense does not warrant complete permissiveness in its use. There are cases in which we have to say that we have absolutely no evidence to support a given claim, and that the nature of the claim does not, by some sort of magic, convert into evidence in its support, what it is quite inconceivable should warrant our affirming it.

In particular, in the concluding section of this paper, I wish to discuss the sense or senses in which an individual may be said, by his life, to provide evidence in favour of the principles, or indeed the faith which he professes. There is no doubt at all that, as a matter of empirical fact, it is an encounter with individuals whose faith manifestly irradiates and rules their lives, which has in many cases disturbed the assurance of those whose formation and experience has committed them to some form of naturalist *Weltanschauung*. That this has happened is a matter of empirical fact, and that this tends to happen is a warranted inductive generalization; but in what sense may the change in outlook be regarded as soundly based upon evidence that will resist dissolution by critical argument?

I

In ordinary life, when we speak of having evidence that this or that is the case, we seem to imply that we are not sure. It is, of course, commonly recognized that, when we state explicitly that we are sure, for instance, that a missing book is in another room, our very use of the word 'sure' shows a certain readiness to argue. When we are sure, as I am at present sure, that the walls of the room in which I am writing are green, I do not have to say that I am. It is something which I just take for granted, and indeed only have to mention if, for some reason, I have to describe the room to a friend, or if in argument I have to mention some fact which I regard as beyond the range of dispute. If I say, however, that there is some evidence, or even that there is conclusive evidence, for a particular state of affairs, then I am, by the very words I use, acknowledging both that I must argue, and that the argument is vulnerable to criticism, or is one which I confidently expect to stand up to any challenge. Thus, if I say of a package which I have received through the post, that there is some evidence that it has been tampered with, and that it has not just sprung open through the carelessness of the sender's packing, I go on to ask the man with whom I am arguing the point, to look closely at the character of the gashes in the paper, suggesting to him that they more closely resemble cuts made by a knife than bursts occasioned by careless handling by the postal authority of a package wrapped in too flimsy paper. But I am not suggesting that I am sure that the package has been tampered with, as I would be prepared to claim if I had seen with my own eyes someone use a knife upon it, with some other person or persons present to corroborate my testimony.

Again, to use another very hackneyed example, there is certainly some evidence for the presence in Loch Ness (in the Highlands of Scotland), of some sort of large, very unusual water creature. Over the years claims have been made by a large number of persons to have seen something they are unable precisely to identify, but which they affirm to be more likely a living creature, than some other floating object. Certainly, some of these witnesses are, or have been, *prima facie* more reliable than others, and one has to discount the extent to which the tradition that there is such a creature has stimulated in the credulous experience, which they have offered as evidence, which they would never have had but for a readiness even to achieve a certain amount of local fame, by experiencing some quite different visual phenomenon at dusk as a seeing of a monster. In recent years, expert zoologists have carried out systematic investigation, aimed at determining whether or not there is such a creature, or are such creatures in Loch Ness. The impulse to undertake such work has been provided by the evidence already available; but it is important to notice that this evidence is treated as part of the total range of facts requiring technically expert evaluation.

Again, to take a very different example from the proceedings of the criminal courts in Scotland. In criminal cases in Scotland the jury is always instructed that three verdicts are possible. The defendant may be found guilty; or he may be found not guilty; or the Crown's case against the defendant may be found 'not proven'. In this last case, the jury implicitly recognizes that there is definite evidence against the accused, of such a sort that they are unable to pronounce him not guilty, as they would, for instance, in a case in which they were convinced, by the evidence led by the defence, that he was in another place at the time at which his alleged offence occurred. But when the Crown's case is pronounced not proven, the evidence is judged *insufficient* to establish the defendant's guilt. It is indeed sometimes suggested by critics of this procedure that a man on trial on a charge which is 'not proven' leaves the Court with the shadow still over him of the likelihood of his actual guilt. But at least this third verdict recognizes that there are cases when there is enough evidence fully to justify the initiation of criminal proceedings, in the first instance, but not enough for the curtailment of the defendant's liberty by a term in prison.

It is tempting, at first, to suggest that there are many fields of human inquiry in which a verdict of 'not proven' is one that can be quite properly passed on claims made on behalf of this or that far-reaching, even revolutionary suggestion. Thus, one who is not technically expert in the field of the controversy may be tempted to say that the claim that certain fundamental, physical laws are irreducibly statistical, and not deterministic in form, is one that is 'not proven'. But here one must never forget that, where criminal courts are concerned, we are dealing with institutions whose function it is to establish whether or not a man's behaviour has been of such a kind as to warrant the drastic curtailment of his liberty, at least for a period of time, or else substantial financial penalty on the ground of offences against the law, committed in full knowledge of what he was doing. The punitive element in the aim of the judicial inquiry inevitably determines the way in which it is undertaken. The very gravity of the consequences for the individual must ensure special precautions against hazardous conclusion, on the basis of evidence which, although strong, even very strong, is still not overwhelming. In such a matter as the form of physical law, we are concerned with a matter most certainly of practical import, but one in respect of which it is possible, even necessary, to maintain a certain theoretical detachment. Indeed, while refusing to abandon a rigorous intellectual seriousness, one can also assume a certain near playfulness of spirit, ready to entertain alternative possibilities, and work out their consequence in assurance that one has time at one's disposal, and that it is better to canvas thoroughly the realm of the possible, than foreclose the discussion in the interest of premature dogmatic assurance. Whereas, when a man is on trial, considerations of common humanity demand a certain expedition in the handling of his affairs. It would be a serious disregard of empirical reality to pretend that these circumstances do not deeply affect the way in which the notion of evidence is received in a context such as that.

Of course, in arguments in fields that seem in part, at least, of purely speculative concern, the temper of the law courts enters in, and affects the character of the argument, and the way in which the evidence is conceived. It is a highly significant fact that the term theodicy is used both to refer to arguments for the existence of God, and also to essays which, taking the existence of God for granted, seek to justify his ways to men, thus acquitting him of those charges of malevolent design to which the many evils, physical and moral alike, encountered in the world around us, lay him open. If one refers in particular to the so-called 'argument from design', one meets an argument in which a whole variety of features of the world are marshalled, constituting not singly, but taken together, evidence alleged to make highly probable, or even certain, the existence of a transcendent designer. Thus one who favours this argument may mention the highly complex combination of environmental factors, necessary to make possible the development of conscious life, as we know it in ourselves. He may go on from there to refer to the equally remarkable fact that natural laws, both those with which we must be familiar in order to survive, and the much more comprehensive regularities established in the exact and observational sciences are, in fact, both alike discoverable by such beings as we find ourselves to be. That such regularities are discoverable is, it is claimed, a contingent matter of fact. One can indeed conceive a universe in which, indeed, there were natural regularities, but ones of such a rarefied sort that they completely defied discovery through the fertility of mathematical invention, and the ever increasing improvement of experimental techniques through advancing technological skill. Indeed one can imagine a world where such elementary regularities as the effect of various foods on the human organism were so elusive that no simple principles of nutrition could be established, and in consequence human life failed to sustain itself for anything but a very limited period of time. So the argument, marshalled in modern times with impressive power by F. R. Tennant of Cambridge, goes on, finding a remarkable pre-determination in the natural environment towards the emergence of spiritual life. The argument is rightly called impressive; for it selects, describes in detail, and emphasizes features of the world which incline the student who is reminded of them towards the acclamation, 'These things are surely not accidental'.

But the critic is immediately able to challenge the advocate of a beneficent author of the human environment, and of human existence, by pointing to a very large number of features suggesting that if, in fact, there is evidence that the natural environment is ordered towards the promotion of characteristically human existence, and indeed to the emergence of spiritual life, there is a great deal of evidence to suggest that it bears the more the mark of a horrifying joke than an ordered vale of soul-making. The case against the alleged beneficence of the Creator is one that can be strongly argued, and while in the argument from design we seem to move at the level of a relatively detached intellectual scrutiny, issuing in a conclusion that we would claim theoretically justifiable, when we pause to consider those features of our environment we are inclined to take as evidence of maliciousness in their architect, the mood is much more that of a court of law. It is as if we ask whether the Creator, if such there be, can be acquitted of evil intent, or whether the evidence is not overwhelming that we must set against the claim that is made for his loving-kindness and wisdom. If we engage in theodicy, it is not the sort of theodicy that provides us with evidence of a transcendent source for the world around us, whose marks we can trace in features of the world we cannot deny. Rather it is theodicy in another sense, the sense in which, in the mood of a prosecuting counsel, we demand that one whom we suppose guilty shall produce, or have led on his behalf, evidence which will show the supposed facts other than they appear to be. The style is that of the book of Job rather than that of a treatise on philosophical theology. It is not that considerations of logic are left behind; rather the mood becomes one of life or death concern, as distinct from one of relatively detached intellectual curiosity. The inquiry is begotten of a sense of outrage, rather than of an eagerness to believe, from which inevitably there springs a quickness to respond to the features enumerated in the premises of the argument directed to establish the reality of a transcendent designer.

II

To turn now to the question of historical evidence. Inevitably discussion of this question raises in the sharpest form the issues relating to the nature and validity of historical interpretation. To say this is not to belittle the crucial significance of questions whether or not an event actually happened, what the detailed constituent elements were of an event concerning whose actual-ity we have no doubt, whether or not a particular individual to whom various actions are attributed actually existed as such. Thus historians of classical Greece will argue whether or not there was an actual 'Peace of Callias' between Athens and Persia, whether a formal instrument was signed, concluding hostilities between the two societies, and de-limiting their respective spheres of influence etc. Again, historians of the last years of republican Rome will argue what exactly happened when Caesar crossed the Rubicon, why this action on his part was the 'casting of the dice', in fact the first action of the civil war between Caesar and Pompey. Again, historians of early Britain will argue whether or not there was an actual King Arthur. They will not be likely to suppose that some of the actions attributed to him by Malory were actually done, or that some of the events in which he allegedly took part actually happened. But they will be concerned to determine whether or not, in the history of Britain, there was an actual individual named Arthur, whose career bore some sort of relation to the elaborate traditions that have grown up around him, so that these traditions could be regarded as having the existence of an historical individual as the necessary condition of their development, and in themselves revealing to critical evalua-tion something of that individual's actual historical achievement. Certainly, discussion of such questions involves the historian in judgments that are interpretative in character, for instance, the critical evaluation of the tradition concerning Arthur. Again,

where determination of the crucial significance of Caesar's crossing the Rubicon is concerned, the historian will draw on his
understanding of the republican constitution at the time of
Caesar's action, and to this understanding interpretation of complex data will have made an important contribution. But in two of
these three cases the historian is concerned with the question
whether or not a particular individual or a particular state of
affairs was actual, whether or not a complete inventory of all the
events that ever happened, or of all the individuals who ever
existed, would or would not include mention of this event or this
individual. To suppose that historians are so absorbed in complex
and subtle interpretation of the past that they can cultivate a kind
of disdainful superiority to brute fact is to obliterate at one blow
the distinction between historical reconstruction and historical
fiction. For historical work the underlying validity of this distinc-
tions is of crucial importance. Where questions of historical evidence are concerned, we have to remember that the historian is
often compelled to ask whether or not such an event could have
happened, whether indeed the physical or economic geography
of a particular area was not incompatible with a claim resting, it
may be, on reasonably reliable written testimony, that a particular success on the plane of power politics was won by this or that
regional group. The historian cannot withdraw into a world of
spiritual activity to whose development physical circumstances
are regarded as somehow indifferent, where indeed it is sometimes claimed that the writ of causal law does not run.

Yet the historian is no mere recorder of the past; he is not
simply concerned to reproduce what he finds in his sources,
much as many crime reporters might reproduce, sentence by
sentence, the argument of the protagonists in a sensational criminal trial or inquiry which they are reporting. It is, however, a
mistake to suppose that the concept of interpretation furnishes a
universal key to all aspects of the historian's work, other than the
task of establishing the record of what happened. In studying the
first two volumes of Richard Ullman's monumental study of
British intervention in the civil war following the Russian Revolution, and in particular the second volume,[1] I found myself force-
fully reminded that one of the professional historian's most significant skills is that of *organizing* extremely complex material. Of
course, he is involved in selection, and here he is informed by
principles of judgment concerning what he supposes to be
important, even though, if he is professionally expert, he must
always be alert to the likelihood that his own pre-judgment

concerning what is, or is not, important may be altered, even shattered, by what is forced upon his attention from his sources. But when I speak of ability to organize, I am thinking not primarily of selection, but rather of a more subtle skill that interpenetrates both selection and interpretation: – the skill displayed in the achievement of such a mastery of material of daunting complexity that the unfolding of the tale which the historian is seeking to tell is achieved effectively, both for the writer himself, and for those who will later read what he has written. Such organization is a highly significant aspect of communication, and we have to reckon with the fact that history, even if we restrict the application of the term to the professional work of critical historians, is always a form of communication. Indeed, it is that form of communication whereby a community is enabled to come to terms with its past. In so far as such a coming to terms with its own past is inevitably shaped and conditioned by the direction of its present experience, the historian is continually poised between a sort of human indifference that will evacuate, in the name of objectivity, the tale that he must tell, of any illuminating power, and the sort of readiness to subordinate historical reconstruction to the demands of homiletic, and even propaganda, that will, in the end, deprive the past of that sort of substantial reality which belongs to it, as a part of that which has actually happened.

III

To write in these terms is to do no more than indicate some of the problems that a proper logic of historical reconstruction would necessarily include. But in so far as we are concerned with questions relating to the extent to which actual contingent circumstances provide any sort of evidence for a transcendent reality, we must take into account the procedures that inform the historian's work. This because of the crucial significance of the question of the sense or senses in which an individual may be said by his life to provide evidence in favour of the principles, or indeed the faith which he professes. Certainly in these, the last sections of the paper, it is with the question to what extent the unity of theory and practice accomplished in the life of an individual may be said to authenticate the theory, especially when the theory involves reference to transcendent reality, that we are concerned. It is, indeed, the question what sort of authentication this is that we are concerned to answer. Here one recalls immediately that the life and death of Socrates set Plato a problem, provided him with one of the points of departure for the mythical construction of his central period. For Plato the manner of Socrates' condemnation and death did not authenticate his life. Certainly Plato could represent him in the *Apology* as pleading a formal innocence of the charges on which he was arraigned; but his failure was more or less complete. Alcibiades, for instance, was a very questionable witness to the quality of his *paideia*. If, in the *Phaedo*, Socrates can be presented as going to his death in a certain self-understanding, it is still to death that he is represented as going, and it is indeed the *memory* of his passing which supplies part of the impulse to Plato to reconstruct the whole fabric of human knowledge. Yet arguably the provision of such an impulse to one who most certainly consorted with him was an important part of the historical achievement of Socrates. Of Plato's work, at least in the 'middle period', Socrates' life was a necessary condition; but inevitably the modern student asks whether Plato saw his mentor aright. And this question must certainly need to be generalized. If we fasten on particular tracts of human history, especially the biographies of individuals, as providing 'arguments' in favour of a transcendent reality, as parables speaking, however indirectly, of the ultimate, we have to face the question whether in speaking in such terms, we refer simply to the subjective impression created in the imagination of individuals, contemporary or subsequent, or to an historical actuality. Of course, as I said at the outset of the paper, such an experience frequently, as a matter of fact, shatters the security of those who have hitherto been contented with a naturalistic *Weltanschauung*. Thus the questions with which we are concerned necessarily include both the validity of the argument here involved, and also the truth of the factual premise that, in fact, this or that individual did live as he is represented as living, did respond to the circumstances of his life in the way he is able to have done, was indeed in those responses animated by the principles he is supposed to have embodied in them.

In order to bring out both the cruciality and the precariousness of this argument, I propose to turn back to the so-called 'argument from design', in order, by such comparison, to bring out factors both of that argument and of the claim that what we may refer to as the claim of the achieved reality of holiness to provide evidence for the transcendent. The throwing of the two arguments against each other may serve to throw light on both alike. If our sense of the total validity of either is not decisively strengthened, at least our self-consciousness concerning what we are about in the use we make of both is likely to be deepened. And this deepening of our self-consciousness may serve to illuminate both the range and the depth, the restlessness, the incompleteness, the fragmentariness and the obstinacy of our metaphysical concern. We may learn something about what we are doing when we pick our way along the frontiers between a world in which the writ of an admittedly flexible, but still authoritative logic is secure, and one in which a quenchless aspiration towards the ultimate is always in danger of a re-fashioning of the harsh outlines of reality, in accordance with its own dreams. We will also inevitably be compelled to face, in a relatively new light, the problem of the authority of revelation, indeed of the validity of faith. For at the level of faith, the kind of confusion, the kind of uncertainty, the kind of facing both ways of which I have spoken, emerges again, only with a new sharpness, a new cruciality, and also a new obscurity. Thus, of course, where the Christian tradition is concerned, the object towards which faith is orientated is a life and death that are regarded as at once desperately needing authentication from beyond themselves, and yet in a way paradoxical and elusive, as so receiving that authentication that in them the Logos is properly affirmed as made flesh, the theory or groundplan of the human world at once achieved and raised to a level beyond the reach of possible unaided human aspiration. It is not, most certainly not, that through the deepening of human self-consciousness of which I have spoken, we shall achieve a kind of solution of the problem of faith; rather the difficulties will emerge with a new sharpness; but at least there may have been an advance in clarity, and definite rejection of premature solution.

IV

It is characteristic of the 'argument from design' that it forces attention on certain features of the world which combine to induce an overwhelming impression of ordered purpose, of careful and attentive arrangement, set in train to provide a setting, arguably the only possible setting, for spiritual experience as we know it in ourselves. The contingent character of the various states of affairs whose compresence, even, if one may speak anthropomorphically, whose co-operation is necessary to provide the conditions of characteristically human experience, is stressed. This even if a measure of validity is conceded to Kant's argument that nothing properly called self-consciousness, the most rudimentary type of awareness of self-identity, is possible without a certain definable minimum of conceptual order. What we know as human experience (if we include the precarious, but none the less undeniable elements of moral progress, the rich variety of aesthetic experience, the partial but still deeply significant mastery over our natural environment), demands very much more than the fulfilment of the most elementary conditions of objective reference. Here, it is claimed, there is evidence analogous to that which entitles a man to say that sudden, unforeseeable, yet interpretable disturbance in his immediate environment speaks of conscious agency, and not simply a remarkable combination of natural forces. The logic of this claim is hazardous in the extreme, and its criticism is in my judgment a fundamental exercise in analytical philosophy of theology. But it lies to a recognizable extent on the circumference of the present discussion, and I must beg leave to do no more than mention it here, while insisting on its great importance.

Yet one has only to turn to the book of Job to find a classical example of a man defeated in the attempt existentially to reconcile experience of personal catastrophe with confession of beneficent and just design; an attempt set in hand because the subject of the experience is, by formation, initially pre-disposed to subsume the hammer blows that rain upon him under some general law which would enable him to receive such shattering experience as, for example, ultimately remedial. We are indeed familiar with the claim that the very ills to which we are subject in consequence of our peculiar human constitution, ensure that in our lives we shall not lack the opportunity to cultivate such virtues as courage on the one hand, and hope on the other, virtues which, in a supposedly more enervating climate of existence, might hardly be brought into play. Yet, in the sharp actualities of bitter deprivation, of physical pain, of sudden bereavement, of betrayal and cruelty, even of personal moral defeat, the individual is hard put to it not to consider his environment as ordered to jeopardize, rather than further, his spiritual progress, to make him sharply aware of contradiction between aspiration and inheritance, between that which he would, on the one hand, seek to realize in his life, and the stuff of which he is made, and the world in which his ways are set, on the other. If we say that suffering is a school in which we learn to know ourselves, we have still to ponder the inwardness of, for instance, the conclusion of Shakespeare's *King Lear*, in which, unknown to her father, Cordelia is dead, even as he speaks of what he has learnt through the terrible experience he has undergone, and the new life which will crown his daughter's fidelity.

No form of the 'argument from design' has ever finally silenced the cry elicited by tragic experience, for instance by the man who has found that his effort to practise *agapē* towards his neighbour, is not expressive of a disinterested concern for that neighbour's good, but rather of his own eagerness to play God. A man, seeking to realize in his life the likeness of Christ may suppose that he is imitating Christ's example in washing the feet of his brethren; yet he may find that because of the lie in his soul, this very act of menial service is at best a conscious pose, and at worst a deliberate essay in a glorification, inevitably destructive, of himself, as well as damaging to those he falsely believes he serves. A 'good Samaritan', by crossing the road to succour the bandits' victim, may put both the victim and himself at risk; his hands may be contaminated, and it could have been better for him to have followed the example of priest and Levite, passing by on the other side in self-disciplined detachment, serving the need of the injured by the recollected intercession for which, by their very seeming disregard of the victim's need, they keep themselves free. Of course, as I have said, we are reminded that we learn by suffering; but it is a school of wasted effort in which the bitter self-knowledge that we gain is often one cause of damage irretrievably done to others rendered cynical, it may be, by their experience of our attempt to show love towards them. It is as if the ways of the world were designed by a *malin génie* quick to laugh mockingly at human beings, caught in consequence of the stuff of which he has fashioned them, in the traps he so skilfully sets.

If we can bear to listen to the simplicities of Christ's parables, in which he bids us glimpse now the likeness of the true neighbour, now that of the man quick to forgive manifold injury, etc., we bear to do so because in his own history Christ has experienced the ultimately tragic consequences of the way he counselled. To practise *agapē* demands, as its condition, that a man shall be broken. Even if we count Christ sinless, even if we say that he alone among the sons of men is fit to wash the feet of his brethren, we still see in him one whirled to destruction by the choice he made, broken in pieces in inevitable consequence of the way he elected to follow. To portray him as a serene heroic figure, always the confident master of the situations which confronted him, always sure and certain of touch in his handling of them, is to trivialize his ordeal, and diminish his significance, to belittle his mystery, and to render inauthentic his humanity. If we speak of evidence in connection with his claim, we find that evidence in the extent and depth to which he is presented as engaged with the human predicament. It is not that his moral teaching, the teaching which is summarized in the Sermon on the Mount, which is presented in the exquisitely memorable narratives of the Lucan parables, authenticates itself as the true style of human living, shows itself as the way in which a man should live his life. There is no teaching that men cannot ultimately bend to the service of their self-glorification. *Corruptio optimi pessima*: the most searching, demanding plea that a man put himself at the disposal of others, may provide the means whereby he imposes upon them a dominion which by its very spirituality avoids recognition for what it is, and is quickly imbued with a sheerly demonic quality. And again, there is no guarantee that any success in the business of living, as human wisdom variously assesses success, will follow on the practice of love.

Its way is the *via crucis*, the way that Christ must take alone, the way indeed with which, in the end, he identifies himself; yet it is the way in which he clothes, with the flesh and blood of his own achievement in defeat, the commandments that he gives his brethren. His teaching is vindicated through his rivetting the question of its validity upon himself.

'To this end was I born, and for this cause came I into the world, that I should bear witness unto the truth. Every one that is of the truth heareth my voice.'[2]

9

Tillich, Frege, Kittel:
Some Reflections on a Dark Theme[1]

Since Karl Popper's book – *The Open Society and its Enemies*[2] – first
appeared in 1945, few have been found ready to defend the
political and social doctrines of Plato's *Republic*. Indeed nine years
earlier R. H. S. Crossman (whose lectures on the *Republic* I recall
attending at New College, Oxford, in 1933, when half-way
through the course, on Friday 16 June, he entered the college hall,
triumphantly brandishing the 'first Nazi book on Plato') had
published a scintillating piece of philosophical journalism – *Plato
To-day*[3] –, anticipating large sections of Popper's attack. Two
years before Crossman's book, Michael Foster, in a study of *The
Political Philosophies of Plato and Hegel*, had shown the depth of
Plato's inhumanity in the metaphysically based tripartite organization of his *kallipolis*.[4] To glance today at, for example, the
ardent pamphleteering of the late Sir Richard Livingstone, who
never tired of commending the study of the *Republic* as a remedy
for contemporary cultural ills (but who also very significantly
deprecated excessively minute attention to its metaphysical
cruces, for instance the interpretation of the 'divided line') is to
breathe the atmosphere of a world at once high-minded, naïf and
ultimately shallow.

Yet where ethics and metaphysics are concerned, this lengthy,
wide-ranging dialogue (the work of a man who was by turns
prophet, logical analyst, reflective moralist, coldly ruthless
draftsman of a supposedly definitive social polity) is often
extremely illuminating. This not least by pin-pointing one central
problem of human existence, namely the relationship of moral
goodness to intellectual insight. It is a gross injustice to Plato to
attribute to him the view that virtue is a form of knowledge.
Rather he would claim (I grossly over-simplify) that completeness of understanding must wait upon an intuitive vision that

demands for its achievement the combination of the most rigorously critical intellectual discipline with a deliberately cultivated simplicity, the one indeed the necessary condition of the attainment of the other. Yet if the vision of the 'Idea of the Good' can only be gained by way of a totally disinterested intellectual ascent for which the detailed study of pure as distinct from applied mathematics supplies the indispensable apprenticeship,[5] its authenticity is only confirmed by the way in which those who have come to enjoy it banish themselves from a merely contemplative existence, and make their way out to live out, in the confused and confusing circumstances of ordinary human life, the sense of that which they have seen.

Very few find Plato's implicit assumption of a single vision supplying necessary, yet adequate guidance for the conduct of life, either public or private, remotely credible. Further, it received most searching criticism at Aristotle's hands in his *Nicomachean Ethics* I.6, a long passage of great density and complexity, but one of permanent significance in moral philosophy (it is also of course one of the sources in the Corpus Aristotelicum of the Thomistic conception of analogical predication). Yet the central metaphysical section of the *Republic* presents with inescapable force (perhaps because it does so indirectly) the extent to which a thinker's intellectual achievement must be judged damaged by grave moral faults in the man. Granted that unmistakable human goodness can make no man or woman a genius, can we suppose that its total absence leaves unaffected any man's claim to be numbered among the master-spirits of our age?

Let us, however, come down to earth. Am I implying that Fellowship of the Royal Society or of the British Academy, Order of Merit or Nobel Prize should be witheld from those who fail to satisfy some ill-defined standard of moral excellence? The student of philosophical logic has much more to learn from study of Russell's *Principles of Mathematics*, his articles on Meinong's theory of complexes and assumptions, and on denoting, and his lectures on the philosophy of logical atomism than from the textbooks of a morally blameless seminary professor, or overworked tutor in a cramming establishment: even if we must concede a certain justice to the view that Russell (for all his reverence for Joseph Conrad, so disconcerting to the *bien-pensants* who invariably imagine him as a Mephistophelean figure) exhibited the detached arrogance in sexual behaviour characteristic of some of the Whig *grands seigneurs* of the eighteenth century among his ancestors. Again we have to reckon with Gottlob Frege, revealed to his brilliant interpreter and commentator, Michael Dummett[6] (a man who with his wife has given years of his life to the struggle against racialist tendencies and racially biassed decisions in our society) by his unpublished *Nachlass* as, for all his logical achievement, a racialist of the most bigoted sort, narrowly nationalist, obsessively anti-Catholic as well as anti-Semitic. He died in 1925: had he lived another eight years, his welcome for the Nazi *Machtübernahme* would have been at least as enthusiastic as that of Gerhard Kittel, initiator of that famous *Theologisches Wörterbuch zum Neuen Testament*, who bent the great resources of his formation in 'biblical theology', his special familiarity with the Judaism of Jesus' life-time, his consummate mastery of the technicalities of New Testament scholarship, to the seemingly congenial task of developing the theological apologia for the Nuremberg Racial Laws. This he did in a notorious book, *Die Judenfrage*, an achievement constituting one of the most terrible *trahisons des clercs* I have ever encountered.[7] After the war, when he knew he was dying, Kittel sent for his friend and colleague Gerhard Friedrich to beg him continue the *Wörterbuch* to its conclusion. One might have preferred to hear that he had asked his friend to help undo (as far as he could) the ill he had done. Clearly the *Neutestamentler* will continue to use the *Wörterbuch* even if he recalls that the insights he may win from its study are (in Plato's phrase) *dunameis tōn enantiōn*, that can be bent to serve a cause that we must judge altogether and irredeemably evil, even as a craftman's mastery of the principles of combination-locks may make him an invaluable recruit to a gang of bank-robbers.

A mathematician's argument is faulted for lack of rigour in proof, not for the financial or matrimonial tangles (however much he may be to blame for them) that have disturbed his concentration and led to the flaws in his argument. His personal troubles are matters for his biographer, or conceivably his obituarist; they will not be mentioned in criticism of his work in professional journals. We may indeed find ourselves ready to extenuate by reason of the scale of a writer's or artist's achievement, the brutal indifference he may have shown to the ordinary, yet always humanly searching and emotionally demanding, claims of wife and family, perhaps even (in his defence) drawing an analogy with Charles Darwin's readiness to forfeit his power to appreciate music by deliberate sacrifice of the time needed to sustain it, to concentration on his biological researches. So we may be prepared to say that it is expedient for the world that some great artists be ready to die morally, even as we allow that a statesman may be justified in unscrupulously devious dissimilation the more effectively to manipulate those he needs to control in service of the vital interests of the community he seeks to serve. We see such dissimulation as continuous with Charles de Gaulle's magisterially ironic comment in the Place in Algiers: 'Je vous ai compris.' We certainly do not suppose such a man innocent of delight in his exercise of power, or of ambition to maintain his personal ascendancy. Rather we admit such motives as necessary determinants for a man to undertake such work, applauding, however, those whom combination of circumstance and self-discipline have made servants of their community as well as of themselves.

But a doubt remains. 'Do men gather grapes of thorns or figs of thistles?' For Plato, Socrates' goodness was one of the points of departure of his speculation. As Plato presents him in the *Apology*, Socrates was a very special sort of teacher, a man who pursued his self-examination, by way of the remorseless interrogation of others. It was this man, condemned by his city in an 'impiety trial' for corrupting the youth, that provided Plato with a very paradigm of human excellence. To Plato he was no impious corruptor: yet the charge that he was such was not *prima facie* absurd, as the flamboyant Alcibiades had not only been his pupil, but had loved him: Alcibiades, so clearly linked in imagination with the débâcle of the Athenian democracy from the moment that his reputation made him the obvious first man to be accused of the mutilation of the Hermae, and the *Salaminian* was sent to recall him from the fleet about to sail for Sicily, depriving him of its command and bitterly antagonizing him against the city that had been thus quick (falsely) to lay the sacrilege at his door. If Socrates had not corrupted, he had failed to secure against corruption the *studiosa juventus* whom he influenced. If thorns do not bear grapes, nor thistles figs, vines may nevertheless bear bitter fruit and fig-trees be found barren. The teacher may fail, fail in his teaching, fail in achieving what he sought by teaching, though as much as Plato's Socrates in this failure he be blameless.

We are today very sensitive of the extent to which the frontiers between intellectual creation and communication are blurred. A fine historian may display his quality by the skill with which he organizes vastly complex source-material, and this is already an act of communication. The hazy concept of interpretation reaches more precise definition by reference to this act in which a genuine mastery of the sources is enjoyed by the man who has studied them and shared the fruits of his study with his readers.

This topic is of peculiar significance at this time, as surely I am not alone in being deeply disturbed by the books treating of the life of the theologian and philosopher Paul Tillich, one by his wife Hannah,[8] and one by an American psychiatrist who was his friend, Dr Rollo May.[9] In fact the latter book seems to support his wife's sombre revelation. Tillich's work is very much discussed, and I was myself among the audience at Aberdeen University who listened to his two series of Gifford Lectures in the autumns of 1953 and 1954. These lectures comprised the second volume of his *Systematic Theology, Existence and the Christ*, and the first, discarded, but in the opinion of many, vastly superior presentation of the field very differently covered in the third.[10] A German who saw service in the 1914–18 war, and who emerged from the experience a Socialist, who was by turns a philosopher in the great tradition of German idealism (he was called to succeed that very considerable practitioner of phenomenology, Max Scheler, at Frankfurt), acknowledging Schelling as his particular *maître*, and a theologian dissatisfied at once by the pre-war liberal theology, associated with the name of Adolf von Harnack, by the 'dialectical theology' of the early Karl Barth and his followers, and by the spurious contemporaneity of his friend Emanuel Hirsch, the theological master of the *'Deutsche Christen'*, he pursued his very individual path in Weimar Germany, and then, as a refugee from the Nazi tyranny, in the USA, at Union Theological Seminary, New York, and finally at Harvard. His boldness in exploration, his frequent insights, his readiness to try to hold together seeming incompatibles – all have contrived to win him praise as well as to occasion exasperation. It is an exploratory quality that has always marked his best writing, and it came through full measure in his lecturing. Yet when I recall now his lectures at Aberdeen twenty years ago, I ask myself what I am to make of the startling contrast between the staid, sombrely dressed, elderly Professor, and the man living in those same years in the USA the life his wife describes.

For what emerges from his wife's book? We have to admit that Tillich emerges as ready to use his unquestioned powers as a teacher, as an intellectual prophet, to attract women into his orbit, whom it would seem that he often seduced. He emerges as wilfully promiscuous, and in his promiscuity coldly cruel towards his wife. As evidence of the reality of this cruelty, the appearance of Hannah Tillich's record is unquestionable evidence.

On one occasion Frau Tillich speaks (p. 154) of asking her

husband after the funeral of one of his mistresses concerning her children. 'He broke into sobs; they hated him.' His tears were no doubt expressive of much more than injured vanity; they bore witness to his sense of injury done. But that hurt could not easily be undone; those children had been his victims.

Again we read (p. 190) than when his wife in desperation made to seek divorce on grounds of infidelity, he threw himself on the floor, begging her not to, enlisting his friends to tell her that it would ruin his career. Sadly we must conclude that at that time the 'courage to be' of which Tillich wrote did not extend to risking his career, his status, his reputation, his security.

Further, Rollo May's apology for his friend, by its curiously muted style, its discernible elision of awkward material, does little to weaken the force of his wife's indictment. To say this is not to acquit her of many inaccuracies of detail, not to deny that in places the frontier between fact and fantasy in her record is blurred. Yet such concession does not in the least diminish one's sense of being compelled by this record to see its subject in a new light. It is simply NOT enough to say that one now sees him 'warts and all'. The flaws of which Hannah Tillich writes inevitably infect the texture of her husband's *oeuvre*. We are aware of an element of fraud, of hypocrisy here as so often 'the tribute vice pays to virtue'. But one is also aware of something that is of deeper significance. Both Tillich and his wife belonged to the often widely experimental period of the Weimar Republic, that period which ended with the Nazi *Machtübernahme* of 30 January 1933. We remember that may theologians of very high reputation (one recalls Karl Heim's preface to the 1934 edition of his *Glaube und Denken*) welcomed the Nazis' attainment of power as the point of departure for the 'moral renovation' of German society.[11] Blind reaction against Weimar was one element in the euphoria which saw in the storming of the homosexual night-clubs in Berlin a sign of the purification of morals that the 'Brownshirts' were bringing. Yet, of course, all was (to speak mildly) very far from lovely, even in this respect, among the book-burning evangelists of a new puritanism: it was significant that when his murderers sought the wretched Roehm on the night of 20 June 1934, they found him in bed with his boy-friend, who inevitably perished with his lover! Paulus and Hannah Tillich belonged to the world of Weimar: but it is not enough to say that Paulus carried its ethos over into the world of his exile. It is the calculated, elaborately defended, yet always equally elaborately hidden perpetuation of a life-style involving an unacknowledged contempt not for traditional churchly forms (the sort of thing that the young Tillich had known as a boy in his father's house), but for the elementary, demanding sanctities of human existence, that demands comment.

Kittel's anti-Semitism was a deadly infection, and every student should be watchful for its distorting influence in his most pervasively seemingly *wissenschaftlich* contributions to the study of the New Testament. Its inspirational source may well be traced to elements in the German national tradition for whose unchallengeable moral autonomy too many German Evangelical theologians had too long argued, bending (it would seem from Törnwall's remarkable study[12] with almost complete disdain for exegetical accuracy) Luther's bifurcation of *weltliche* from *geistliche Regiment* to serve their deeply religious commitment to *Reich, Thron, Wehrmacht*. But where Paul Tillich is concerned, we have to reckon with the built-in risk of a deep corruption in a theology that would cultivate a temper of exploration.

The temptation that must beset the theologian whose temper is that of the explorer of the unknown, even the forbidden territories of the world of ideas, is not to be identified quickly with a superior disdain for the proved simplicities of traditional wisdom. Rather it is one of self-dramatization, of seeing himself in his own eyes as one taking upon himself the most demanding and most frightening tasks, emancipated both by the aims, and indeed by the content of his enterprise from the discipline of a self-questioning that reaches the very substance of what he is in himself. He is always a romantic: it is worth remembering that Tillich's intellectual master was Schelling, a speculative intelligence profoundly different from Kant (surely the supreme German philosopher) and indeed from Hegel, whose outlook was formed through criticism not only of Kant, but also of the much less critically self-conscious first dividers of his inheritance, Fichte and Schelling: this though Hegel himself could be charged with a failure to assimilate the depth of Kant's criticism of the early German Romantics! The German-Swiss Catholic theologian Hans Urs von Balthasar gave the subtitle *Prometheus* to his early study of the sources and achievements of the German Idealists, *Die Apokalypse der Deutschen Seele*.[13] As a theologian Tillich saw his work and himself in apocalyptic terms, saw his achievement as authenticating itself as a tremendous exploration of the unknown: or as a leap into the abyss, where self-justification or total destruction must be the outcome. There is no middle way, and a failure to which a shattered human corpse would be witness, would have a kind of immediately heroic quality, in its scattered fragments a gesture of contempt to those who lacked the courage thus to leap, their hesitant, sometimes frightened patience contrasting with the reckless self-giving of the heroic leap. But the self-giving is surely counterfeit, and one has further to ask how far the heroic is a Christian category.

It has often been remarked that Christ's temptation to cast himself from the pinnacle of the temple (the climax of his desert ordeal in Luke's record) was ultimately one of presumption. 'And he shall give his angels charge over thee to keep thee in all thy ways: in their hands they shall bear thee up lest at any time, thou dash thy foot against a stone.' By this leap into the abyss he would arguably prove himself to himself, wresting from his Father by triumphant vindication *coram populo* the overt certification of his sonship that he sought. And if it were not forthcoming, all would surely be over. We could not deny an element of heroism to such an attitude expressed in deadly risk, a kind of revolt against the circumstances he was seemingly constrained to accept which we are ourselves tempted to regard as authentic. Yet the ambiguous alternative had its own quality of endurance: humanly the secret remains undisclosed awaiting the Father's hour. Yet so hidden even from the open perception of Jesus himself, it admits him to the intimacy of the outcast, by his own acceptance of unbearable ambiguity at once their judge and their advocate, their healer and their fellow. Heroic flight from the costly penetrating realities of Incarnation as that enfleshing is defined by the *via crucis*, the way that is at once acceptance and revolt, Yea and Nay to the unbearable and unintelligible, is refused, and very dimly we can glimpse God's unity itself put at risk in this interrogation, yet triumphantly affirmed by Jesus' answer.

At first this reflection may seem an irrelevant footnote to the preceding comments on Paul Tillich's history. Yet it is just possible that to ponder Christ's refusal to accept the 'either/or' of total emancipation from ambiguity issuing inevitably in failure, or equally total annihilation, provides a key to unlock Tillich's failure at the level of faith. All human faith depends upon, and is hardly decipherable *mimēsis*, of the *fides Christi*, the faith of Christ, that is itself human expression of God's total fidelity to himself and to his creation. And this faith of Christ we have most painfully to see as something that if we rest our hope upon it, and find in it the source of our flickering charity, we must affirm for what it was, and through the Resurrection, eternally is: response after the manner of God's being and of human need, no wilful wresting of an unambiguous triumph over circumstance that will, by its seeming transparency, satisfy our own conceit.

10

Idealism and Realism: an Old Controversy Renewed

In his recent writings on the philosophy of logic, Michael Dummett has insisted that the dispute between idealism and realism is the central issue of metaphysics. Although it is always dangerous to refer to philosophical cruces as if they were contests between hypostatized abstractions, there is no doubt at all that Dummett is referring to issues of central importance. Moreover, they are issues which continually recur in new forms, even in forms startingly unlike previous, even supposedly classical formulations. Thus problems raised by the apparently inescapable implications of part of Wittgenstein's later philosophy, especially his philosophy of mathematics, are a very long way from the sorts of question that beginners in philosophy first encounter in the study of Berkeley. Yet several writers on Wittgenstein have found it profitable and illuminating to trace analogies between his thinking and that of Kant, who devoted a celebrated passage in the Analytic of Principles to refuting what he called 'idealism', encountered in 'dogmatic' form in Berkeley, and in 'problematic' form in Descartes. Kant's refutation is interesting in itself; but in his work it is a necessary part of his subtle and strenuous effort to have the best of both worlds, to hold together a view which treated learning about the world as a finding, with one that regarded such learning as a constructive act. It is partly in response to this dual claim that the analogy between his work and that of Wittgenstein is to be found, and far though Berkeley may be from Wittgenstein, it is worth remembering that it was by reference to Berkeley that in part at least Kant defined his own position, and that the position of a man sensitive as Wittgenstein was to the pull of hardly reconcilable considerations.

Do we invent, or do we discover? If we are at all sensitive to etymology, we may suspect that this is no genuine dichotomy;

for the sense of the Latin *invenire* lingers in the title of the ancient feast of the Invention of the Cross, commemorating Helena's alleged finding of the instrument of Christ's execution. The inventor achieves, and by achieving discloses possibilities. The frontier between inventing and discovering does not coincide with that between 'knowing how' and 'knowing that'; rather it suggests that there are important areas of border dispute between these allegedly contrasted opposites. I learn unguessed secrets by manipulating a situation to bend its potentialities to the purposes of my enquiry. Collingwood pointed out how often causal enquiries were practically determined;[1] the identification of one feature in a situation rather than another, as the cause of difficulties that confront us, is determined by that feature's amenability to practical treatment. Thus a motorist will blame his difficulties on the state of his brakes, rather than on the gradient of 'Rest-and-be-Thankful' or Porlock Hill; this because his brakes are, within limits, under his own control (if he is no expert, he can seek technical assistance when they are clearly out of order); whereas he can do nothing about the gradient of the hill. Again if a 'do-it-yourself' enthusiast blows up his bungalow, and nearly kills his wife, his two children, and himself, we find the cause in his belief that he could effectively service his gas-fired central heating installation himself, and not on the properties of natural gas. In both these cases, attribution of cause is expressive of selectivity, conditioned by our interest and the skills available to us.

Our knowledge of the world about us is directed, and enlarged and advanced by our concerns, and it assumes the kinds of form that it takes partly by reason of its permeation by such interests. We are part of the world, and when we hold it at a distance from ourselves, as we do when we seek to enlarge our understanding of its order, the very act of doing so constrains the world to assume a different look from the one it has when we are living, breathing, eating, what you will. Yet when we recall the extent to which we are unquestionably part of the natural world, we find that we can do no other than acknowledge the authority of the objective. The world is as it is, and not as we might want it. We can surmount the hill, and keep ourselves and our families alive by having our brakes mended, or by admitting that gas-fired installations demand the skill of the professional. Yet it is because hills are as they are, and natural gas as it is, that we must adjust in the way in which we have to. It is the way in which things are that sets us the problem of practical adjustment, and certainly we often learn sharp lessons concerning their order through the defeat of early initiatives and of unreflective interference.

Again, when we turn to consider the most significant and fertile styles of conceptual innovation, we certainly find our horizons enlarged, it may be by the resources of more powerful sorts of mathematics or by such developments as electron-microscopy and sheer virtuosity in their exploitation. But there remain horizons. There are conceptual constants which make possible the assimilation of the most novel advances, either in suggestion of theoretical order, or in manipulative technique. Yet it was Kant who, with an unexampled delicacy and subtlety of intellectual perception, insisted that these constants were *our* constants, and that where that *our* is concerned, it is most difficult to draw the line between what is imposed from the side of the subject, and what from that of the material with which the subject has to do. If these constants are expressive of the form of the world, they are so expressive as realizing the inescapable limits of our understanding.

The term *anthropocentric* is not infrequently used to characterize the point of view that insists on the relativity of most, if not all, forms of conceptual order to the human experient. Kant's doctrine was anthropocentric is so far as he argued that the objective world from which the subject differentiated himself and by so doing achieved self-consciousness, was, in respect of its most pervasive structural order, expressive of the way in which that subject necessarily came to terms with what was thrust at him. What we called our world, we had assimilated by imposing on the matter of sensation, a shape that we could only confidently affirm to characterize it within the limits of our experience.

The constants of spatial location, and of temporal date, of substantial permanence, and of causal determination, inter-woven one with another as they are, are constants of a human world. Yet there is nothing arbitrary in our use of them. Indeed it is on the ground of his totally uncritical attachment to the funda-mental laws of Newtonian physics that Kant has been most frequently charged with lapse into the sort of dogmatism he disliked in others. His own vaunted apparatus of 'transcendental proof', ingenious though its conception may be, does not in the end (we are told) deliver him from bondage to the illusions that the cosmology he knew was of final authority, and that the sorts of natural law that he was concerned to insist to be of universal scope,[2] were alone admissible as patterns of change, etc. Such dogmatism (illustrated, for instance, by his belief that he has proved *a priori* the 'law of the conservation of mass') is at least evidence of the extent to which any suggestion that conceptual order was a matter of arbitrary choice was inimical to Kant. If he regarded the experiential constants he sought so painfully to extract and to vindicate (at his most profound, differentiating them by rarefied abstraction from the fundamental laws of classical physics) as expressive of the characteristic styles of the human experient, they were significant not as belonging in any sense to the inner life of the subject, but to the constitution of his world. It was as conditions of objectivity that their sense lay.

'How are objects of experience possible?' To ask such a question is to direct attention away from the sort of consideration that would encourage a man to treat intellectual activity as if it were a prolonged essay in imaginative or inventive ingenuity. Certainly imaginative boldness, conceptual as well as experimental innovation, are both alike indispensable. Indeed if one moves from study of nature to that of human history, or indeed human behaviour, the extent to which advance of understanding depends on the fusion of careful study of available material with the kind of intuitive perception which may succeed in unlocking the secrets of complex situations of seemingly impenetrable density cannot be denied. Any slavish adherence to supposedly secure, itemized atoms of alleged certainty without the inevitable risk that must accompany an essay in constructive understanding dooms the adherent to the sort of safe success, wherein security is purchased at the cost of fundamental advances both in insight and practical mastery.

In his book, *The Logic of Modern Physics*,[3] P. W. Bridgman summarized Einstein's analysis of the concept of simultaneity by claiming that he was insisting that the statement that two events are simultaneous was equivalent to the statement that two events satisfy the conditions required for us to pronounce them simultaneous. In other words, simultaneity is reduced to terms of the criterion or criteria for the application of the concept, and two events are properly judged simultaneous when we judge ourselves justified in so regarding them. The standard or standards by reference to which we think ourselves thus justified are of our own devising. What we mean when we claim two events to be simultaneous is not that the statement that they are simultaneous accords with the facts, but that the use of the concept of simultaneity in respect of their occurrence is justified.

But what of the principles by which it is justified? And what is involved in the attempt to formulate them? If we approach the analysis of the concept of truth by way of examples of proposition to which the application of the picture-theory is not *prima facie* implausible, we come to think of questions concerning acceptability or inacceptability as settleable by comparison of proposition and fact in a way analogous to that in which, for example, the features of an 'identikit' picture may be compared with those of the man the police believe likely to be able to help them with their enquiries. What is more important, we are sure that the question whether or not one proposition is true or false can be settled independently of the question whether or not another proposition is true or false. Thus the question whether or not there is a thunderstorm in Barcelona on 1 July 1976 can be settled without reference to the question whether or not there is a Spanish tresure-ship sunk in Tobermory Bay in the Inner Hebrides. Thus, without committing ourselves to the logical mythology of 'atomic propositions' corresponding with 'atomic facts', and the implied ontology of ultimate simples, we are enabled to make sense of the view that there are a number of propositions of whose truth in the sense of correspondence we are assured which are genuinely independent one of another.

At this point inevitably we are reminded of controversies concerning the so-called externality or internality of relations to the terms they are said to relate, which were closely interwoven with the arguments between protagonists of the so-called 'coherence' theory of truth and those who like Russell and Moore, in the first decade of the present century, sought to rehabilitate the classical Aristotelian doctrine of truth as 'correspondence'.[4] Indeed the thesis that at least some of the relations in which some states of affairs in the world stood to other states of affairs left the states of affairs in themselves totally unaffected was an ontological assumption (defended, for instance, by Moore in his very influential paper, 'External and Internal Relations'[5]) that was seen to be demanded by any form of correspondence theory.

The coherentist would argue in reply to the claims made for the alleged correspondence of structure as well as of features between proposition and fact in the examples taken that the alleged separability of these statements from the continuum of the world of experience was far less clear cut than we might suppose. Thus in the two examples taken assumptions concerning date and location involving quite sophisticated methods of chronology and cartography were in use. Further, the frontiers between events (and *fact* in the context of these discussions has been effectively defined as an event or set of events regarded as making a given proposition true or false)[6] are blurred: they cannot be endowed in their individuality with the sort of self-containedness that must be found in them if they are to fulfil the role which the referents of true propositions must play.

'It is in the stream of life that an expression has meaning.' This remark of Wittgenstein's is often quoted as embodying the fundamental insight underlying a so-called 'holistic' theory of meaning. According to this view, to understand what we say when we utter any sort of sentence, we must do justice to its total context in language. If we claim that we know what individual language-fragments purport to refer to and that therefore we know what must be the case if the propositions these fragments frame are to be accounted true, we fail to do justice to the extent that the force and significance of such fragments reside in their total setting. Further it is only in regard to that setting that we know what it is that we are doing when we use this or that sentence. Even such relatively simple factual statements as the two mentioned in illustration above (viz., concerning the weather in Barcelona, and the sunken treasure-ship in Tobermory Bay) cannot be treated as if they were somehow detachable from the whole business of living in which they have their home. The claim that to grasp the meaning of an expression we must attend to the intricacies of its role in our language as a whole is clearly bound up with the emphasis on justified assertibility or use as distinct from truth-conditions, that I illustrated above by reference to Bridgman's comment on Einstein's definition of simultaneity. In Wittgenstein's later work, it is arguably in his treatment of problems in the philosophy of mathematics that his emphasis on assertibility as the ground of legitimate use comes full-tide, and with a wealth of examples, concerned now to cure hearers or readers of the illussion that 'pure mathematics is the physics of the intelligible realm' and by revealing the special roles of calculation in advancing knowledge of the details of our world, to throw light on the relation of pure to applied mathematics; now to bring out for the whole theory of necessary truth, the implications of regarding mathematics as invention rather than discovery; now to criticize Russell's work on the foundations of mathematics, he seems to ground every sort of necessity in an arbitrary *fiat* of the subject. Yet what he is doing only begins to become clear when viewed in relation to language as a whole.

The phrase 'holistic theory of meaning' may recall the metaphysical slogan of the thoroughgoing coherentists that 'nothing is true, but the whole of truth'. The palpable absurdity of speaking of the 'whole of truth' as true has often been pointed out: but those who, for instance, heard the late Professor Harold Joachim lecture in Oxford as late as the mid-thirties will recall the incantatory quality of his diction as if he would communicate a vision in which the familiar would emerge transformed, but with its many contraditions eliminated (a strict Hegelian would say *aufgehoben*) by this transformation.

Certainly those who champion the 'holistic' solution to the problem of meaning are innocent alike of indulgence in absurdity and of invocation of an incommunicable absolute. And again for the most part they eschew the generous ambiguity with which such notions as coherence and system were employed by co-herentists enabling them to blur the differences between very different sorts of system and between equally different examples of coherent discourse. Thus we speak of the system of Euclidean geometry, of Leibniz' metaphysical system, of systems of book-classification in libraries, of so-and-so's system for betting on horses, or playing roulette; we characterize a search or investigation as systematic when we intend no more than that it is conducted according to a plan. Again we blame a lecturer for incoherence when we mean that we have been unable to grasp the relations between different phases of his argument, or the design informing the presentation of items that seem to have been mentioned almost at random. Further when we acquit a man of the charge of being under the influence of drink on the ground that his speech was coherent, we refer to the fact that his statements were intelligible and consistent both internally and one with another.

In practice we do use the notion of coherence, invested with a certain 'openness of texture', in admitting or disallowing the claim of assertions made concerning matters of fact to our accept-ance, or at least to our consideration. Thus in the claim recently made that the recovery from a terminal cancer of the intestines of a Glasgow dock labourer named Fegan was miraculous (effected allegedly by the intercession of a seventeenth-century Jesuit martyr, James Ogilvie, who was executed for refusing to ac-knowledge the supremacy in matters ecclesiastical in Scotland of James VI), the general practitioner, who was attending Fegan in what he confidently expected to be the last stages of a lengthy illness, while admitting such surprise that he momentarily ques-tioned his diagnosis (he was not, I suspect, speaking seriously), disallowed the possibility that the sufficient and necessary condi-tion of his patient's recovery should be found in divine intervention (whether or not elicited by the Jesuit's prayers, those prayers having themselves been as a matter of fact invoked by a group, including Fegan's wife and parish priest). Even if the doctor could be accused of a metaphysically and theologically unsophisticated attitude to the relations of primary to secondary causality, we can hardly deny the good sense he showed in seeking to explain Fegan's recovery naturalistically. A specialist indeed suggested that in this very remarkable recovery, there was possibly a paradigmatic, certainly a highly dramatic, instance of the spontaneous regression of a cancer: of such regressions there are now a sufficient number for their occurrence to constitute a phenomenon urgently requiring investigation, not least to find ways in which such regressions might be effectively induced. Such characterization is not explanatory: Fegan's recovery has been tenatively identified, and (it may be) the concept through which it has been so identified enlarged. One might even say that its significance has been defined, and that in a way that at once banishes substitution of self-indulgent mystery-mongering for understanding while at the same time emphasizing fields in respect of which explanatory concepts are not available, but must be sought.

This example illustrates the extent to which in a properly sophisticated everyday use of the notion of coherence, a balance is struck between insistence on the fluidity of any sort of confidently embraced conceptual system and refusal to disallow the relative authority of certain experiential constants. Yet these constants, often conceived much more loosely than through a quasi-Kantian 'transcendental deduction', are never by the coherentist invested with any sort of inviolability, whether by appeal to alleged rational intuition or to a supposedly unchallengeable common sense. It is certainly the case that for the coherentist this fluidity (if I may continue the metaphor) belongs to the waters of a river or ocean whose pattern is ultimately both stable, all-embracing and all-reconciling. But the analogies between the coherentist's attitude and the principle implicit in the attitude of those who subscribe to a 'holistic' theory of meaning is worth exploring; and it is arguable that both agree in a determination, if not to abandon, at least radically to depreciate concern with what is or is not the case in the sense in which such concern if affirmed as central by those who identify truth fundamentally with correspondence: this though they realize the need for the utmost sophistication in analysis of that correspondence.

If truth, however, is identified with correspondence with fact, it should be clearly recognized that correspondence is to be regarded as the 'focal meaning' of the term 'truth'. That is, we most certainly do use the term 'truth' when it would be a sheer mistake to suppose that we could substitute for it 'correspondence with fact'. For instance, if we claim that one physical theory has displaced another, and are not content with analysing that displacement in terms of greater conceptual economy, comprehensiveness, simplicity, even aesthetic quality, but wish to insist on a more secure purchase-hold on what is the case, we immediately recognize the inadequacy of the notion of correspondence to convey the advance achieved. Again,[7] if we allow that it makes sense to speak of truth in connexion with a system of non-Euclidean geometry, it is obvious that here truth must be analysed in terms of the internal coherence between axioms, postulates, theorems, etc. It is as if the spread of the notion of truth enables the notion to comprehend relationship between propositions that seem to have little or nothing to do with its 'focal' sense.

So indeed in the classical instance of forms of being in Aristotle, *sterēsis* or deprivation may be thought to have nothing significantly in common with substance. And again, to develop an example used by Professor J. L. Austin,[8] forms of Fascist polity may be noticed that cannot be regarded as inspirationally derivative from the political ideas and enterprises of Benito Mussolini (for instance that of Charles Maurras and l'Action Française which antedates by a considerable period the preparation of the so-called 'March on Rome'), but which are none the less, properly classified as Fascist by reference to the paradigm of Mussolini's movement. The conceptual unity is established through the tracing of the relationships to the 'focal' realization; we may say that sometimes it is the positing of the 'focal' case, as distributing its sense *kat' analogian*[9] through the quasi-derivative realizations, that enables us to group together what otherwise might fall apart.

The issue with which this paper is concerned can now be restated in terms of the extent to which we allow the notion of truth in the sense of correspondence to pervade and control the way in which we understand our thinking to relate to what is the case. Or must we see our coming to terms with our world as something that is pervaded less by bringing our thought into submission to what is the case than by continually adjusting and revising standards of the acceptable of which we are in the last resort ourselves the authors?

It is a commonplace to claim for the so-called 'anti-realism', inspired by Brouwer's rejection of the 'law of excluded middle', that it does justice to the very many propositions of which it is impossible for us to say decisively whether they be true or false. Admission or rejection is a matter for our own decision. And what may be claimed in respect of universal propositions of unrestricted generality must also be said where very many, if not all, the most important, indeed exciting things we say about the past are concerned. It is not simply that where, for instance, the study of such a period as seventeenth-century English history is concerned, characteristically Marxist assumptions serve to direct the attention of historians, already cognizant of the variety of source-materials available, to tracts of that material they have hitherto neglected; nor is it also simply a matter of setting the constitutional and religious conflicts of the age of the Civil War in the context of contemporary economic conflicts and changes, and seeking to understand the former by reference to the latter. Rather it is a sense that no frontiers can easily be set to the corrigibility of historical judgments, and that revolutions of perspective at least as great as the one mentioned may occur, altering our most elementary sense of what it is to come to terms with the past as historians.

To one concerned with questions in the philosophy of theology today, these issues are necessarily raised very sharply where the question of the so-called 'essence of Christianity' is concerned. It has been a commonplace to insist that if truth or indeed falsity is to be claimed for Christianity, this claim demands that certain statements shall be defensibly made concerning the life and teaching of its alleged founder. Thus Bertrand Russell insisted that the claims made for the supreme moral excellence of Jesus fell to the ground in view of the fact that he is represented in the gospels as threatening everlasting torment to those whose behaviour failed to conform with the standards he proclaimed, or indeed refused to adhere to him.[10] Similarly others have been moved to a very different judgment from Russell's by the way in which (from their reading of the gospel narratives) Jesus is represented as going to his death, disdaining any and every sort of violent intervention to attempt to extricate him from his predicament, praying for the executive agents of his brutal execution, indeed by his whole endurance, expressing in deed the inwardness of the reply to his flatterer, which so much impressed Kant: 'Why callest thou me good? One only is good: namely God.'

Yet it is very often insisted to-day that Russell and the believer whose attitudes I have contrasted with his are alike guilty of the same errors both in supposing that from the gospels (and other New Testament writings) it is possible to extract a portrait of the so-called 'founder of Christianity', and also in supposing that, if it were so, the features discernible in such a portrait would be of fundamental importance to the question whether or not Christianity is true or false. The question whether or not such a portrait can be extracted from the New Testament writings is a highly technical question, involving, in particular, an answer to the question not whether or not the gospels are biographies (in the sense in which, e.g., Xenophon's *Memorabilia Socratis*, Plutarch's *Lives*, Suetonius' *Lives of the Caesars*, etc. may be so regarded) but whether or not they may be judged in any sense properly biographical in character, whatever other purposes, even other primary purposes, they may have served. There is, however, no doubt at all that the very genuine difficulties involved in treating the gospels as biographical sources have proved very congenial to those who would argue the total or near-total irrelevance of the historical reconstruction of the likeness of Jesus of Nazareth to the question of the truth or falsity of Christianity. Indeed they would argue that when we come to see gospel-writing as an episode or a set of episodes in the development of the Christian movement, we will come to see that it is that movement to which we may (if we choose) adhere which gave the gospels their significance, and in which indeed in their contemporary use they continue to find significance. Their sense resides not in what they purport to describe as having happened, but in the uses to which they may be put.[11] We should not seek to conceive what it is that they say in order to decide whether or not it is the case, but rather to find them acceptable by constraining them to translation into terms of our own situation.

It is claimed for such an attitude that it acknowledges both the corrigibility of any and every historical reconstruction of the past, and at the same time, by emphasizing the priority of questions of use over reference in determining whether or not certain alleged vehicles of meaning may still be given free currency, it allows significant sources to continue to exercise a special authority. But in all this we make ourselves and the laws concerning what may be permissibly said, which we are for ever fashioning and refashioning, the ultimate arbiters.

Yet the distinction between historical reconstruction and historical fiction remains. The past may be something that we regard ourselves as continually refashioning. But there are irreversible advances in historical understanding. Yet certainly such advances are necessarily limited in scope to the human scene; for historical work (unless one regards geology, evolutionary biology, and cosmology as historical in character) is necessarily and innocently anthropocentric. It is a sheer mistake to infer from the proposition that many disputed questions are today incapable of settlement and likely to remain so, that no questions here are capable of decisive settlement. For there are constants which help to define the area of the problematic.

Yet what of the more deeply pervasive anthropocentrism mentioned at the outset of this paper? Have we not in the end to reckon with the extent to which standards, which are necessarily human standards, pervade and determine the very structural constants through which we seek to let that which is the case have its way with us? Is not the very concept of the world whose order is as it is and not as we would have it, a concept framed in terms of our seeking to distinguish the world from ourselves and thereby to enter more deeply on the irreducible uniqueness of our selfhood? It may be that as a result of empirical investigation, whether cosmological or directed to the close study of animal behaviour and communication (e.g., among dolphins) some of the constants which we employ (e.g., time, space, communication itself) will be delivered from part of their anthropocentric taint. Yet the idealist's claim that we decide what questions are answerable or how questions should be understood that they may be made answerable, continues to infect our confidence that we know what must be the case if this or that proposition is to be accounted true, even if we shall never ourselves be able to determine whether or not it is so. In knowing the truth-conditions of a statement, do we or do we not leave behind or disregard built-in limitations of our human condition? It is as if at this point another question begins to emerge: namely, what limitations we may suppose one day likely or conceivably to be overcome, and what we must accept as built-in to the very possibility of asking whether or not something is the case. It may well be that a part at least of the enquiry traditionally named 'ontology' is concerned to lay hold of the latter and to give an account of them as comprehensive and as free of counter-intuitive paradox as possible. It may indeed also emerge here that the very discontent with idealism, to which reference has often been made in this paper, is expressive of a recurrent sense that to abandon concern with what is the case, and to allow all that one can justify oneself in accepting in the sense in which one can render it acceptable, is to convert awareness of anthropocentrism from a problem into a solution, or rather into a recipe for dissolving a multitude of problems. Yet through continual worrying at these problems, some insight may be won, even though that insight be very different in nature and content from what we might anticipate.

11

The Conflict between Realism and Idealism

Remarks on the significance for the
philosophy of religion of a
classical philosophical controversy
recently renewed

I

The impact of general philosophy on the philosophy of religion
must appear at first sight a somewhat artifically conceived and
unrewarding topic. In writing in these terms I am in fact introducing a paper that is concerned not with a method or set of
methods, let alone with a body of doctrine, but rather with a
controversy that is continually reappearing in new and unexpected forms. In contemporary philosophy (as I understand it)
this controversy has emerged again stated in terms of a sharp
division of view in the theory of meaning:

Should the meaning of a statement be defined in terms of its
truth-conditions, that is: with respect to what must be the case if
the statement in question is to be regarded as true?

or Should its meaning be defined in terms of its use, that is:
with respect to the conditions that must be fulfilled for its proper
assertion?

The formulation of this question shows very clearly the influence of Wittgenstein's later works,[1] in particular that part of it
which may interpreted as concerned with one of Frege's most
important theses in the philosophy of logic. It derives its shape
from the critical assimilation of Wittgenstein's demand: 'Do not
ask for the meaning; ask for the use.' Does this demand embody a
universal principle that can at one blow resolve a whole number
of problems relating to the validity of very many sorts of state-

ment? Certainly in the lectures on the foundations of mathematics given at Cambridge in the first half of 1939[2] that have recently been published, we have very striking illustrations of the way in which Wittgenstein himself obeyed his own prescription in treating such problems as those of the sense in which we can properly speak of the existence of natural, rational, irrational and transfinite numbers, and of the relations of pure to applied mathematics. He has much to say moreover of the central crux in the philosophy of mathematics, namely whether a new piece of mathematics is to be regarded as an invention or as a discovery: much also with the aid of very illuminating examples that throws a great deal of light on such problems as the nature of logical and mathematical truths as he came to conceive them in his later period. Because he worked out in detail the consequences of Brouwer's rejection of the so-called 'law of excluded middle', Wittgenstein's standpoint in this period has been characterized (in the title of studies devoted to it) as 'strict finitism'.

While it is obvious that discussion in detail of these developments in the philosophy of logic calls for a great measure of technical expertise, even those whose deficiency in mathematical training keeps them aloof from such close evaluation of the arguments involved recognize the extent to which, in these investigations, old arguments concerning idealism and realism are re-activated. Sometimes indeed this realism arrogates to itself the proud title of Platonism, with reference in the first instance to the doctrines of Plato's 'middle dialogues' (e.g. *Meno, Symposium, Phaedo, Republic*): doctrines which even when Plato criticized them with devastating effect in the first part of the *Parmenides*, he yet claimed to be a far more serious option than the suggestion that the so-called 'Forms' (including here the objectives of the mathematicians' study) could be relegated to the status of *noēmata* or thoughts. One catches the resonance of this sharp rejection of a view of mathematical conceptions as mind-dependent creations in Frege's polemic in *The Foundations of Arithmetic*[3] against any form of 'psychologistic' account of the origins and nature of arithmetic, illustrating his argument by discussing very actutely the status of such concepts as the Equator and the centre of mass of the solar system, rejecting any view which would assign to these concepts a mind-dependent status akin to that of a succession of mental images. In the philosophy of mathematics the 'Platonist' is concerned to insist that in coming to know something new, we discover, we do not bring into being what we then possess as knowledge.

It will be realized that an analogous problem arises in the world of the experimental and observational sciences; this though there are important differences between the ornithologist patiently watching for hours birds coming and going in the vicinity of a sewage farm, and the experimental physicist working with others in the artificial environment of his laboratory, invoking the assistance of highly sophistical laboratory technology (whose absence, maybe on grounds of financial priorities which have compelled the allocation of sparse research funds to the equipment of other chemical, bio-chemical or biological investigation, must hobble the progress of his researches). Where the bird-watcher is concerned, we may say that he finds what flies into his sight. So on Sunday afternoon, 9 February 1978 at the estuary of the River Don on the north side of the city of Aberdeen, after more than twenty-four hours of weather almost unique in the area in its combination of snow, frost and gale-force winds, the Professor of Natural History at that time (Professor V. C. Wynne-Edwards, FRS, a most distinguished student of bird behaviour) insisted that he had seen birds he had never seen before outside the Arctic Circle. It was through perception (with its built-in ability to recognize birds of any and every species) that he was enabled to see (I use the word advisedly) the birds that were so surprisingly there. But they were brought there by the state of the weather, the sufficient, necessary conditions of their presence specifiable in terms of the state of the weather, their response to it (whether or not teleological conceptions are involved here), and the nature of the estuary whither they had arrived. (I write as an amateur.) Whereas where theoretical physics is concerned it is quite different. While Einstein, criticizing the style of the dogmatic empiricist, who is always tempted to reduce knowledge of the external world to the registration of patterns of sensation, concedes that it would be wrong to attribute to thinking a *Durchdringungskraft*, a penetrative power through which it might reach behind the supposed veil of sense to an intelligible reality, graspable by pure intellection, he is even more emphatic in insisting on the extent to which fundamental scientific progress must wait on the development, by spontaneous intellectual creativity, of more powerful branches of mathematics. Such innovations may suggest new sorts of theory, may even enable the *impasse* Einstein himself reached in attempting to unify field theory with the general theory of relativity to be overcome. Admittedly it is with Sir Arthur Eddington in his Tarner Lectures, *The Philosophy of Physical Science*,[4] that we seem to hear again the voice of René

Descartes, when, as on occasion he would seem to do (though at other times he acknowledges the importance of experiment), he identified physics with an extension of speculative geometry.

We may indeed summarize the demands which the above examples help to articulate as comprising in the first instance a request for the analysis of the notion of fact; this because if the meaning of a statement is thought to reside in its truth-conditions, then in framing the conception of the fulfilment of those conditions we cannot avoid sooner or later invoking the notion of fact. This though we eschew the crudities of the picture-theory of the proposition and of the truth-functional view of the relation of all complex to simple propositions. The notion of correspondence must be freed from any sort of involvement with the attempt to establish a one-one correlation between terms of proposition and constituents of fact.

No one can suppose that in the natural sciences, let alone the historical study of human economic, social and political institutions, one can easily draw up the frontier-lines between observation (and its counterpart in historical study) and imagination, the flash of intuitive perception that is one of the marks of genius, inventive virtuosity in choice of questions to be attacked and of the means to seek their answer etc. Always we have to recall what may be termed a pervasive anthropocentrism. The enquiries we prosecute, whether parochial or cosmological in their import, are *human* enquiries. God, if he exists, has no need to raise questions nor to devise the syntax of their most fruitful articulation. Yet if we are realists, we see such questioning as always orientated towards what is; it is correctly experienced as a questing. For a realist the right to affirm what he believes he may affirm is not won through ability to site the expression in question on the map of language as a whole, as if it were that whole which alone, but without external challenge, authorizes us in saying what, by subtlety of understanding, we can place within its compass. Right to affirm depends also on an element of external reference, of *fit* between statement and what is the case. (Of course in this short exposition, I must plead guilty to very serious charges of slackness in treating such major *cruces* in the philosophy of logic as the relation of word and concept, sentence and proposition. But I have aimed only at providing enough background for the discussion of theological issues that follows to be intelligible.)

Does the meaning of what the religious believer says consist in its agreement with established rules for the use of the expression in question, or indeed in the fulfilment of the ritual act to which it belongs? Is its meaning something to be found in its relation to the complex reality of religious behaviour in the same way that one speaks of finding the meaning of that behaviour in its relation to human life as a whole? Is religion an activity which is ultimately its own justification? Are religious beliefs themselves simply an isolatable aspect of this activity? If we define significance in terms of assertibility, we are no longer bound to speak of such beliefs as beliefs *about* something any more than we should speak of theorems, as for instance the theorem that every even number is the sum of two primes, as a description of acutal arithmetical realities. The meaning of such a theorem is found in its role in mathematics. So where religious *credenda* are concerned, their meaning is found by specifying the part played by profession of faith in the life of religion. We can count such beliefs valid by the extent to which the process to which they belong and to which by their profession they contribute is an acceptable human activity.

On such a view the horizons of religion remain always open. The frontiers of the concept of religion are undefined, and we are justified in regarding it as something that is continually being brought into being. It is indeed a *faciendum* rather than a *factum*. We can completely misunderstand the religious life, including the important part of that life which consists in the dialogue between different religious traditions, if this life is construed as being concerned with what is the case. To accept the classical conception of truth as correspondence of proposition with fact and to apply this conception to religious *credenda* is from the point of view I am trying to expound totally to misunderstand the nature of these *credenda*, treating them as if they were referential statements, as if one were right to treat them as true or false in the same way as a statement concerning the weather today in the north-west of Scotland.

We must not forget that those who identify meaning with conditions of assertibility emphasize the rejection of the 'law of excluded middle'. There are very many propositions about which one cannot confidently say whether they are true or false. What for instance should be said of universal propositions of unrestricted generality? In everyday life, as in the exact sciences, these propositions play a very important part. A mother warns her child not under any circumstances to eat certain fungi, giving a very careful description of their appearance. She is fully aware that she is offering something very different from the warning she may also give that a neighbour's dog is a vicious animal.

Propositions concerning the distinction between the edible and the poisonous we must learn in order to survive. They help us to frame our responses to the conditions of our biological existence and we do not doubt their claim to universality. Yet are we at ease in speaking of them as if they must be either true or false? If we suppose truth to consist in correspondence with fact and falsity in its absence, what of the relation between the universality and necessity we suppose belong to these propositions and identifiable constituents of the world?

If we pass from daily life to the much more complex world of the exact sciences, the problem becomes even more acute. What must be said concerning the truth of Newton's inverse square law or of Mendel's ratios in respect of biological inheritance? Such universal propositions of unrestricted generality cannot be treated as truth-functions of singular proposition. If we say that all readers of this paper are interested in philosophical problems, what we say is true if and only if all readers are interested in such problems. If someone reads the paper out of affection for the author, while finding it unspeakably boring, then the statement that all its readers are interested in philosophy is unquestionably false. But we can say this because where such a statement is concerned its generality is restricted, and we are therefore able in principle at least to specify the conditions of its truth or falsity. It is unquestionably the case that universal propositions of unrestricted generality are also falsifiable; indeed, we know that where progress in the sciences is concerned, falsification is of the greatest significance, and it is commonly insisted that vulnerability to falsification differentiates the scientific hypothesis from the attractive, even exciting speculation. But what of the peculiar status that belongs to that for which we claim unrestricted generality? We are totally unable to conceive the sort of infinite verification that would be needed if we were able to specify the truth-conditions of this sort of proposition.

A solution is inevitably sought by reference to the role of such propositions in respect of an activity whose limits cannot easily be defined. We learn to banish from our minds any sort of scruple that a nagging concern with their supposed reference keeps alive. Where very many convictions essential for the progress of human knowledge and indeed the maintenance of the human life are alike concerned, we allow weight to fall on the side of the subject. It is the subject who in sovereign decision, pronounces one assertion justified and another unjustified. It is in fact for the subject to decide what is to be affirmed or denied. The obvious congruity of this sort of philosophizing with a more ancient traditional idealism is sufficiently clear in what I have just said. We must now turn to catch the resonance of this philosophical controversy in one of the most important and intractable discussions in the philosophy of religion today, namely that which is concerned with the notion of the transcendent.

Is the transcendent a *datum* or a *dandum*? A *factum* or a *faciendum*? I am tempted to suggest that if one is a realist in philosophy of religion, one is not inclined to the view that supposed reference to the transcendent is to be regarded simply as the preliminary condition of the believer's life, and as that which gives that life its form. The transcendent is not a notion which emerges in that life nor one that finds in that life its proper context. Rather it is manifested by its intrusive presence as something continually demanding that we transform our understanding of its content more and more rigorously, as if every articulation of that content were precarious and necessarily incomplete, in order that we may *begin* to grasp what we seek to refer to. Yet although our speech, such as it is, concerning the transcendent belongs necessarily to the 'negative way', we are compelled all the time to insist that we are not enjoying play with the creation of our own imagination. We are in fact not simply invoking this notion as a tool that advances our own self-interpretation. To speak in such terms is to claim too much and too little at the same time. It is to claim too little for such a fragment of an individual's confession of faith to say that in this confession he is in the last resort concerned simply with self-interpretation. To suppose that this is the sole significant concern of such a confession is in fact to identify the boundaries of every human life with the boundaries of what is, and thus also to claim too much. We have only to look at such confident anthropocentrism coolly to recognize its inadequacy, an inadequacy as evident to atheist as it is to theist.

II

To make this discussion less abstract I want now to turn, even somewhat abruptly, to suggest the 'presence' of this central controversy between idealism and realism in an area of dogmatic theology, namely that of the controversy between the 'subjective'[5] and 'objective' conceptions of the atonement.

The champions of the 'subjective' conception emphasize the manner in which the individual makes the work of Christ his own; indeed they go so far as to suggest that this work must not

be conceived in any way, which contradicts the supreme significance of its appropriation. It is by reference to the ways in which
Christ's work is appropriated that the work itself is to be conceived. To conceive the work in ways that diminishes the significance of its appropriation is to suggest that its form, the *that which
it is to be*, contradicts its *telos* or end. Therefore let the work be
conceived as that which, in this way, rather than that, or better, in
this way *through* that, is made its own by its intended
beneficiaries. Its essence, even its *esse*, lies in its being appropriated, in its being received by those beneficiaries in terms that
may, or may not, be objectively preferable by reference to this or
that level of achieved moral perception, but which none the less
are adequate for the purpose they fulfil in the lives of the reci-
pients in question. One may liken a doctrine of the atonement to a
tool. Now the tools in a large toolbox are very different. The role
of a screwdriver is different from that of a hammer, and it would
be absurd to use a highly sophisticated machine-tool as if it
were made to open a jammed door or drawer! We need to see
doctrines of the atonement as tools in the appropriation of its
deepest sense. Further, we have to recognize the extent to which
these tools differ one from another, and draw from this recognition renewed awareness of the diversity and complexity of the
activity of appropriation in which, on the subjective side, the *esse*
of the work of Christ consists.

The situation is altogether different, if we suppose that what
makes the appropriation of Christ's work significant, lies in its
being in itself what it is, namely the extrojection *in conditiones
humanas* of the threefold being of God. If we find in Christ's work
the accomplishment of a verdict on the human scene, and beyond
that the completion or fulfilment of the act of creation, God-
grounded, God-defined, God-orientated, it is altogether different. Certainly Christ's work does not ignore the subjective par-
ticularities of the human scene, let alone the windings of human
experience, both individual and collective. Initially, indeed, it is a
verdict on their self-destructive potentiality, and it is in the
whirlpool of deviously conflicting human purposes that the work
is accomplished, and the still centre of its steadfast reality
achieved.[6] Do we suppose that the faith which it elicits is primarily a response to its accomplished actuality? Or is it a series of
spontaneously initiated exercises, whereby we make our own
that which these events, as we have received them, seem to us to
suggest; and by this response constitute them what they are?

Most certainly, to follow the 'objectivist' tradition in soteriol-

ogy, is not to belittle the rich complexity, and indeed the dark
perversity, of human engagement with the mysteries of redemption. There are forms of 'objectivist' doctrine which are morally
monstrous, suggesting sometimes that crime and its retributive
punishment are the most fundamental forms of being at the
human level, and at others that God is the abiding enemy of his
creation, needing the incessant multiplication of supposed ritual
sacrifices to deflect his fury from this or that target of his supposed inexpiable anger. (Thus, the recognition of a 'middle place'
of growth and purification, even through suffering, regarded as
the lot of the vast majority of the departed, became perverted[7]
into the anticipation of a penal 'purgatory', wherein the departed
allegedly endured the punishment due to them for the so-called
venial sins which they had failed to expiate. If prayer for the
departed is always a cry for mercy, it should be mercy sought
from one who is the healer of the wounded, rather than a
prison governor who, with minute accuracy, computes the duration, and the attendant severities, of his charges' stay in their
appointed jail.) There is certainly a sense in which the history of
the doctrine is a part of the story; but is it the whole story? More
important, does it do justice to the central theme? Again if we
judge it the whole story, what place do we leave for the correction
of admitted perversions?

III

To return now to the general theme of this paper. One of the
metaphysical doctrines, characteristic of the theology of Aquinas,
which has given rise to most intellectual and indeed spiritual
scandal, is his insistence that while creation is related to God in
such a way that without him it is an *Unding*, none the less he
is not *really* related to it. There is something intensely paradoxical in seeking to maintain the divine aseity and absolute transcendence of all else, by thus denying any relation of the transcendent to his creation. After all, it might be said that in so far
as any form of theism whatsoever involves reference to God *and*
the world, the theist has insisted on a relation of conjunction between the two and that we must suppose this conjunction significant for God as well as creatures. Further, if we seek to do
justice to the absolute dependence of creatures upon Creator, by
using, for instance, the analogy of the dependence of a melody on
the singer who is singing it, can we suppose that the singer is
totally unaffected by the melody he is singing, its interruption for

instance before he has sung the last two verses of his song, a matter of absolute indifference to him, so that he could not care less whether song was sung in part or whole, or not at all? If we elaborate our example by thinking of a trivial popular melody (let us say the 'Pick of the Pops' at the top of the 'charts' for a week in June 1978), altogether ephemeral, almost forgotten well before Christmas, we still find it impossible to suppose that where the singer's individual biography is concerned, his short-lived relation to this song is unreal. Certainly we would want to say that the relation was external to one of its terms, namely the singer, in the sense that his short-lived relation to the song in question was something that did not touch the substance of his musical achievement, that which made him the singer that he was, in the way in which, for example, the late Kathleen Ferrier's schooling by the great *maestro* who continually encouraged her in the performance of Mahler's *Lieder*, went some way to make her the great singer that she was. Where the individual 'melody-event' of the pop-singer's singing of his melody is concerned, we rightly say that its reality as part of the furniture of the world depends upon the singer's singing on this occasion. Yet of course the melody as a *Gestalt-qualität*, exemplified in numerous singings of the song in question, making them singings of that melody and not another, is unaffected by this individual performance. Here, indeed, as an analogy of the world's relation to God, this image breaks down, inasmuch as for the theist the world as single, unique, all-embracing event or set of events in its or their unique and unrepeatable particularity, depends absolutely on its Creator. For 'the world is everything that is the case', and the properties of that which makes it up do not somehow survive its non-actuality.

This relatively detailed discussion may have thrown some light on the relevance to my central topic of the sort of ontological analysis concerning the status of relations that followed in England the publication in 1903 of Russell's *Principles of Mathematics*, and of the several important papers in which Bertrand Russell and G. E. Moore criticized the monistic doctrines of Francis Herbert Bradley and others affected by his highly individual genius, or at least developing doctrines sometimes more than superficially akin to Bradley's, even if lacking his strange and elusive subtlety. Both Russell and Moore strongly championed the so-called 'correspondence' theory of truth, and linked their defence of this theory with an assault on the thesis that the relations into which a term entered with any other term, substantially affected the being of the term in question. Moore indeed saw the continuity of these issues with mediaeval debates concerning the relations of substance and accident, and the status of the individual. Although, where Wittgenstein's *Tractatus* is concerned, we acknowledge now the crucial importance of his study of Frege on the one hand, and of Schopenhauer on the other, we cannot possibly neglect the background influence of these discussions on the texture of his logical atomism. For him the externality of individual facts, one to another, is an axiom of first order importance. (What is a fact in this context if it is not an event regarded as making a given proposition true or false, to borrow a suggestive comment of H. H. Price?)

Although the theist regards the world as a unity by reference to its total dependence on God, we are perhaps coming to be able to see why, for St Thomas, the presence of God to the world, conceived as a relation in which he stands to the world, must be represented as *notional*, not real. It is an attempt to understand the dependence of the world in respect of the resonance of that dependence on the divine being, as something approaching asymptotically the limit of that sheer externality which virtually passes over into a complete absence of relatedness. For God the world in itself is of no significance. Yet – and here is the deepest paradox – this ontological indifference (if we may so express it) is posited as the authentic foundation on which we may base his complete engagement with the world's history in self-giving love.

No section of the traditional philosophical discipline of ontology demands more rigorous and careful treatment than that of relations. Controversy concerning their status is a recurrent issue of metaphysics (in my remarks above I have concentrated on the controversy aroused by the nineteenth-century British Idealists; but I do not forget Leibniz's engagement with the question of the reducibility of relations to qualities). Certainly in a different, but still related sense, the concerns of the philosophy of religion today, and the ways in which it is pursued, throw into clear relief the issue of the status of the 'relational'. The word 'dialogue' is currently everywhere heard. But what are these 'dialogues' and what are we to say of the participants? How are they to be understood, and how is the enterprise on which they are engaged to be esteemed? And what of the relations between them through which the enterprise is carried on? Are we to understand dialogue as in fact the current phase, or *a* current phase, in the development of religious actuality in its totality – a totality that is regarded as self-justifying and by reference to which the work of those taking part is justified through the contribution made by the roles they fulfil in its articulation? To resume the earlier analogy provided by the notion of tool: are we to treat the individual contributions made by participants in 'dialogue' as so many tools, or even to envisage the enterprise to which they contribute, as itself a most powerful instrument, akin perhaps to a 'thermic lance' by whose power access can be gained to the most allegedly impregnable strong-room, and the valuables it contains (provided proper skill is exercised in its use)? Yet the analogy of the tool may well be judged by some to break down inasmuch as 'dialogue' may be conceived as itself belonging to an activity whose significance resides in the *telos* or end, immanent in it from the beginning, and by its full articulation giving the whole process its shape and justification. A 'thermic lance' is under the control of the man who uses it (provided, of course, that he is technically competent to do so), and he uses it to gain access to valuables that he believes all the time secure in a strong-room; his use of this tool in no sense brings into being what he seeks. Whereas 'dialogue', in this respect far less akin to the dialectic of Plato, whether the Socratic dialectic of the early dialogues, the method employed on the *hypotheseis* in the 'middle dialogues', or that illustrated differently in the *Sophist* and the *Parmenides*, than to that of Hegel, is regarded as in some sense creative of, or contributory to the being of, its own objects.

Thus we find it plausible to suggest that in modern inter-religious dialogue, the dialectic in play is more nearly Hegelian than Platonic in that the objects sought in and through the exchange or confrontation are brought into being by the meeting. It is a commonplace of modern study of Hegel's writings, by authorities as different as Jean Hyppolite, George Lukacs, and even the theologian Hans Küng in his remarkable, impressionistic appraisal of Hegel's Christology, to emphasize that for him the sources of his dialectic are to be found as much in Greek tragedy as in the Academy: that its structure shows the depth of the impact made on him by the tri-logical structure of, for instance, Aeschylus' *Oresteia*, or indeed (an example that made a great impact on him) by the *stichomuthia* between Antigone and Creon in Sophocles' *Antigone*. Hegel's reflections on the issues raised by that great play are part of the patrimony of European literature and thought; yet even while one acknowledges the depth of his insight, one is aware that the teleological element in his dialectical vision, while it did not occlude, even promoted, his profound sensitivity to the reality of human conflicts, and their role in men's and women's collective and personal history, somehow softens the sharpness of his engagement with the issues he has uncovered. Does he measure up to the terrible conclusion of Sophocles' play? Or does he adequately face the paradox that Antigone's obsessive, near-incestuous preoccupation with her unburied brother Polyneices undoubtedly activates in Creon an obstinate arrogance in which a threat to his own dignity is a threat to the *polis*, and in which all sense of the need for the ruler, even in a time of crisis, to govern by consent of the governed, is lost, that she is indeed the destroyer of her uncle as she is of his son Haemon, to whom she is betrothed, and whose loss she contemplates as retrievable in a way a dead brother's cannot be; and yet that this woman remains incomparably the nobler human being of the two? This although one could continue the catalogue of charges against her to include her Amazonian contempt for her sister's hesitation, even for her sister's sense that Eteocles, the brother who fell in defence of Thebes in obedience to his uncle, has also his place in the scheme of things. We are faced not with the promise of a reconciliation somehow achieved, as if human differences could have their sting drawn by conversion into near-academic arguments, but with a terrible end, in which by her death Antigone redeems herself, but in which very many loose ends are left untied. Hegel's besetting optimism needs to be offset by the treatment the play has received in Germany from Heinrich Weinstock, in America from Cedric Whitman, and in Switzerland from André Bonnard in his excellent short book: *La Tragédie et l'Homme*.[8]

How do we regard what we are pleased to call dialogue? Do we see it as an end in itself in which indeed its end is somehow immanent? Or is it a seeking together that may end in what is hardly bearable, even as Oedipus' relentless investigation, involving him, as Sophocles' play proceeds, in a remorseless search for self-knowledge, issued in a knowledge that he could not bear? So now that he sees his little human world as it is, he can bear no longer to look upon it, but rushes out to blind himself, that, seeing, he may no longer behold. Dialogue may run into the earth of the humanly intractable. For religious conflicts do not happen in a nicely protected academic vacuum, but for instance, in the way in which they threaten the precarious stability of the world in the Middle East today, in the bitter division of Jew and Arab, with the so-called Christian West rendered impotent by the guilt of centuries of vindictive persecution of the Jewish people (if at times subtle, remorselessly pursued policies of social exclusion replaced the fury of the pogrom), and by the memory of such monstrous perversions of Christ's gospel as found expression in the so-called 'Crusades'. We have to reckon with the tragic dimensions of what we are pleased to call 'dialogue'; this even while as Christians we acknowledge that to seek such conversations, and to pursue them, is binding on us as an imperative. Here arguably we have much to learn from the complex and searching argument of Kant's *Religion within the Bounds of Reason Alone:* a work in which the lessons that Christians should always seek to learn from the *Aufklärung* are presented with an unforgettable rigour by the philosopher who, more than any other, had purged those lessons of every taint of facile optimism. Again it is one of the marks of Hans Urs von Balthasar's greatness as a theologian that in his meditations on the Stations of the Cross[9] he saw the theme of the rejection of the old Israel as very near the inescapably tragic centre of the paschal mystery. Thereby he achieved that very rare thing – a short masterpiece of Christian devotional writing in which depth of theological insight is constrained to serve and to purify spiritual vision.

It is the fault of the idealist always to seek escape from the authority of the tragic, to avoid reckoning with the burden of inescapable fact, to find in the supposed whole constituted by the history of the spiritual life of mankind the context not only within which individual essays after the Absolute leave their meaning, but also their justification. Reference to an external standard is gone; meaning is defined in terms of conditions of assertibility, not in terms of truth-conditions. Yet what of the situation in which we must confess the latter unknown? What escape is there from the resulting impasse? Here I would revert to the conflict between 'objective' and 'subjective' understandings of Christ's work to which I referred earlier. For those who favour the objective conception there is no escaping the admission that they are thrust towards the acknowledgement of that which in its inmost essence must remain unknown: that is to acknowledge the actuality of a work wrought by God in which the self-limitation involved in creation reaches its ultimate term. In his recent study of Christ's agony in the Garden of Gethsemane,[10] André Feuillet has rightly followed his minute discussion of the divergent synoptic narratives, of their possible echoes in the fourth gospel and the letter to the Hebrews (including scrutiny of the precise sense of the words employed by the writers) by a study of Pascal's *Le Mystère de Jésus*. He is justified in my judgment by thus admitting that the work of the *Neutestamentler* must be complemented (if understanding is to be enlarged) by the kinds of insight that may be achieved by the intuitive vision of the religious genius. It is arguably not the least service that the metaphysician can do for the theologian that, by his critical discipline, he enables the latter to articulate what it is that pulls him up short, that compels him at once to acknowledge that what he says is significant only if certain truth-conditions are fulfilled, and yet that the secret of the manner of their fulfilment lies with God, with the Father indeed to whose will Jesus in his agony abandons himself, leaving indeed to him the final and the only ultimately valid judgement on his mission. 'There was a Calvary above that was the mother of it all.'

12

Parable and Sacrament

Since Bonhoeffer's *Letters and Papers from Prison* were first published in 1953,[1] we have been familiar with the phrase 'religionless Christianity' and its cognates, and with the explicit rejection of the presentation of Christianity as the *vera religio*, or indeed as a religion at all, Although Bonhoeffer in these letters rejected Barth's 'positivism of revelation', no student of the second edition of Barth's great commentary on the epistle to the Romans[2] would have found much in Bonhoeffer's insistence that was unfamiliar to him except (and this, of course is a great deal), the boldness with which he developed its implications for the understanding of the life of faith in the world that he knew. It was Barth who, in his sustained radical criticism of the methods of nineteenth-century *Religionsphilosophie* (and in this commentary Barth wrote as a prophet converting to his own uses lessons he had learnt from masters as varied as Plato and Kant, Kierkegaard and Dostoevsky, etc.) had made familiar rejection of the thesis that there was an extractable essence of religion. Even if there were such a study, or such an essence, it was quite irrelevant to the understanding of the Christian faith. Indeed, concentration of attention on such a supposed human endowment might encourage the illusion that by its disciplined cultivation men and women could achieve for themselves a kind of spiritual maturity that would entitle them to be regarded, and indeed to regard themselves, as masters in much that pertained to the relations of creature to Creator.

Barth rejected the whole long tradition of successive attempts to lay bare the essence, or authentic form, of the religious consciousness, which was inaugurated by Kant's characteristically complex and nuanced study *Religion within the Bounds of Reason Alone*, and which had in the period to which Barth's writing belonged received a very influential late expression in Rudolf Otto's work *Das Heilige*.[3] With the devastating but often illuminating unfairness characteristic of the prophet, Barth would seem to dismiss every contributor to this long enterprise as guilty of achieving little more than a fresh variation on a nearly valueless theme. In later writings, for instance in his lengthy studies of eighteenth- and nineteenth-century Protestant theology,[4] Barth went a long way toward redressing the balance lost in the fierce prophecy of his first great work. Thus his own essay on Hegel is an impressive confirmation of Henri Bouillard's judgment[5] that in the *Dogmatics* Barth's intellectual master is much more Hegel than the latter's critic Kierkegaard, to whom he is so obviously indebted in sections of the early commentary. But if scholarly conscience makes it impossible for one to regard the critical judgments passed in the commentary as fair to the writers criticized, its devastating insight remains for those who would avail themselves of its resources, not in the style of slavish disciples, but rather in the manner of those who would allow their own thinking to be disciplined by the critical interrogation of one who, in an extraordinary work, offered the world a unique fusion of exegesis, theological and metaphysical analysis, and prophecy.

The temper of the commentary was often that of a prophetic style of *theologia negativa*; indeed many passages in it recall the brilliantly argued metaphysical agnosticism of the first part of Plato's *Parmenides*, in which the philosopher submits to extremely acute critical analysis the three notions he had invoked in characterization of the relation of the particulars revealed to us by sense perception to the transcendent forms, namely presence, participation, and *mimēsis* (copying). Yet at the same time the reader cannot escape hearing sound a clear note of liberation, even in the context of the author's harsh rhetorical rejection of so much familiar to the student of Schleiermacher, Ritschl and the rest. Barth continually insists that we must not set frontiers to the sort of human situation or experience through which God may declare himself. And here, inevitably, one thinks of the parables of Jesus.

Jülicher's elaborately argued insistence on the generic difference between parable and allegory clearly breaks down. Thus, whatever solution we favour of the critical problems raised by the climactic Matthaean image of the 'sheep and the goats' (Matt. 25, 31ff.), it would seem definitely allegorical in that its interpretation demands that we suspend disbelief concerning the elaborate apocalyptic apparatus which the author invokes, and that we attend closely to the precise significance of each detail (even to the extent of asking whether the Son of Man of v. 31 is to be identified with the king of v. 34). Yet when this utterance is spoken of as a parable of the 'sheep and the goats', the term is not being used equivocally. It is rather that the concept of the parabolic possesses an 'openness of texture', allowing us to subsume under it pieces of discourse as different one from another as the parables of the sower, the tares, the ten wise and ten foolish virgins, the marriage feast, the labourers in the vineyard, the talents, the lost sheep, the lost coin, the two brothers, the good Samaritan, the prayers of Pharisee and tax-gatherer, the unjust steward, etc. Although Jülicher's distinction between parable and allegory cannot be sustained, his work remains a landmark in the study of this form of discourse, in that he compelled the serious student to recognize how many of the parables presented fragments of ordinary human life, sometimes trivial, sometimes obviously presenting crises in human relationships, often disturbing by the questions which they left unanswered. Thus, in the parable of the two brothers, the hearer or reader is left at the end quite properly wondering concerning the later outcome of the affair. The wayward brother's return will be duly celebrated; but what then of his relations with his disciplined, industrious elder brother, who could surely claim that only by his management of their father's estate has a home been preserved for his younger brother to return to? It was not he who had converted the part of his father's inheritance which was his due into hard cash, and squandered it; rather he had sacrificed himself, even allowed himself to become the somewhat hard, and censorious individual that he is suggested as being, because he had preferred unromantic hard work to the more colourful life which, for a while, his brother had enjoyed. And again, what of the damage that the prodigal had done? What of the women with whom he had consorted? We need not suppose that he had himself corrupted them; no doubt they were professional prostitutes, who had embraced their profession for the sake of the material rewards it brought them. Yet, in his use of them, he had in some measure connived in their debasement of the currency of their lives. There are a great many loose ends, and one is not simply indulging a philistine curiosity if one reflects upon them. Rather one is treating the tale with the seriousness that it demands, realizing that it is not offered to us as matter for our edification but (if one regards it, to use the idiom of J. L. Austin, as a perlocutionary utterance) as something that is only effective in a manner proper to its form if we are deeply disturbed by what it says. Certainly it presents the superiority of the way of acceptance over that of rejection, suggesting indeed that the former is more nearly akin to, or at least less totally dissimilar from, the way of God with his creatures, than the latter; but woe betide us if we interpret acceptance too lightly, if in a facile anthropomorphic way we ignore the torturing ambiguities of human life. If the parable counsels simplicity, it is a simplicity of which *simplisme* is the mortal foe.[6]

What is true of the parable of the two brothers is, of course, true of many other parables. For instance, the parable of the lost coin speaks immediately to those who (like the present writer), are chronically guilty of mislaying, not only money, but articles in daily use. Anyone with a tendency to this sort of carelessness knows only too well the experience of finding himself obsessed by the thought of the object he has lost, unable to turn back to other business till he has found it, experiencing a quite exaggerated relief when his sight falls suddenly on what he is looking for. Experience may tell him that he is more likely to find it if he turns back to what he was doing, and waits till the object surfaces. But such profound counsel very often proves powerless to overcome distraction and until the lost object is found he can think of little else. There is manifestly nothing here which seems even remotely suggestive of the holy, as Otto conceived it. We are a long way removed from the sort of experience that undoubtedly a great many visitors to the shrine of Our Lady of Walsingham in Norfolk (to mention only one instance) claim to have enjoyed in that place of pilgrimage (in spite of the garish shoddiness of the imitation baroque of its adornment). In the sort of incident mentioned in the parable, there is nothing of *mysterium tremendum atque fascinosum Deitatis*. Yet it is in this sort of incident that Jesus bids his hearers discern an analogy of the relentless, almost obsessive quest of the Creator for the creature, of the movement of God to man, which he himself, in his ministry, including indeed the speaking of such parables as the one referred to, has effectively embodied.

Again, what of the extremely obscure parable of the unjust steward? Its exegesis is certainly baffling and it is not insignificant that a few years ago a very devout and certainly well educated Anglican layman wrote a letter to the principal English church newspaper,[7] in which he pleaded for an alternative to this 'most unhelpful passage' as the liturgical gospel for the Sunday on which its reading is prescribed as such in the Book of Common Prayer. One is tempted to answer by saying that it is no part of a parable's purpose to be 'helpful', as if such utterances belong to the same *genre* as five-minute-long religious talks on the radio. A parable must disturb, rather than edify. Yet one must concede that where the parable of the unjust steward is concerned, its precise force remains more than usually obscure. But one thing that it seems to thrust upon the attention alike of hearer and reader is the need for a kind of remorseless energy in the affairs of the kingdom of God, at least as great as the quick unscrupulous skill displayed by the steward in the story, to extricate himself from the disastrous consequences of his dishonesty. A question-mark is set against the kind of piety that confuses passive acquiescence with authentic humility, that needs to learn the sorts of lesson conveyed rather less harshly in the parable of the talents.

We may seem to have moved a long way from Barth's influence on Bonhoeffer, to which reference was made at the beginning of this paper, and indeed from the criticism of *Religionsphilosophie* embodied in the former's great commentary on Romans; but it could be said that Barth's prophetic utterance has helped to make possible this sort of response to the parabolic, this sensitivity (if I do not use the word improperly) to its profoundly theological, yet deeply non-religious, dimensions. No one who is at all familiar with the range of Bonhoeffer's writings can fail to recognize that he was a most considerable theologian, often severely professional in his choice of the categories he used, and of the problems which he elected to discuss. If he criticized religion, his criticism was the criticism of a man who found that certain sorts of religious concentration, in consequence of their intense preoccupation with the supposedly special experiences that brought men before God, neglected the wide-ranging complexity of the human reality. In his teaching by parable, Jesus illustrated ways in which very various aspects of this reality could, if seen aright, convey, with devasting effect, the ways of God with man.

In the argument of this paper, the emphasis has fallen hitherto on the parables regarded as vehicles of representation. At the outset Jülicher's hard and fast differentiation of parable and allegory was rejected; but it was argued that many parables treated simply as short narratives, or as brief evocations of familiar routines of human behaviour, are simply naturalistic. Employers of labour have, as a matter of fact, behaved in the sort of high-handed way exemplified in the parable of the labourers in the vineyard. The dull, worthy, hard-working man (who by his industry and his stubborn integrity preserves a business enterprise from disaster, or an estate from rotting) is capable of the sort of exasperated outburst with which the elder brother greets the elaborate celebration of his worthless, but arguably more colourful junior's home-coming. Yet, as the reference to Jüngel's book suggested, appreciation of their precise character as vehicles of representation is inevitably incomplete without attention to the parables' role, to what it was sought to achieve by their delivery and by their recording.

And here, of course, we must reckon with the arguments advanced in such works as C. H. Dodd's *The Parables of the Kingdom*,[8] and Joachim Jeremias' *The Parables of Jesus*,[9] which have insisted on the distinction between the setting of the parables' actual delivery by Jesus (frequently irrecoverable) and the context in which their delivery is recorded in the individual gospel. Recent work in the field of *Redaktionsgeschichte* has stressed the extent to which the four gospels, very far from being 'scissors and paste' compilations, embody carefully distinct presentations of the teaching ministry and work of Jesus, ordered in accordance with serious theological presuppositions, differing in important respects from one evangelist to another, and issuing in highly individual, if significantly complementary handling of traditional material, material which is sometimes common to more than one of the four writers, but which also is often preserved for posterity in the writing of one, and not another. In attempting to assess the role of a particular parable (and therefore its precise meaning) in the teaching of Jesus himself, we have therefore very often to assess the extent to which the redactional construction of the context corresponds in some measure to the setting in which the tale was originally told, and from which again in some measure its force as a parable was derived. If we say that it is part of the function of parabolic teaching to disturb, we have still to ask concerning the sort of disturbance such teaching was intended to effect. Moreover we have to distinguish very carefully the sort of disturbance effected by the parable as first delivered, from the kind of disturbance it is represented by individual evangelists as effecting (and this, of course, is relative to the writer's over-all conception of the significance of Jesus' teaching ministry, etc.) and both alike from the sort of disturbance we experience from finding such forms of teaching, with their apparent implications concerning the relations of creature and Creator so deeply embedded in the records of Jesus' ministry. For us what is startling in the parables is their total freedom from any quasi-numinous quality, the kind of quality that one believes one finds in, for instance, great liturgical texts. Again, they are totally free,

for the most part, from the sort of pregnant religious imagery, of
the kind with which traditional preaching is saturated. And here,
by way of illustration of the point made, I wish to turn again to the
parable of 'the sheep and the goats'.

This parable invokes a solemn apparatus of traditional apocalyptic; but to the modern reader the use of this apparatus is
almost immediately subordinated to the sharply interrogative
style of a devastating irony. It is sometimes suggested by New
Testament scholars (for instance, with variations of emphasis, by
T. W. Manson, J. A. T. Robinson and Enoch Powell), that the
parable seeks to suggest that in the hour of the judgment of the
nations, their peoples are revealed as standing or falling by the
extent to which they have discerned the presence of the Son of
man in his humble missionaries. But in my judgment, Théo
Preiss, in his remarkable essay 'The Mystery of the Son of Man'[10],
penetrates aspects of its sense more deeply by insisting that we
construe the parable at least as it is offered to us in the gospel
according to St Matthew, in ethical and theological, as distinct
from narrowly ecclesiological terms. It is only such an exegesis as
Preiss offers that, to *the modern reader*, does justice to the profound moral irony with which the tale is suffused. For Preiss the
parable is certainly theological in that it treats of the presence of
the Son of Man in the midst of the world, and it is important that
the Son of Man of which it speaks is one who is initially presented
in apocalyptic terms, viz., as the mysterious pre-existent being to
whom a very special, if sometimes ambiguously defined role, is
assigned in the final judgment. Yet what the parable insists is that
this mysterious figure is present all the while in the needy, the
hungry, the naked, the prisoners, etc. It is those who serve him in
this real objective presence who are his confessors, and moreover
– this surely is the crux of the parable – their service is as little
self-conscious as the bland neglect of his presence by those who
pass him by is deliberately intended. Both sheep and goats alike
are totally bewildered, one by hearing of their authentic, spontaneous discernment of the Son of Man's presence, the other by
realizing that in spite, no doubt, of their strenuous piety and
unremitting eagerness in good works, they have failed to perceive his crying need of their succour. The irony is devastating.
For all the parable's implicit praise of a spontaneous simplicity
of response, it seems also to confirm such other *logia* as those
which stress the narrowness of the gate, and the elusiveness
of the path which leads to eternal life. Almost the judgment of
the nations in its amazing *peripeteia* is presented as a comedy.

So in different ways, as we receive the parables at our level of self-consciousness with the burden of very many centuries, marked by the betrayal of Christ by the churches heavy upon us, we receive them as devastating correctives of our cultivated religiosity. Yet we only receive them effectively as such correctives, if we take most seriously the total context to which they belong, which indeed by their deliverances they may have helped to realize. Their quick and varied invocation of the ordinary and not so ordinary routines of home life is powerful because their diverse concern (and their concern is diverse in so far as, regarded as vehicles of meaning, they must be seen to operate on a number of different levels), is always somehow with the movement of God towards his people. One can even say that one does not fail in exegetical insight if all the time one recalls that they are part of the human *lalia* of the one in whom without mixture and without confusion, yet without possibility of division or separation, divinity and humanity are united. It is fitting that the speech of the Incarnate should be human, even desperately human. If, as he went before his disciples on the way to Jerusalem, they were afraid, and if that fear was occasioned by aspects of his bearing that could be subsumed under Otto's concept of the numinous, yet his secret was not disclosed in such discernible, isolatable numinosity (discernible and isolatable as the texture of his skin, or the colour of his beard), but in his person, in the totally unique union in him of human and divine. If none spoke as he did, and if in such speech he is revealed as Word made flesh, that speech must have achieved (at least within terms of the cultural relativity to which, as a man, he was committed) a human completeness that alone fitted it to be the instrument of his self-declaration.

In the fourth gospel it is only after the elaborate transcendent metaphysical prolegomena of the introduction that the evangelist turns by way of the interrogation of John the Baptist by an oddly assorted delegation of the Jerusalem 'establishment' to introduce Jesus to his readers as one standing among men of whom they are ignorant, his conformity to the human condition so complete that, unlike his flamboyantly colourful and fiercely controversial forerunner, he is completely indistinct from his peers. It is only against the background of a speculative theological thrust beyond the very frontiers of the created universe, that the ordinariness of Jesus can be seen for what it is; that same ordinariness which later, when he has avowed that 'Before Abraham was, I am', and by his avowal inevitably incurred a blasphemer's death by stoning, will enable him, by the simple device of merging with the temple crowds, to evade the fury of those whom he had offended. (It is a sheer mistake to read into the last verse of John 8 any suggestion of a supposed supernatural evasion of his foes. If exegetes read more detective stories in which men on the run dodge their pursuers, by the simple device of, for instance, thrusting themselves into the rush-hour crowd at a busy underground station, they would not make the mistake of failing to see the fourth evangelist's eagerness to emphasize the sheer ordinariness of the man who alleged that in respect of that which he is fundamentally, they have to do with what, in its changeless atemporality, pre-existed not only Abraham but the coming to be of time itself.)

By emphasizing the extent to which, in parables, we encounter a religious idiom which (to use a modern phrase) has been rigorously 'desacralized', we are not therefore even for one moment abandoning continued reference to the dimension of the transcendent as belonging to the very essence of religious faith. The ways in which, by parables treating of human life as it is lived, men and women are compelled to engage with the dimension of the transcendent are various. After initial emphasis on their representative or informative function, we have gone on to speak of their role in disturbing acquiescent unreflective piety, and this it may be, as in the case of the parable of the unjust steward, by introducing a kind of perplexity, even creating a mood of resentment (as seemingly in the case of the devout English layman whose plaintive letter I have mentioned earlier in this paper) that the comforting world of accepted routines of communion between creature and Creator be rudely interrupted by the suggestion that one can discern, across the self-regarding sharp practice of a man who has cheated his master across the years, that which should be expressed in the violent energy of those who take the kingdom of God by storm.

Yet has the sacral no place in the ministry of Jesus? Jüngel (and indeed other German scholars, whose names are more closely linked than his with the so-called 'new quest of the historical Jesus'), have stressed the great significance in Jesus' ministry of his readiness to eat and drink with those on the very circumference of decent society, for instance harlots and tax-gatherers. His studied refusal to refrain from table-fellowship with those from whom a prophet would surely hold himself aloof, was occasion at once of profound gratitude, and of profound scandal. Even more than the cursing of the fig tree, it was a 'prophetic sign', a symbolic action in which the reality it suggested was actively present, its energies at work. If his teaching by parable was deed as much as word, his readiness to eat and drink with the outcast was word as well as deed. Thus, to Zacchaeus, Jesus' readiness to invite himself to a meal at his house was a sign of God's acceptance; to Simon the Pharisee (a somewhat reserved host), Jesus' behaviour at his table was, if not scandalous, at least indicative of a sad failure of prophetic discrimination. One can, indeed, in the parables in which invitation to a banquet plays a significant role (whether they are attributed to Jesus himself, or treated in the forms in which we have them as compositions of his disciples), see something of the nature of a reflective transcription into the medium of a sometimes slightly dramatized narrative of what had been one of the most characteristic marks of Jesus' ministry.

To speak of such meals as 'sacral' is almost certainly out of place. Yet, in the tapestry of the gospels, they are necessarily woven together with the obviously very significant narratives of the feedings of the four thousand, and the five thousand. With the important question of the factual component of these miracle-stories, we are not concerned. It may well be that Jesus' shrewd judgment of human reaction enabled him, by distributing what he could lay his hands on from suddenly available sources, to shame others present into sharing their carefully concealed personal provisions among their fellows. Yet the impact of his initiative is obvious, and it is not for nothing that the fourth evangelist (in whose narrative Jesus' meals with all and sundry play no part) suggests that the crowd which was then fed, their thoughts already at passover time turned towards the exodus, saw in the satisfaction of their hunger a renewal of the gift of the manna, and in wild, ill-judged acclaim of Jesus as Messiah, sought to crown him king, thus compelling him to escape the destructive bondage of their devotion by a quick withdrawal. From his hiding place he returns to speak enigmatically of the flesh and blood of the Son of Man as 'meat and drink indeed', insisting in one and the same discourse both that men and women are without life unless they are nourished by this food and drink of the Son of Man's flesh and blood, and that the flesh is of no avail: for it is the spirit that makes to live and his words are spirit and life. Understandably men drift away bewildered, if not shocked; but Peter emerges as spokesman for those who are compelled to stay with Jesus, as he 'has the words of eternal life'.

It was of the messianic banquet in which the Leviathan would

be given them for food that the Jews sang as the death-trains
rolled on their way to Auschwitz, Maidanek and Treblinka.
Whatever Jesus' motives in the wilderness-feedings, and they
certainly included anxiety lest improvidence should induce collapse in some of those who had gathered around him, the gospels
suggest that it was in terms of the commanding image of the
messianic banquet, as well as the more limited particular image of
the manna, that the faithful came to view his action. The highly
controversial eating and drinking that marked the restless life of
one who was content to be called glutton and hard drinker, who
was in his way of life strikingly indifferent to his roots and origin,
imposing upon his family, including his mother, the hard task of
accepting his cultivated rejection of every familial tie, was itself
seen in terms of the imagery in which such actions as his performance in the wilderness encouraged men and women to view his
life and work. 'I have come not to call the righteous, but sinners':
in Mark's version that to which they are called is left unstated. It is
an implicit variable to which the reader must supply the value
himself. The Matthaean addition 'to repentance' reduces the
force of Mark's deliberately opaque language of invitation. One
could say that one possible value of this variable must surely be
'to eat and drink with me'. Such invitations to meals that are seen
as anticipating the messianic banquet, indeed help to correct any
crude conceptions of that splendid repast, by insisting that at its
centre there lies acceptance that is redemptive.

Yet if we find ourselves at a loss whether to speak of such meals
as sacral or not (and, if pressed, we would have to answer
negatively), the problems raised by the Last Supper are of a
different order. Whether or not (with Jeremias) one supposes the
synoptic tradition correct in presenting it as a paschal meal (even
if one resolves the difficulties left unresolved by his arguments by
use of the very ingenious suggestions concerning divergent traditions of passover celebration advanced by Annie Jaubert in her
celebrated monograph[11]), the problems with which one would
have to deal in a full treatment of this issue are almost without
number. Apart altogether from problems of chronology, there is
the crucial question of the precise nature of Jesus' innovation in
the ritual observed by his disciples and himself (whether paschal
or not), in the designation of the bread as his Body, and of the
authenticity of the language attributed to Jesus by Paul, and
included in one textual tradition of Luke's narrative (which is
almost certainly rightly rejected on textual-critical grounds)
commanding the action to be repeated as his anamnesis. The

fourth evangelist, who does not record the action over bread and cup, would seem, by the structure of his sixth chapter (if one is justified in treating that chapter as a unity,) to wish his readers to regard the eucharist as simultaneously the negation and fulfilment of the feeding in the wilderness. In a measure, it is a kind of warning against misunderstanding the only sense in which Jesus can be regarded as Messiah. There is a perilous ambivalence in the way in which men who are right to acclaim the wonder of his generosity and the mutual generosity one to another he evokes in those he addresses, may construe the wonder which they are moved to acclaim.

Lietzmann's *Messe und Herrenmahl*[12] remains one of the great landmarks of this century in the study of eucharistic origins. His central thesis is too well known to require summary, and whatever one's verdict of its ultimate tenability, there is no escaping the effectiveness with which he has called students' attention to factors in the background of the eucharist with which a serious theology must reckon. I refer to the duality he emphasizes between the supposedly miraculous feedings in the wilderness, the tradition embodied in the Emmaus narrative, and the 'breaking of bread' of the primitive church on the one side and, on the other, the Pauline teaching concerning a rite commanded by Jesus at the Last Supper, following in its form the actions there performed by Jesus and most closely related to his death and passion. So Paul speaks of the eucharist as a proclamation (*kērygma*) of the Lord's death 'till he come'. A simple student of the New Testament would be hard put to it to find in the experience of the two disciples at Emmaus anything which could *immediately* be construed in terms of a proclamation of the Lord's death 'till he come'. The question with which Lietzmann leaves his readers is inevitably the question whether Paul by his personal authority succeeded in imposing his own shape on the practice which he found in the communities which he visited, giving to that practice a relation to Jesus' last meal with his disciples which it did not have essentially, and incorporating in the tradition concerning his actions at that supper a command to repeat those actions which Jesus himself never gave.

Earlier in this paper reference was made to Juñgel's very illuminating references to the force of Jesus' parabolic teaching, in which he drew on the resources of modern analytical philosophy of language. In the upper room on the threshold of his betrayal, Jesus performed actions whose manifestly symbolic character demanded that they should be understood in ways comparable to that in which a highly contrived parable might be said to demand understanding, or more simply in ways comparable to those in which we understand or fail to understand, or half fail to understand, what a person is saying who for instance is deliberately rendering himself vulnerable in our presence by self-revelation, or what we ourselves are actually doing when by promise or other verbal performance we commit ourselves in the future or arouse in others expectations concerning our behaviour which we bind ourselves to fulfil with only a partial discernment of what is involved. To say that by his actions over bread and cup Jesus committed himself to what was coming upon him can hardly be disputed. Indeed, Maurice de la Taille[13] insists that by his self-commitment to death (he speaks of the action in the language of his own theological notation as *oblatio hostiae immolandae*) Jesus so disposed of his future that to withdraw afterwards would be intolerable blasphemy; it is the ruling out of the possibility of withdrawal that gives to the narrative of Gethsemane its peculiar poignancy. What is clear is the depth of meaning with which the action is endowed. It is not for nothing that in Luke as well as in the fourth gospel the private teaching of Jesus to his own is brought to focus in the upper room; and if John omits the actions over bread and cup his presentation concludes with the long prayer of self-consecration in which Jesus consecrates himself for his disciples in order they too may be consecrated in the truth.

When we ask ourselves whether the actions of the last night throw light backwards as well as forwards, we are faced with one of those questions in which the genetic study of origins passes almost imperceptibly into the very different task of theological construction. Is one or is one not justified in supposing a kind of teleology in the ordering in relation one to another of the various meals of Jesus? On such a view one would have to say that the end is not yet; but, in saying that, one would already be seeking to order these exchanges in relation one to another, refusing to dodge the issue of the relation of the one and the many. There are of course issues here of critical history that thrust themselves sharply upon our attention. But at the same time one is entitled to allow one's understanding to be illuminated by one's own sense of the problems that in a long and tortuous history reflection has enabled us to discern as present in the tormenting mutual involvement of sacred and human, religious and moral, focused in the eucharist. One cannot escape acknowledging that Jesus' actions in the upper room have a ritual character; one may even suppose oneself justified in saying that we are here face to face with liturgical foundation. Yet the context is desperately human; it is a moment of confident glory that passes immediately into prolonged bewilderment, fear, pain, defeat. Indeed, ritual actions point mercilessly to such an outcome; one could even say that they lack the innocence of earlier feastings even as they are without the seemingly effective presence of that which is made known at Emmaus, when the ultimate frontier of death itself has been crossed. Yet those to whom the mystery is revealed at Emmaus remain in that space and time in which the awful things were done that were the necessary condition of their experience.

We are all of us aware of the extent to which historical churches, even in the manner in which they are sought to renew their vision, have failed by making liturgy an end in itself, by erecting the sacred into a place of allegedly triumphal authority over the human. Whereas the authentically sacred is the servant of the human, but always on its own terms. For the authentically human can be lost if we fail to allow our imaginations to be opened by the frightening possibilities of the transcendent that presses upon us, if we belittle the dimension of contemplation where we are schooled to perceive tragedy without loss of hope.

We need to imbue that which belongs to liturgical tradition with a deeply interrogative quality, compelling questioning of the very substance of the liturgy itself as we have received it. Yet without liturgy, without religion, we too quickly lapse into a mood that trivializes parable by making what it would communicate an easy lesson, somehow complete in itself, not requiring continually to be complemented, even corrected by reference to authentic human existence. It is in context of the dialectical reality of that existence that the relations of sacred and human have to be worked out, and of the manner of this working out we have a pattern, hard though it may be for us to maintain firm grasp of it, in the image of Jesus. At Emmaus, the stranger opened the understanding of the two disciples to the sense of the scriptures, to the light that those scriptures, properly understood, threw on the dark riddle of the previous days' events. If it is a manifest weakness in this paper that it fails to do justice to the resurrection-faith, I can only plead that that faith is in fact the base on which its development and its total argument is rested. It is only in its light that this kind of understanding is possible. Indeed a highly critical theology would insist that it is Jesus' resurrection that makes it absurd to suppose that the eucharist as celebrated in Christian communities is a mere *mimēsis* of the Last Supper. It is very much more; but the end is not yet, even as the sense of Jesus' readiness to eat and drink with the outcast awaited a revelation, indeed the actualization of that love to God and man which was its ground, declared in prayerful action but achieved in the rawest human setting.

This paper may seem over involved, even as it is certainly too long. It may also seem merely to repeat what has long been familiar. In fact the procedure of its argument may seem simply to provide one more illustration of the familiar enterprise of seeking to reduce the bewildering to terms other than itself. In the history of analytical philosophy in this century the method exemplified in Russell's definition of a cardinal number as 'the class of all classes corresponding to a given class' has been generalized and employed, for instance in attempted definition in experiential terms of physical unobservables. The enterprise has been generally thought to have failed; what men hoped to reduce proved irreducible. Yet it would be a mistake to suppose that the attempt to eliminate had been a waste of time. The move had to be made in the name of an advancing understanding.

One could say that in this paper we have been concerned with a comparable attempt at reduction. But what we sought to reduce touched at the most intimate levels the posture proper to human beings under the sun.

Thus the peculiar indirection of parabolic communication alerted those to whom it was made to the unnoticed deep significance of the ordinary, even the trivial. They were set free from the illusion of supposing that the sacred could be isolated or set apart from life as a whole, treated as object of special experience or quality of special time or place. One had to learn to reckon with the unexpected intrusion of the transcendent and not by self-induced reverence diminish the reach of that which knows no limit. We must learn all that is involved in refusing to say that the dominion of God over his world is manifested here but not there. For unless we learn such lessons it is not only our understanding that will be inhibited, but our aims also that will be distorted. We will come to suppose that the sacred is something which we can protect, an area of life that we can fence in and preserve inviolate. It is no accident that it is with reference to Bonhoeffer that his paper began. For by his life, and especially of course by its closing years, he made tremendous protest against the suggestion that the sacred was a kind of human territory that could be preserved whatever happened, that might indeed be put in danger by the very attempt to intervene perilously with the circumstances of its historical environment. So in his last years the pastor involved himself in conspiracy directed towards the murder of the tyrant to whom his people had submitted. This was no romantic self-indulgent affirmation of violence as somehow a way of spiritual liberation; such a mood would have involved the substitution of one illusory sacred for another. Yet in the confused occasion of his last months of freedom most certainly the God whom he sought to serve was present to him.

But Bonhoeffer remains most significantly a man who was professionally a theologian, attentive, even after war had begun, to distinctive technical theological issues, including for instance questions concerning the eucharist which had long divided Lutheran and Reformed. At first this must seem a contradiction; but rather it is one expression of the fact that the kind of complexity which belongs to human life as through Christ we know it to be is often, if not always, the only road to an authentic simplicity. It is moreover a reflection of the sort of complexity which earlier in this paper it was suggested we must acknowledge when we face the question of the presence of the sacral in the ministry of Jesus. That sacral is not eliminated, nor reduced to terms of anything other than itself in such a manner that it is made to vanish away. It remains as that which must always be nearly eliminated but which must none the less remain as protection against triviality, and is a sign of the ultimate mystery.

In the argument of this paper it has been suggested that it is in the eucharist that these questions received their sharpest definition. For by its centrality in Christian practice men and women are continually tempted to make its performance an end in itself, and then, as if reacting violently against their own misunderstanding, to evacuate its form of any import on their little world. But such reaction, even if it justifies itself by reference to the sharp worldliness of the parabolic, fails altogether to do justice to what is of the essence of that parabolic, namely its incompleteness. Once that incompleteness is forgotten then the force of parable as indirect indication of the transcendent is gone. If eucharistic worship is a strangely dangerous reality, it is so because when effort is made to reckon with its many dimensions we are compelled to see that if it is the place of understanding, it is also the place where misunderstandings of many sorts may assume an obstinate permanence in the life of the spirit.

13

Ethics and Tragedy

I

Some years ago a book appeared on the plot against Hitler, which misfired so disastrously on 20 July 1944, and whose misfiring cost many brave men their lives. This work, entitled *The July Plot*,[1] was reviewed in *The Observer* by R. H. S. Crossman, a very well known Labour minister and journalist, who is also remembered by many of my generation at New College, Oxford, as a highly provocative teacher of moral and political philosophy, and indeed of history, both ancient and modern. He said that he only knew one work in the English language which might be said to deal with the problems of political obligation which von Stauffenberg and his fellows faced, and that work was Shakespeare's *Julius Caesar*. (Had he recalled Scottish experience, he might have referred to arguments conducted by such men as Knox, Buchanan, and Montrose, in the sixteenth and seventeenth centuries, and had his attention strayed to the Continent, he might have added that the sixteenth and seventeenth centuries were rich in pamphlets on tyrannicide, for instance the French Protestant literature which followed the massacre of 'St Bartholomew', and the writings of Mariana and the Jesuits who followed him. Yet Crossman's claim that in the English tradition in the narrow sense, there is one work, and only one, and that the tragedy by William Shakespeare which he mentioned, is strongly defensible.) Certainly Shakespeare's play stresses the gravity of the tyrannicides' act. Written against the background of an absolute monarchy, precariously asserted and sustained with royal control of all causes, as well ecclesiastical as temporal, throughout that monarch's dominions, painfully maintained with aid of rack, thumbscrew, axe and noose, and backed by theological sanction, it belongs to an age always tempted in the last resort to accept such authority as the only effective dyke against anarchy, against what Hobbes later characterized as the ever-present threat of relapse into a state of 'incipient war'. Something indeed of this sort of attachment to royal supremacy of the kind first asserted by Henry VIII and continued, although in subtly modified form, by his daughter Elizabeth, is projected back in the poet's imagination on to the master of the Roman world, in the months that followed Munda.

So we have Brutus' long argument with himself, ending in his conversation with Portia, his insistence that Caesar alone shall perish, '[carved] as a dish fit for the gods'. Antony must be spared, even receiving permission for the famous panegyric whereby he inflamed the city against Caesar's murderers. (Cassius, with whom, of course, before the end Brutus quarrels sharply, is a shrewder hand in conspiracy.) But Brutus goes further than indulge his scruples; thus critics of the play have remarked how by his language he seeks to invest the assassination, both before and after it is done, with the character of a sacrifice. 'Let's carve him as a dish fit for the gods.' His blood is shed as if to expiate by its flow the city's sin in contemplating too lightly the bestowal on him of the dreaded royal dignity, as if also to atone for Caesar's own fault in allowing the enthusiasm of foolish supporters to distract him from his fidelity to the standards of Rome. Indeed, there is more than a hint that his death may be for him both merciful release, and in a measure reparation. His memory is safeguarded. He will live in the recollection of those who came after him, with his image untarnished by recall of an ageing man's indulgence of his flatterers.

One may indeed call what I am now referring to masquerade, an elaborate essay in self-deception, whereby a man is enabled to ensure that he does not know what he is doing. But it is an essay in the sort of self-deception that issues from an intense scrupulosity which yet does not shrink before the projected, deliberately contrived, and cunningly executed murder. And this emerges with overwhelming clarity if we contrast with Brutus' scruples the mood of the triumvirs, including the stripling Octavius, as they prick down the names of the representatives of the old order whom they will proscribe, and whom they will thus leave without protection of law, fair game for any killer. The scene is very short; the number of those whose fate is sealed is very large. In a recent film of the play, it was set in the *calidarium* of one of the public baths, which emphasized what the playwright had sought, by the device of an almost casual brevity, to bring out. While Brutus was eaten up by uncertainty before decision, and by his sense that every restraint must be observed in that decision's execution, and shows himself ready to use quasi-liturgical language to suggest that what he was engaged in was immolation, rather than murder, Antony, Octavius and Lepidus were out to settle old scores, or to remove from the Roman world all representatives of the old order capable of providing any sort of reflective political rallying point for their opponents.

There is certainly much in that play which spoke to the condition of men, many of whom, as serving army officers, were bound by the special oath that bound them personally to Hitler as commander-in-chief (following Hindenburg's death in 1934). But what might it have said to such men? In a very obvious sense it did not deal with their situation, but rather deployed, with a classical penetration, the predicament of men, of one man in particular, similarly placed, offering less advice than illumination. For it was in a situation remotely comparable to this one that the problems facing those who decided that they must have done with the Führer arose. What this play offered such men, and indeed continues to offer others similarly placed, is the representation of the *inwardness* of the dilemma facing any man who finds himself compelled to consider playing a part in such an enterprise It is a representation achieved with all the insight of a supreme genius, informed also by a deep sense of the necessity of an unchallengeable political authority as arguably the only effective dyke against anarchy. With this sense he is able to combine remarkable power in tracing the windings of human thought and imagination in men compelled to make such a decision, even indeed imposing upon their understanding of that decision, once it has been made, the form of their spontaneous inquiry in the making of it.

A traditional moralist would say that here we have an example of the conflict of duties. Men have a duty to obey those in their society in whose hands government, in so far as it exists at all, rests, who do *de facto* if not *de jure* (in a time, moreover, of supreme external emergency), monopolize that society's coercive resources. There was also a special duty incumbent upon serving soldiers, bound by such an oath as the one mentioned, not to imperil the lives of men engaged on active service by overthrowing, with no effective alternative governmental authority in view, the central executive power of the state at a moment in the history of their country when both in the western and still more in the eastern theatres of war, those men were hard pressed. Inevitably such conditions gave special force, in the minds of the sorts of conspirators we are writing of, to the claims of the old rule that tyranny is better than anarchy, or the risk of anarchy. Yet, on the other side, one need only ponder quickly the nature of the tyranny at issue here. It was a régime that had consigned, or was in process of consigning, six million Jews to the gas chambers, etc. Again, if one thinks of the special problems of serving soldiers, one has only to read the letters written from the eastern front to their former teacher, by men whom Dietrich Bonhoeffer had trained at Finkenwalde, to realize the intolerable moral choices facing such men as part of their daily lives; thus they were in a situation in which repeatedly they must choose between merciless extermination of partisan forces, and of those who gave them shelter, and exposure of the men serving under them to continual risk of death, or wounds. The conspirators sought to create a situation in which the public authority should no longer force men to face such intolerable burdens. In old-fashioned language, they sought to convert the state from a beast of prey into a beast of burden. Therefore, as men who have willed this end, they must also will the means of effecting this conversion, and indeed of effecting it, at a time when, since the decision of the Casablanca Conference to impose 'unconditional surrender' upon Germany, its successful achievement must rob their country of all rights of self-disposal.

To men facing such issues as these certainly *Julius Caesar* speaks. From it they must learn to count the cost, and to see that they may go forward only when they have counted it. Part of that cost is to acknowledge the intractable for what it is. Murder is murder, is murder. The proposition which these words express is far from trifling. What does a man do to himself by participation in such conspiratorial action? He is committed to the use of means that must inevitably jeopardize the ends those means seek to serve. Here indeed Dietrich Bonhoeffer's biography[2] has much to say that is said in clearer tone when heard by those who begin to ponder its lesson against the background of a knowledge of Shakespeare's play.

II

We have here a fundamental theme of tragic drama. It is a commonplace of very old-fashioned moral philosophy to insist that 'ought implies can'. A man has an obligation, if, and only if, he has the means of fulfilling that obligation, of fulfilling it without, in fact, jeopardizing himself, as he must, if he finds the act of fulfilment self-destructive. Tragic exploration of the human condition makes men aware of the reality of this jeopardy. What our responses make of ourselves is not what we foresee. So, in the case of Hamlet seeking to right that which is rotten in the state of Denmark; he has to pay a terrible price, both in the currency of his own life, and that of others bound to him in various ways, for instance Ophelia. It is irrelevant to say that a more resolute man would have handled the situation differently, even much less destructively. The man on whose shoulders the task was laid, was the man who was predictably, being the sort of man he was, exposed by its undertaking to the sorts of conflict which, in the play, are revealed as almost destroying him, and most certainly, through their impact upon her, destroying Ophelia. Hamlet is a 'revenge tragedy'. No man should be judge in his own cause. Hence men have recourse to the impersonal arbitrament of court procedure, following a charge grounded in the results of disinterested investigation, or in cases of civil dispute, as part of an action judged by men expert in the law to be reasonable, in terms of existing legally established rights and duties. But can men all the time be spared the sort of ordeal laid on those who must be judges in their own cause, and in a cause that is at once their own, and that of others, whose rights, or indeed whose health and safety can only be secured by their action? Such an extreme situation as the one with which Shakespeare's play is concerned enables us to see what it is that may confront us. In its action we are enabled, in fact, imaginatively to understand the actuality of human action; we are prevented from treating it as something which we can look at from a distance, as if the stuff of individual life were not often at stake in its accomplishment. To write in these terms is not to allow a kind of existential self-indulgence to inhibit action; rather it is to protect ourselves against the sort of self-deception to which, in our action, we may find ourselves exposed, and indeed from which we may suddenly seek to escape by turning aside from what we must do, by passing by on the other side lest, by our intervention, we imperil not only ourselves, but those who have none other than ourselves to give them succour.

It would be a very grave mistake to generalize about tragedy as if there were an 'essence' of the tragic that we could extract and capture in a manageable formula. The world of Racine is very different from that of Shakespeare, and both alike from the worlds explored by the ancient Greek tragedians. Yet if one bears in mind Plato's searching criticism of tragic drama as a suitable form for the presentation and exploration of ultimate issues, one finds that the most important aspect of what he repudiated was the sense that from tragedy we continually renew our sense of the sheerly intractable in human life. The issue of the day is not within our power, even if there are no other human agents than ourselves to undertake it. In part this intractability issues from the situation which confronts us as it develops; in part it issues from ourselves as we are revealed to ourselves in the action which we have to undertake, cast as it may be to a shape vastly different from the one intended, by circumstances foreseeable or unforeseeable, which yet themselves are partly what they are, in virtue of what we do, and partly in virtue of what is in no sense in our power. Certainly here we touch the frontiers of the rational, if the rational is identified with the prudential. We also touch the frontiers of the rational where rationality is conceived in the metaphysical sense of a creative Logos, whether immanent, or transcendent, or both at once powerful to make all things expressive of its creative purpose.

III

The kinds of issue with which we have been concerned were also treated in classical tragedy; I think, in particular, of Sophocles' work, interpreted by such scholars as Heinrich Weinstock and Cedric Whitman.[3]

Thus, in Sophocles' *Electra* the central figure of the tragedy is presented as one who has allowed herself to become a harridan in consequence of her very fidelity to the realities of the situation at the court of Aegisthus and Clytemnestra. Her behaviour towards her more accommodating sister, Chrysothemis, is frankly Amazonian. When the circumstances of Orestes' return lead her to suppose him dead, she is overcome by despairing fear, her ration of courage exhausted by the ordeal which she has faced for so long; as a person she seems to disintegrate, only to be brought to terrifying life again by the realization that her brother is not only alive, but returned to his home to exact that vengeance for which she had saved him as a child. The monstrous character of the events that followed is excellently brought out by the sharply different treatment which Euripides gives to this whole episode in his *Electra*, seeking to impress upon the spectators the morally outrageous quality of matricide.

Again, let us consider the *Antigone*, which notoriously furnished Hegel with the classical illustration of his conception of tragedy as residing essentially in the conflict of right with right. For him the essential conflict of the play concerns the issue between the claims on the invididual of the laws and ordinances of the city-state, represented by Creon, and the claims of those mysterious 'unwritten' laws of which Antigone constitutes herself the champion. The theme of the play cannot, however, be adequately captured in this formula. Antigone is markedly Creon's superior as a human being; she is a genuine heroine, although (in an interestingly different way from Electra), she is also brutally Amazonian in her behaviour towards her sister, Ismene. Certainly her preoccupation with the burial of her brother, Polyneices, has a frankly obsessive character; this though the text of the play reminds reader and spectator of the physical horror of a corpse lying unburied for even a short time in the sort of climate in which the scene is set. Yet Antigone's preoccupation with Polyneices makes her oblivious of her other brother, Eteocles, who had died in defence of their city; more impressively, for a period she seems totally indifferent to the devotion of Haemon, Creon's son, to whom she is betrothed. At one moment she speaks of a dead brother as irreplaceable, in a way in which a dead husband is not. But it is not only such extreme sentiments that make anyone who attends closely to the text of the play vividly aware that the curse on the house of Labdacus, which hangs heavily over its characters, includes the burden of incest, which the children of Oedipus, begotten by their father on the body of his own mother, must bear. Antigone is the child of a monstrous union, and it is impossible, in the play, to escape the sense of a sheerly incestuous element in her preoccupation with her brother. One is aware of the destructive force of this obsession. In her exchanges with her uncle, she activates the very worst in him, compelling him to identify inextricably the welfare of his city, for which he bears executive responsibility, with his own image of himself, which deteriorates as their exchanges proceed. It is not only that he is betrayed into a blasphemous contempt for the gods; it is also a fact that he makes himself ridiculous, a small man cast by fate for a role far greater than he can play, clinging with a kind of furious obstinacy to the form of his office. His catastrophe follows inevitably with the death of his son, and at the end of the play he is a broken man. Yet towards its beginning he showed himself one who would seek to consult with those over whom he bore rule, to govern by consent, and not as a tyrant. One could say that he was unfortunate in having to deal with Antigone; one could even say that he, too, was broken by the curse upon the house of Labdacus. Yet in the play it is Antigone's obsession, and the manner in which it was expressed, that robbed him of prudence, and that destroyed his sense of moderation.

Yet in this play Antigone redeems herself. However confused her motives at the outset of her campaign, however more deeply they become confused as that campaign proceeded, the heroic quality of her death is beyond question, and one is made aware that before she faced the last stages of her ordeal, her tenderness had returned, manifested in a very human regret for the world she was leaving, for the experiences of marriage and motherhood, of which she was irrevocably deprived.

The play certainly explores at a very deep level conflicts of personal duty. The exploration is in the portrayal, compelling the reader and spectator to recognize that not only in the circumstances of actual life does it very frequently prove impossible to reconcile such conflicts by recourse to a formula, but more importantly, when an individual makes a right choice, the motives of that choice may be muddied beyond his or her full, or even partial awareness. Consequently, human action comes to seem ambiguous; or it may be that while we continue to applaud what men or women do, we find that in the doing of it they have revealed themselves as flawed, not only in the actual performance, but in the springs of their response to the situation confronting them – springs which we acknowledge to be at least a necessary condition of their acting as they did. This even when, as in Antigone's case, they are in a measure vindicated by the manner in which, before the end, they have overcome some of the worst manifestations of the destructive flaws, whose power has been revealed in their actions.

Again, in the *Trachiniae*, we have in Deianira a woman of a tenderness and compassion very rare in classical Greek drama. She is presented as Heracles' wife, plunged by her marriage into a monstrous world of heroes, demigods, etc.; yet she remains ultimately gentle, a figure of mercy, a woman who loves her husband, and who is guilty in her sending him the 'shirt of Nessus', certainly of folly, but equally certainly of nothing worse than imprudence. A more ruthless action would have had less horrifyingly destructive consequences. For the play ends with Heracles on the pyre, cursing his wife, even as he dies; it is she who has destroyed him, and although some commentators on the play would see in the manner of his death a kind of assumption, such interpretation betrays a sheerly sentimental refusal to attend to the last lines spoken by Heracles' son, in which (in a manner that Plato clearly found outrageous), he lays reponsibility for these inexplicable horrors on the arbitrary will of Zeus. There is no rhyme nor reason discernible in what the spectator has seen. Here, in an extreme and, indeed monstrous situation, those who have attended this play have been compelled to reckon with the element of the utterly intractable in the human environment, whereby men and women are tricked into destructive courses by their very virtues. As we admire and applaud these virtues, refusing to abdicate from acknowledging mercy and pity the superior of ruthlessness and cruelty, we have to recognize that the practice of the former, and not only in the sort of supernatural environment in which Deianira is placed, may issue in destructive consequences. And thus the play concludes on a note of unrelieved pessimism, because against the divine order no protest is availing; it is at once inexorable and to our discernment morally indifferent.

It may seem surprising that these references to Sophocles' tragedy should not have included, before now, some reference to the greatest and most complex of them all, *Oedipus the King*. But comment on this very difficult but extraordinarily impressive play has deliberately been left to the end, because in this play Sophocles engages with the problem of self-knowledge. Too often discussion of the *Oedipus* has been dominated by Aristotle's very influential treatment in the *Poetics*, and has, in consequence, concentrated on seeking out the 'tragic flaw' in Oedipus. Wherein is he guilty of *hubris*? In his behaviour towards Laius on the occasion of their fatal encounter? In the manner in which he fulfils the responsibilities of kingship? Or in a brash self-confidence manifested in both alike, portrayed during the action of the play in his treatment of Teiresias? The extent to which the play is concerned with self-knowledge was, of course, remarked by Sigmund Freud, who, in his dictum 'the poets knew it all already', must surely have had in mind this most remarkable of Greek tragedies, on which he himself wrote an essay. It is very striking indeed that a play concerned with a man who murders his father, and takes his mother to wife, is so largely presented as a prolonged interrogation, an investigation which the man who conducts it as part of his public responsibility, gradually comes to acknowledge most intimately concerns himself. In an essay on the detective story, published in 1928, the late Miss Dorothy Sayers included this play of Sophocles (together with the tale [in the Apocrypha] of Susanna and the Elders), as examples of the detective story in ancient literature. Anyone fortunate enough to see the production of Sophocles' play in translation in London in 1945/46, in which, against the background of an extraordinarily impressive décor, Lawrence Olivier played Oedipus to Sybil Thorndike's Jocasta, will have been made vividly aware of the extent to which sight is emphasized in the play, that sense regarded, for instance by Plato, as the most akin to intelligence. It is the blind Teiresias, who knows things as they are explicitly and self-consciously from the beginning; but when Oedipus, for so long seemingly self-confident in fulfilment of his executive responsibilities, acknowledges the truth, and looks upon the world of his family as one no longer able to disguise from himself the reality of its relationships, the sight is more than he can bear, and he rushes out to destroy his eyes, returning a blind man, but one in no sense any longer estranged from the truth.

One is tempted to say that the self-knowledge he achieves is more than he can bear. The plague in Thebes, occasioned by his guilt, has made it necessary for him as king to uncover the truth about himself; by his resolution in this pursuit he destroys himself, deprives himself, not only of illusion, but of the capacity to act. He has helped to make a world so terrible that the realization of his partial but crucial responsibility for its creation robs him of any power, of any capacity for further action. There is, of course, a savage irony in the fact that it was only through learning his destiny from the oracle, and leaving his home with Polybus and Merope in Corinth, to avoid the terrible guilt prophesied for him, that he involved himself, first with Laius, and then with the affairs of Thebes. In an extremely impressive recent study of the play,[4] Philip Vellacott insists that we must go further than this, and recognize that Oedipus in some sense *knew* all along who it was whom he had killed at the crossroads, and therefore whom it was that he took to wife. Whatever the final verdict on Vellacott's argument, he has not only called attention to features of the play of which any serious interpretation must seek to give account, but also related the theme which it treats in the medium of tragic drama to the sorts of epistemological investigations with which students of some of Plato's dialogues are very familiar, i.e. those dialogues concerned with the relations of knowledge and right opinion etc. (e.g. *Meno*, *Republic* V–VII and *Theaetetus*), part of whose impulse came from Plato's reflection on the Socratic imperative 'Know thyself'.

The theme of self-knowledge is one of daunting complexity. Certainly men are often, very often, betrayed by failure to understand their motives, by their capacity to deceive themselves through casting themselves in roles for which they are very ill suited, seeking by their performance to disguise from themselves their human reality. But what of the man exposed, as Oedipus was, when he left Corinth, to a situation in which (following the death of Laius, for which he may be judged partly guilty), he is compelled to act on behalf of his fellow men because (in reading the riddle of the Sphinx), he is able to deliver them from a terrifying bondage? From there he goes on to assume responsibility, the responsibility of king, and to confirm his status by taking to himself as wife the king's widow. Vellacott argues that he must have suspected the truth, for instance, that the circumstances of Laius' death must have recalled to him vividly the details of his own encounter with the arrogant old man with whom he had brawled on the road. How far, again in terms of this latest interpretation, are we to suppose that he consistently suppressed from his conscious mind what he knew (though ready enough to face, in the half-angry, half-confident way in which he did, the process of public investigation in which – again on this view – what is brought out is something which he knew already)?

The reference to *Oedipus* comes fittingly last in these inevitably brief comments on some of Sophocles' plays. This because self-knowledge is something which we would, in different ways, wish for Electra, Deianira, Antigone and, indeed, to return to an earlier section of this study, for Brutus, most certainly scrupulous, but equally certainly quick to seek to hide from himself what he is actually about. Hamlet, indeed, is a man who certainly knew, or half knew enough for the awareness sometimes nearly to destroy him and others, to make him a sheerly destructive force for those involved with him.

IV

A gushing woman once remarked to the great Duke of Wellington, 'A victory must be a supremely exhilarating and glorious experience.' The old man replied: 'A victory, Madam, is the greatest tragedy in the world, only excepting a defeat.' There is a profundity in this comment by a great soldier which, in the world of theology, is sadly absent in the writings of those theologians who write and speak glibly of Christ's victory. In the tragedies at which we have glanced, it may be said that there is very little which one would describe as victory. Yet, in *Hamlet*, retributive justice is done. So, too, in *Electra*. In the *Trachiniae* the end is profoundly pessimistic, and in *Julius Caesar* the victory of the triumvirs leaves room for a tribute to Brutus, but a tribute paid by men who have shown themselves quite innocent of the sort of scruple displayed tragically by the man whom they are praising. In the *Antigone*, the heroine achieves a genuine victory over herself, and goes to her death with the deep flaws revealed in her, as she faced her ordeal, purged away. Yet, as we have seen, there was a destructive quality in her action. Oedipus leaves to find his way, in Sophocles' last play, to Colonus, and there to peace. But as a man he is broken, and he leaves his city in hardly retrievable disorder. It is sometimes said that in *King Lear*, a play which has not been discussed in this essay, the terrible events it portrays are justified by the old man's achievement of self-knowledge; but in his monograph, Nicholas Brooke[5] has shown (in my view conclusively), that the play's ending (the death of Cordelia and Lear's ignorance of it), makes such comment superficial. Lear finds his way to a kind of self-knowledge, but precariously, and at a most terrible cost, involving the destruction of the one he really loved, and who really loved him. If men and women find their way to what we call victory, whether over circumstances or over themselves and the bitter consequences of their inheritance and nurture etc., too often such victories are won at cruel cost to others. And again, the services which men do for their fellows, for which they are rightly esteemed, are very often made possible only at a cost, both to some of those with whom they have to deal, and indeed to themselves, because of what they are, that must be recognized for what it is, namely total disaster. In concluding this study, I wish finally to comment on the sheerly tragic quality in the life of Christ, finding in the profound reply of the Duke of Wellington, quoted at the beginning of this section, a fitting point of departure.

V

It is not chance that the so-called Manichaean heresy awoke in the defenders of Christian orthodoxy emotions of savagery such as received terrible expression in the Albigensian crusade. The questions which that heresy raised in a metaphysically confused, and indeed vulnerable form, have never been fully answered. The so-called 'problem of evil' remains intractable by any of the methods traditionally employed to solve or dissolve it. The relevance of the issues raised in this essay to that problem is too obvious to need comment. It has been very often (though not

exclusively) in the medium of imaginative literature that the
questions which refuse to be answered in terms of a facile teleology have persistently intruded themselves. But very few have
been bold enough to attempt to read the gospels as tragedies, at
least until comparatively recently.

There have been various obstacles to inhibit such an exercise,
and in particular the way in which, in popular piety, both
Catholic and Protestant, the extremely complex and elusive
resurrection narratives have been read. Certainly these stories
are the literary projection of a victory, even of a victory that
is conceived as absolute and final, where the human condition is
concerned, in which, indeed 'death is swallowed up'. Jesus is
presented as entering upon a life that, unlike human, and indeed
animal life as we know it, does not move towards an inescapable
horizon of death, a life over which death is affirmed no longer to
exercise any sovereignty. What is suggested concerning that life
and its modes cannot concern us here. Rather simply we should
allow ourselves to raise the crucial question whether this victory
is free of the tragic quality which the Duke of Wellington insisted belonged necessarily to all victories. To this the answer
must surely be a clear negative. The surd element remains. The
Son of Man had gone his appointed way, and the one who made
it possible for him to take that journey 'has gone to his own place'.
Further, the steps which Jesus might have taken in respect of
the rapidly approaching catastrophe of the Jewish people, to
whom, in the first instance, he came, remain untaken, and can
no more be set in hand. 'Daughters of Jerusalem, weep not for
me, but for yourselves.' Those words occur in Luke's account of
the passion, which is often regarded by critics as the presentation
of a serene human sufferer accepting his destiny, with no damage
to his continued fidelity to his Father and his unbroken tenderness towards mankind. Yet the actuality of irretrievable disaster
is as sharply present in Luke's narrative as in that of Matthew,
Mark, or John. The victory of Jesus is certainly absolute in this
respect, that his way is affirmed as uniquely that of God himself,
both in respect of that which is accomplished through his taking
that way, and its inexhaustible suggestion of an example to be
followed in utterly different circumstances. Yet it remains mys-
teriously and inescapably tragic. Indeed, increasingly one sees
that the reality of Christ's humanity resides partly in the fact that
as he lived he was confronted with real choices, fraught, in
consequence of the way in which he chose, with disaster as well
as achievement in their train. His prayer to be spared the ordeal

that in the end was drawing mercilessly upon him was no charade. If, in retrospect, he is seen to dominate the rapidly changing scenes of his passion, it is not the contemptuous domination of men who, by combination of self-regard and blind folly, compass in different ways their own destruction by the execution they combine to make sure takes place. It is the domination of a judge who would, if he could, descend from the seat of judgment, but who knows that the way of mercy compels him to occupy it till the bitter end, to probe to the bottom the reality of men's rejection, not only of the ways of God, but of the very substance of their humanity.

The ambiguity remains in the victory of Jesus. Therefore, in an essay concerned largely to raise the whole question of the significance of tragedy for ethics, it is permissible to end by insisting that there are lessons of the greatest importance to be learnt here by Christian theology, and not least in the field of Christology, which is arguably itself its heart and centre.

Notes

1. The Future of Man

1. Henri de Lubac, 'L'Homme Nouveau', *Affrontements mystiques*, Éditions du témoignage chrétien, Paris 1950.
2. P. Teilhard de Chardin, *Le Milieu Divin: an essay in the interior life*, ET, Collins 1964, Harper & Row 1965.
3. Heinrich Ott, *Wirklichkeit und Glaube* I, Göttingen 1966.
4. Ulrich Simon, *A Theology of Auschwitz*, Gollancz and Doubleday 1967.

2. Lenin and Theology

1. The centenary fell on 22 April 1970.
2. G. Lukacs, *Lenin: a study on the unity of his thought*, ET, NLB, London 1970; D. Shub, *Lenin: a Biography*, rev. ed., Penguin 1966; L. Fischer, *The Life of Lenin*, Harper & Row 1964, Weidenfeld & Nicolson 1965; A. Ulam, *Lenin and the Bolsheviks: the intellectual and political history of the triumph of Communism in Russia*, Macmillan, New York 1965, Secker & Warburg 1966.
3. A fragment of Deutscher's work has been published: *Lenin's Childhood*, OUP 1970. Of earlier accounts, A. V. Lunacharsky's famous vignette of Lenin is much admired (*Revolutionary Silhouettes*, ET, Allen Lane, the Penguin Press 1967, pp.35–52). *Encounters with Lenin* by Nikolay Valentinov (N. V. Volsky), ET, OUP 1968, and *Impressions of Lenin* by Angelica Balabanoff, ET, University of Michigan Press 1964, contain extraordinarily interesting material on Lenin the man, and his ideas. Valentinov's book also includes (pp.152–68) an account of Fr Serge Bulgakov's breach with Russian Marxism, surely of the greatest interest to historians of twentieth-century Christian thought.
4. J. P. Nettl, *Rosa Luxemburg*, 2 vols., OUP 1966.
5. K. J. Kautsky was the author of what was for long the best known and most thorough Marxist account of the origins of the Christian movement (*Foundations of Christianity*, ET of 13th German ed., Allen & Unwin 1925), and also of a less well-known but more permanently valuable study of Thomas More (*Thomas More and his Utopia*, originally 1890, ET, A. & C. Black 1927). E. Bernstein pioneered the Marxist interpretation of the seventeenth-century English Puritan Revolution (*Cromwell and Communism: Socialism and democracy in the great English Revolution*, ET, Allen & Unwin 1930).

6. It is interesting to note that Luxemburg's murderer was enabled to evade justice by the intervention of a naval officer named Canaris, who during the second world war was head of the section of the *Abwehr* which found employment for Dietrich Bonhoeffer. Canaris' role and attitude during the Nazi period remains obscure; but he was in some sense committed to resistance to the régime, as he was executed in 1945. He was clearly not a man of the quality of General Ludwig von Beck, who after 1938 grew enormously in stature, as his moral perception of the iniquity of the Nazi régime enlarged. Indeed, Helmut Gollwitzer has recorded a conversation with Beck in the darkest days of June 1940, in which the general, drawing not only on his knowledge of the sort of strategic problems (of communications etc.) that Napoleon had been unable to master, but also on his recognition of the wisdom of Plato's insistence that the tyrant carried within him the seeds of his own destruction, predicted Hitler's downfall, and partly restored the confidence in the future of Niemöller's curate in his Dahlem parish. See Nicholas Reynolds, *Treason was no Crime: Ludwig Beck: Chief of the German General Staff*, William Kimber, London 1976, pp.207f.

7. V. I. Lenin, *What is to be Done?*, ET, Martin Lawrence, London 1933; *The State and Revolution*, ET, Allen & Unwin 1919.

8. Lenin, *Materialism and Empirio-Criticism*, ET, Foreign Languages Publication House, Moscow 1947.

9. See the account of Archbishop Davidson's involvement in this affair in G. K. A. Bell's *Life of Randall Davidson*, 1st ed., OUP 1935, vol. 1, ch. XXVI, pp.474–80.

10. L. Trotsky, *History of the Russian Revolution*, ET, Gollancz, 3 vols. 1932–3, 1 vol. 1934, Simon & Schuster, New York 1936.

11. Sir John Wheeler-Bennett's book *Brest-Litovsk: the Forgotten Peace* (Macmillan 1938, reissued 1963) still richly repays study. Deutscher's account in *The Prophet Armed: Trotsky 1879–1921*, OUP 1954, of Trotsky's attitude in the negotiations is also important. See also the wealth of material in the companion volumes to Martin Gilbert's *Winston S. Churchill*, vol. 4, Heinemann 1975.

12. Theodore Dan (F. I. Dan), *The Origins of Bolshevism*, ET, Secker & Warburg and Harper & Row 1964; D. W. Treadgold, *Lenin and his Rivals: the struggle of Russia's future, 1898–1906*, Methuen and Praeger 1955; Israel Getzler, *Martov: A Political Biography of a Russian Social Democrat*, CUP 1967.

13. To say this does not imply indifference to the fact that Geneva was the scene of some of the most crucial debates!

14. On this see M. Lewin's invaluable study, *Russian Peasants and Soviet Power*, ET, Allen & Unwin 1968.

15. I owe this phrase to Alan Bullock. See his account of the Nazi *Machtübernahme* in his *Hitler*, Odhams and Harper & Row ²1964.

16. Maurice Merleau-Ponty, *Humanisme et Terreur*, NRF, Paris 1948. See also Artur London, *L'Aveu*, ET, *On Trial*, Macdonald 1970.

17. Plato, *Republic* II: Socrates' summary of Glaucon's and Adeimantus' questions.

18. But see Bell, *Life of Randall Davidson*, vol. 2, p.746.
19. Yet in a sermon preached in Great St Mary's Church, Cambridge, a few years ago Trevor Huddleston, then Bishop of Stepney, said that in the area of East London in which he lived there were those who remembered Lenin in his days there.
20. It should be remembered that this paper was first written in 1970.
21. I am concerned to criticize Knox as a theologian, not as a *Neutestamentler*. As a writer on narrowly New Testament topics, he is no doubt very good indeed, as the attention paid to his work by the greatest experts certainly implies; as a theologian, I find him thoroughly slipshod in conceptual analysis.
22. This article was written *before* the controversy over the decision of the executive of the World Council of Churches to allow funds to support those fighting racism, and the publication of the report: *Violence in Southern Africa*, SCM Press 1970.
23. *Christian Faith and Communist Faith*, ed. D. M. MacKinnon, Macmillan 1953.
24. Bastiaan Wielenga, *Lenins Weg zur Revolution*, Chr. Kaiser Verlag, Munich 1973.
25. Rosa Luxemburg and N. Bukharin, *Imperialism and the Accumulation of Capital*, ET, Allen Lane, the Penguin Press 1972.
26. Richard Kroner, *Von Kant bis Hegel*, 2 vols., Tübingen 1921, 1924.
27. Josiah Royce, *Lectures on Modern Idealism*, Yale University Press 1919, reissued 1964.
28. S. Bulgakov, *Du Verbe Incarné*, Aubier, Paris, 1943. Bulgakov was exiled from Russia in 1923.
29. *Christian Believing*, SPCK 1976.
30. H. Vogel, *Christologie* I, Munich 1949.
31. Michael Dummett, 'Biblical Exegesis and the Resurrection', *New Blackfriars* 58, February 1977, pp.56–72; Fergus Kerr, OP, 'Exegesis and Easter', ibid., March 1977, pp.108–21.

3. *Law, Change and Revolution*

1. In this paper I have done no more than offer certain prolegomena to a study, much more directly theological in character, of the ethical and religious problems raised by the use of coercive force in human affairs. It was, necessarily, written primarily out of British political experience.
2. Rohan Butler, *The Roots of National Socialism*, Faber & Faber and Dutton 1941.
3. Alfred Rosenberg, *Der Mythus des 20. Jahrhunderts*, Munich 1930.
4. G. W. F. Hegel, *Theologische Jugendschriften*, ed. H. Nohl, Tübingen 1907; ET, *Early Theological Writings*, trs. T. M. Knox, introduction by R. Kroner, University of Chicago Press 1948; W. Dilthey, *Die Jugendgeschichte Hegels*, Leipzig 1905.
5. Gerhard Ritter, *Staatkunst und Krieghandswerk. Das Problem der 'Militarismus' in Deutschland*, 4 vols., Munich 1965–68; ET, *The Sword*

and the Sceptre: the Problem of Militarism in Germany, Allen Lane, the Penguin Press 1972–73.

6. L. S. Amery, *Thoughts on the Constitution*, OUP 1947. Amery, a well-known British Conservative politician, in his early years was deeply under the influence of the formidable proconsul and theorist of empire, Lord Milner.

7. C. H. McIlwain, *Constitutionalism: Ancient and Modern*, Cornell University Press, Ithaca, 1940, ²1947.

8. This passage was first written before the crisis of Nixon's resignation.

9. On the significance of the 'separation of powers' in the operation of the distinction between *gubernaculum* and *jurisdictio* in the American Constitution, see Arthur Schlesinger, *The Imperial Presidency*, Houghton Mifflin, Boston 1973, André Deutsch 1974.

10. On this whole issue see A. J. Marder's remarkable essay 'Oran 3rd July 1940' in *From the Dardanelles to Oran*, OUP 1974, pp.179–288.

11. Jacques Havet, the author of a valuable study of *Kant et la Problème du Temps*, Paris 1947, was in 1951 working for UNESCO.

12. I think, for instance, of the Jesuit theologian, Père Yves de Montcheuil, executed by the Germans in 1943, who in July 1940, preaching to students, arraigned Vichy's anti-Semitism.

13. This in spite of the debt admitted by General Guderian to the works of Basil Liddell-Hart and Major-General J. F. C. Fuller.

14. Friedrich Meinecke, *Die Idee der Staatsräson*, Munich 1924/25.

15. See T. E. Hulme's *Speculations*, Routledge & Kegan Paul 1924.

16. Aldous Huxley, *Grey Eminence*, Chatto & Windus and Harper & Bros. 1941.

17. To say this is not to excuse Richelieu's indifference to issues of distributive justice. On Richelieu's concept of *raison d'état*, the long study by William F. Church, *Richelieu and Reason of State*, Princeton University Press 1972, is invaluable. It is worth noting that Church was McIlwain's pupil.

18. Reinhold Schneider, *Philipp der Zweite oder Religion und Macht*, Cologne ²1957.

19. Compare also Shakespeare's exploration of the tragedy of Henry VI of England in his three plays on the reign of that monarch.

20. Peter Laslett, ed., *Locke's Two Treatises of Government*, CUP ²1967.

21. Edmund Wilson, *Patriotic Gore*, OUP, New York, and André Deutsch 1962. The chapter on Alexander Stephens is pp.380–437.

22. Adam Ulam *Expansion and Co-existence*, Praeger and Secker & Warburg 1968.

23. J. P. Nettl, *Rosa Luxemburg*, 2 vols., OUP 1966.

24. Richard Ullman, *Anglo-Soviet Relations 1917–21*: vol. 3, *The Anglo-Soviet Accord*, Princeton University Press and OUP 1972.

25. J. L. Stocks, 'Locke's Contribution to Political Theory' in *John Locke. Tercentenary Addresses*, OUP 1933.

26. Melvin Richter, *The Politics of Conscience*, Weidenfeld & Nicolson and Harvard University Press 1964.

27. G. Kitson Clark, *Churchmen and the Condition of England 1832–1885*, Methuen and Harper & Row 1973.
28. So Rousseau finds the springs of authentic social inspiration in such figures as Solon, Moses, etc.
29. Thucydides II 63, translated by H. T. Wade-Gery in 'Thucydides, Son of Melesias: a Study in Periclean Policy', in *Essays in Greek History*, Blackwell 1958. Pericles' target of *apragmosunē* is crucially significant in respect of all the issues treated in this paper.
30. N. M. Sutherland, *The Massacre of St Bartholemew and the European Conflict 1559–1572*, Macmillan and Harper & Row 1973.
31. This rather than an obsessively malignant Catholic fanaticism probably determined her course, however agreeable the massacre might be to men of the temper of Pius V (who was of course by then dead).
32. Jacques de Bollardière, *Bataille d'Alger, bataille de l'homme*, Desclée de Brouwer 1972.
33. Reinhold Niebuhr, *Nations and Empires: Recurring Patterns in the Political Order*, Scribner's 1959, Faber & Faber 1960.
34. I hope to deliver this as the Martin Wight Memorial Lecture at the London School of Economics in March 1979; it will be entitled: 'Power Politics and Religious Faith: Aldous Huxley's *Grey Eminince* reconsidered after thirty-seven years'.

4. *Absolute and Relative in History*

1. Hans Küng, *Menschwerdung Gottes*, Herder & Herder, Freiburg 1970.
2. John Knox, *The Death of Christ*, Abingdon Press 1958, Collins 1959.

5. *The Problem of the 'System of Projection'*

1. Friedrich Waismann, 'Verifiability' and 'Language Strata' in *How I See Philosophy*, Macmillan 1968, pp.39ff. and 91ff.
2. Jonathan Bennett, 'Entailment', *Philosophical Review* 78, 1969, pp. 197–236.

7. *Finality in Metaphysics, Ethics and Theology*

1. Henri de Lubac, 'L'Homme Nouveau', *Affrontements mystiques*, Éditions du témoignage chrétien, Paris 1950.
2. Dietrich Bonhoeffer, *Widerstand und Ergebung*, Munich 1951; ET, *Letters and Papers from Prison* (1953), revised and enlarged edition, SCM Press and Macmillan, New York 1971.
3. The theme of the Rome Colloquium in 1970 at which this paper was read was, fittingly enough, 'Infallibility'.

8. *Evidence: Preliminary Reflections*

1. Richard Ullman, *Anglo-Soviet Relations 1917–21*: vol. 1, *Intervention and the War*; vol. 2, *Britain and the Russian Civil War 1918 – February 1920*, Princeton University Press and OUP 1961, 1968.
2. John 18.37.

9. Tillich, Frege, Kittel: Some Reflections on a Dark Theme

1. An address given at the Perse Commemoration in the Chapel of Gonville and Caius College, Cambridge, on 12 December 1975. It has been expanded, but it should be emphasized that these additions do not alter its fundamental sense.
2. Karl Popper, *The Open Society and its Enemies*, 2 vols., Routledge and Kegan Paul 1945; 2nd ed. revised, 1952.
3. R. H. S. Crossman, *Plato Today*, Allen & Unwin 1937, OUP, New York 1939.
4. M. B. Foster, *The Political Philosophies of Plato and Hegel*, OUP 1935.
5. It hardly needs to be said that for Plato the pure mathematician *discovers*: he does not invent. The temper of this realism is excellently conveyed by G. H. Hardy in *A Mathematician's Apology*, CUP 1940, reissued 1969, and more technically in his Rouse Ball lecture on 'Mathematical Proof', published in *Mind* 38, 1929, pp.1–25. The very important, exceedingly technical issues involved have been much discussed in recent years, following the publication of Frege's *Foundations of Arithmetic* in an English translation by J. L. Austin (Blackwell and Philosophical Library, New York 1950), and of Wittgenstein's *Remarks on the Foundations of Mathematics* (Blackwell and Macmillan, New York 1956), and most recently of the text of the lectures he gave on the same and related subjects in Cambridge in Lent and Easter Terms 1939 (see ch.11 n.2 below). Wittgenstein's position, developed in conscious criticism of Frege's realist tendency to treat number as 'objects' (a highly technical term in his philosophy of logic), has sometimes been characterized as 'radical finitism', even as suggesting that we make up our mathematics as we go along. While Brouwer's influence cannot be denied, some liaisons with realism remain. What is impressive in Plato is his acceptance of pure mathematics, realistically interpreted, as an indispensable moment in the intellectual *askēsis* of the individual. Hence Whitehead was moved to entitle a late essay 'Mathematics and the Good' [published in *Essays in Science and Philosophy*, Philosophical Library, New York 1947, pp.97–113; Rider, London 1948, pp.75–86], as if to emphasize the significance of Plato's (to many moderns) paradoxical linkage between the characteristic preoccupation of the pure mathematician and the quest for an all-illuminating ultimate 'in whose light we see light'. (Cf. Plato's own analogy of the sun.) A modern must, however, concede that while it is impossible to accept Plato's intellectual ascetic as it stands, today the philosophy of mathematics is one of the areas in which arguably the central and ultimate issue of metaphysics, viz., the controversy between realism and idealism, is most sharply raised. On these matters I may be allowed to refer to my Presidential Address to the Aristotelian Society in October 1976, entitled 'Reflections on the Controversy between Idealism and Realism', and its sequel given at Rome in January 1977 on the resonance of this controversy in philosophy of religion (the next two essays in the present volume).

6. See the introduction of Dummett's *Frege: Philosophy of Language*, Duckworth 1973, Harper & Row 1974.

7. Gerhard Kittel, *Die Judenfrage*, Stuttgart 1933 (two editions in one year). On Kittel's attitude see Richard Gutteridge's recent important book, *Open thy Mouth for the Dumb: the German Evangelical Church and the Jews 1879–1950*, Blackwell and Harper & Row 1976. See also Robert P. Ericksen, 'Theologian in the Third Reich: the case of Gerhard Kittel', *Journal of Contemporary History* 12, 1977, pp.595–622.

8. Hannah Tillich, *From Time to Time*, Stein & Day, New York 1974; Allen & Unwin 1975.

9. Rollo May, *Paulus*, Harper & Row 1973, Collins 1974. In the biography by W. and M. Pauck, *Paul Tillich* (2 vols., Harper & Row 1976, Collins 1977) these issues are again necessarily raised.

10. Paul Tillich, *Systematic Theology* I–III, University of Chicago Press 1951, 1957, 1963, Nisbet, London, 1953, 1957, 1964; reissued SCM Press 1978.

11. Karl Heim, *Glaube und Denken: Philosophische Grundlegung einer christlichen Lebensanschauung*, Berlin (¹⁻²1931) ³1934, p.5; ET, *God Transcendent: Foundation for a Christian Metaphysic*, Nisbet 1935, Scribner's 1936, p.xvii.

12. Gustaf Törnvall, *Geistliches und weltliches Regiment bei Luther: Studien zu Luthers Weltbild und Gesellschaftverständnis*, Chr. Kaiser Vērlag, Munich 1947.

13. Hans Urs von Balthasar, *Die Apokalypse der Deutschen Seele*, 3 vols., Salzburg 1937–38.

10. *Idealism and Realism: an Old Controversy Renewed*

1. R. G. Collingwood, 'On the So-called Idea of Causation', *Proceedings of the Aristotelian Society*, 1937–38, pp.85–112.

2. I am not forgetting his great interest in teleological explanation, expecially in biology.

3. P. W. Bridgman, *The Logic of Modern Physics*, Macmillan, New York 1927.

4. In his valuable article on the correspondence theory of truth, contributed to the *Encyclopaedia of Philosophy*, ed. Paul Edwards (Macmillan and Free Press, New York 1967), A. N. Prior rightly emphasized the permanent value of this early twentieth-century discussion as a contribution to the philosophy of logic.

5. G. E. Moore, 'External and Internal Relations', *Philosophical Studies*, Routledge & Kegan Paul 1922, pp.276–309.

6. E.g. by John Wisdom in his series of articles on 'Logical Constructions' in *Mind*, vols. 40–2, 1931–33, and by H. H. Price.

7. I am much indebted here to discussions with the late Dr Friedrich Waismann.

8. See J. L. Austin, 'The Meaning of a Word', *Philosophical Papers*, OUP 1961, pp.23–43.

9. Mediaeval students of Aristotle spoke of such predication as 'analogy of attribution', and some, for instance Cajetan, in his *De Analogia*

Nominum, depreciated its importance in metaphysics *vis-à-vis* 'analogy of proper proportionality'.

10. See Bertrand Russell, *Why I am not a Christian and Other Essays*, Allen & Unwin and Simon & Schuster 1957, pp.12–14.
11. These uses may, of course, differ profoundly from one gospel to another. Indeed in answering the question 'What is a gospel?' we may find a classical illustration of four works grouped together by reason of analogy or 'family resemblance'.

11. The Conflict between Realism and Idealism

1. By Wittgenstein's later works I mean the *Philosophische Bemerkungen*, Blackwell 1964, the *Philosophische Grammatik*, Suhrkamp Verlag, Frankfurt 1969, the *Philosophical Investigations*, Blackwell 1953, and the lectures given at Cambridge between January and May 1939 on the foundations of mathematics (see next note), and not only the very remarkable reflections *On Certainty* (Blackwell 1969) written in the last weeks of his life, the very last indeed five days and four days respectively before his death in April 1951.
2. L. Wittgenstein, *Lectures on the Foundations of Mathematics*, ed. Cora Diamond, Harvester Press, Hassocks, Sussex 1976. In the philosophy of mathematics, the term 'Platonism' is used to stand for the doctrine according to which there are determinate mathematical objects, e.g. cardinal numbers, sets, etc.
3. See ch.9 n.5 above.
4. Arthur Eddington, *The Philosophy of Physical Science*, Tarner Lectures for 1938, CUP and Macmillan, New York 1939.
5. I do not here have in mind the great mediaeval theologian Peter Abelard. The density of his logical and philosophical work and of his theology demand purely concentrated study.
6. Here I have in mind the various roles fulfilled by such individuals as Peter, James, John, Caiaphas, Pilate, the unknown soldiers and the unnamed women, and also by the three Maries of the Johannine tradition, Mary of Bethany, sister of Martha and Lazarus, Mary the mother of Jesus and Mary Magdalene. In a haunting study included in his collection of papers *Creator Spiritus* (Einsiedeln 1967), Hans Urs von Balthasar, engaging with the question: 'Die Messe, ein Opfer der Kirche?' (op. cit., pp.166–217), treats of the indispensable contribution made by these three women to the completion of the work wherein the Son, giving glory to the Father, himself received from the Father in his final hour the substance of that glory he had received from the Father ere ever the world was. We must never forget the way in which the sombre tapestry of the Lord's passion is woven: the manner wherein throughout its course the ultimately mysterious and the humanly familiar are interwoven one with another.
7. I am emphatically not thinking of the tradition represented by the posthumous work of an English member of the order of 'Helper of the Holy Souls' entitled *The Divine Crucible of Purgatory* (Burns, Oates

and Washbourn 1940). The English Roman Catholic philosopher, E. I. Watkin, called my attention to this remarkable book in 1941 as a classic of the spiritual life, which was also deeply significant in respect of the problem of the state of the departed. He regretted that the preface to this work had taken the shape of a brief dogmatic statement of the penal conception of purgatory by a somewhat insensitive and unintelligent English Jesuit. *The Divine Crucible of Purgatory* was well appreciated and commented upon by the French Dominican theologian Yves Congar in his essay on 'Le Purgatoire' in the collection entitled *Le mystère de la mort, et sa célébration chrétienne,* Editions du Cerf 1951.

Neither in referring to penal conceptions of the atonement have I in mind the soteriology of R. W. Dale (open to criticism though I hold it to be), whose ministry at Carrs Lane Congregational Church, Birmingham, will never be forgotten. Dale's work was a *point de départ* for much important English work in this area, and neither R. C. Moberly and Henry Scott Holland (for all their debt to John MacLeod Campbell), nor P. T. Forsyth nor Hastings Rashdall can be fully understood except in relation to his near-classical statement of the penal theory. By criticism of his work one can indeed approach the *arcana* of the Christian doctrine of redemption.

8. Heinrich Weinstock, *Die Tragödie des Humanismus*, Heidelberg ²1954, ⁴1960; Cedric Whitman, *Sophocles: a Study of Heroic Humanism*, Harvard University Press 1951; André Bonnard, *La Tragédie et l'Homme*, Neuchâtel and Paris 1950. See also 'Ethics and Tragedy', the concluding paper in this volume.

9. Hans Urs von Balthasar, *The Way of the Cross*, ET, Burns & Oates and Herder & Herder 1969.

10. André Feuillet, *L'Agonie de Gethsémane*, Gabalda, Paris 1977.

12. *Parable and Sacrament*

1. See ch.7 n.2 above.
2. Karl Barth, *Der Römerbrief*, Munich 1919, ²1922; ET, *The Epistle of the Romans*, OUP 1933.
3. Rudolf Otto, *Das Heilige*, Stuttgart 1917; ET, *The Idea of the Holy*, OUP 1923, ²1950.
4. Karl Barth, *Protestant Theology in the Nineteenth Century* (originally 1952), ET, SCM Press and Judson Press 1972.
5. See Henri Bouillard, *Karl Barth*, 3 vols., Aubier, Paris 1957.
6. In this section I would acknowledge a deep debt to the discussion of Jesus' teaching by parable in Eberhard Jüngel's *Paulus und Jesus*, Mohr, Tübingen, ²1964. This book was at the time of its publication the only one known to me, treating of the gospel narrative, that availed itself of the important work done on the theory of speech by philosophers along the lines pioneered by J. L. Austin. Jüngel's achievement in this early work is all the more impressive in that he does not in it display direct familiarity with, or indebtedness to,

Austin's posthumously published writings. But in his treatment of Jesus' teaching ministry he illustrated the kind of light that might be gained from a careful study of Austin's work on performatory and performative use of language. Jüngel has recently taken the discussion of these issues further in a major theological work: *Gott als Geheimnis der Welt*, Mohr, Tübingen ²1977, which is (rightly in my opinion) regarded as one of the most important works of recent German theology, and of which surely we may hope for an early translation to make it available to those unable to read it in the original. Finally, I realize that this paper would have been much improved, had I been able to read, before writing it, C. F. Evans' excellent Ethel M. Wood lecture, 'Parable and Dogma' (available in his *Explorations in Theology* 2, SCM Press 1977, pp.121ff.): this though I am unconvinced by his remarks (op. cit., p.130) on the parables of the lost sheep and the lost coin.

7. The writer was Uvedale Lambert, and his letter appeared in the correspondence columns of the *Church Times*.

8. C. H. Dodd, *The Parables of the Kingdom*, Nisbet 1935, Scribner's 1936; rev. ed., Collins and Scribner's 1961.

9. Joachim Jeremias, *The Parables of Jesus*, ET (1954), 3rd ed. revised, SCM Press and Scribner's 1972.

10. This paper by Théo Preiss is included in the collection entitled *La Vie en Christ*, published posthumously by Delachaux & Niestlé in 1951, and in the selection from it published as *Life in Christ* (Studies in Biblical Theology 13), SCM Press 1954. The French edition also includes a transcript of Preiss's lectures in the Faculté de Théologie Protestante at Strasbourg in the late forties on 'The Son of Man', containing in germ the great work he hoped to write on the subject.

11. Annie Jaubert, *La date de la Cène: calendrier biblique et liturgie chrétienne* (Études Bibliques), Paris 1957.

12. Hans Lietzmann, *Messe und Herrenmahl*, Bonn 1926, Berlin ³1955; ET, *Mass and Lord's Supper*, Brill, Leiden 1954.

13. Maurice de la Taille, *Mysterium Fidei . . .*, Beauchesne, Paris 1921; ET, *The Mystery of Faith: Regarding the Most August Sacrament and Sacrifice of the Body and Blood of Christ*, Sheed and Ward 1941. I also venture to refer to a paper of my own given to the Sixth Anglo-Catholic Congress on 9 July 1948, and published in the Report of the Congress (Dacre Press 1949, pp.130–7). There are several things in this paper that I would wish to correct (including the misleading impression that Bar-Kochba's revolt came before, and not after, the sack of Jerusalem by Titus's legions), but also matters of considerable substance. Indeed, to rewrite that paper in the light of the lines of thought adumbrated here might be a profitable exercise, especially if I included a revision of further thoughts on the eucharist included in a short, rather concentrated essay, 'Sacrament and Common Meal', contributed to the volume in memory of R. H. Lightfoot, *Studies in the Gospels*, ed. D. E. Nineham, Blackwell 1955, pp.201–7. I venture, however, to mention these pieces here as, 'dated' though they may be, especially the first, they raise issues

closely related to some of those approached in the essay on 'Parable and Sacrament' included in this volume.

13. Ethics and Tragedy

1. A. R. Manvell and H. Fraenkel, *The July Plot*, Bodley Head 1964 (*The Men who Tried to Kill Hitler*, Coward-McCann, New York 1964).
2. Eberhard Bethge, *Dietrich Bonhoeffer: a Biography*, Collins and Harper & Row 1970.
3. See ch.11 n.8 above.
4. Philip Vellacott, *Sophocles and Oedipus*, Macmillan 1971.
5. Nicholas Brooke, *King Lear*, Edward Arnold 1963.

Index